Free-access higher education

Warren W. Willingham

74762

College Entrance Examination Board, New York, 1970

Orders for this book should be sent to the College Entrance Examination Board, Publications Order Office, Box 592, Princeton, New Jersey 08540.

Editorial inquiries concerning this book should be directed to Editorial Office, College Entrance Examination Board, 475 Riverside Drive, New York, New York 10027.

Library of Congress Catalog Card Number: 70-130310

Printed in the United States of America

For Anna

Contents

Maps

Tables

Tables for Chapter 5 (*each state profile*)
1. Number of recognized colleges at different levels of accessibility
   (fall 1968)
2. Percentage of different populations within commuting distance
   of a free-access college (fall 1968)
3. Estimate of additional colleges required to put
   specified percentages of the state's population within commuting
   distance of a free-access college

Preface

The principal intention of this study was to provide some bench marks that would give some quantitative indication of how accessible higher education is, in order to improve understanding of the current status of educational opportunity. The method involved an analysis of the populations living near an inexpensive, nonselective college in various geographic areas. It brought together three divergent components — people, communities, and educational institutions — into a sort of educational demography.

The study was undertaken at the College Board's Access Research Office, which was established in Palo Alto, California in 1968 to prepare reports on the status of access to higher education. As Chapter 1 describes, the geographic aspects of access to college have taken on new importance, especially during the past decade. Since the implications of such geographic data are particularly important to the statewide development and organization of higher education, the findings for each state are reported individually in the 50 state profiles of Chapter 5.

Many readers will respond to natural curiosity and turn immediately to favorite states, wondering after a while what the terms mean, where the data came from, and what the study is all about anyway. This is a good place to say that such questions are taken up in the first four chapters. Impatient browsers would be wise at least to read the first few pages of Chapter 5, which explain briefly what the state profiles contain.

The final three chapters will convey, I hope, the important impression that access to higher education is a far more complicated matter than the availability of free-access colleges. A much larger task is the development of programs that have personal relevance and economic utility for diverse populations under different conditions. It is very likely that in the next decade we shall see the development of second-generation state models of coordination and governance that will have profound and lasting effects upon the form higher education will take. It seems especially important that educational leaders and planners be sensitive to the state's responsibility to provide equal educational opportunity and, at the same time, be wary of the constricting danger of centralized coordination for both institutions and students. With respect to these problems, this volume contains much data, some suggestions, but no confident prescriptions.

Those readers who like maps and numbers will correctly guess that this work was thoroughly enjoyable. But the study does include a great deal of troublesome detail which, though checked several times, is still subject to error or different interpretation by those more familiar with local circumstances. Of course, the lapses are my responsibility, as are the interpretations that are made in these pages.

I am greatly indebted to a number of friends and colleagues who were kind enough to read all or part of this report in manuscript. The criticisms and suggestions of Edmund Gleazer, Lyman Glenny, Dorothy Knoell, and Lewis Mayhew were especially helpful and appreciated. The manuscript was read by College Board staff members too numerous to mention individually, though I owe each my gratitude. Their generous and careful attention helped to avoid misconceptions, but it must be acknowledged that my colleagues do not agree with all interpretations retained in this final version.

Others are due special thanks for their more direct involvement in the production of the report. Donna Kofnovec and Becky Daniels carried out most of the analytic work; Nancy Lambert typed the various drafts in the midst of other responsibilities. I am grateful for their excellent work and good humor. I also express appreciation to Richard Ferrin who contributed valuable suggestions and assistance throughout the study. And the final report has been greatly improved by the special interest and skill of the College Board publication staff, particularly Diane Olsen and Brenda Jones.

Finally, I owe a debt of gratitude to Ben Cameron Jr. who was a constant source of support and assistance during the course of this work. But most of all it was my wife, Anna, who provided the stimulus to begin, the good judgment along the way, and the encouragement to complete the task.

Warren W. Willingham

June 1970

1. The new meaning of equal opportunity

Higher education can no longer be regarded as a privilege for the few, but must be seen as a right for the many.

Julian Bond

Infrequently a writer succeeds in making simple a problem so subtle and fundamental that it affects much of our daily lives. In his essay *Excellence,* Gardner (1961) confronts such a problem—how to nurture the rare talents so badly needed by society while, at the same time, giving all individuals equal rights and a fair distribution of privilege. No social system has solved this riddle satisfactorily, but the main shortcoming of democratic free enterprise is the devastating effectiveness with which competition brings some to the top and leaves too many at an unacceptable bottom.

The suggested answer is that society must be so organized that all individuals have unfettered and continuous opportunity to pursue their interests and utilize their individual talents. During the past decade equal opportunity for higher education has become an important manifestation of this philosophy. As Coleman (1969) notes, equal opportunity is an evolving idea not subject to easy definition. It has many facets and is subject to many conflicting frames of reference. Nevertheless, one important barometer of equal opportunity is the accessibility of higher education to its potential clients. It is the extent and nature of this accessibility with which this report is concerned.

One useful way to study access to higher education is to examine data describing the characteristics of those high school graduates who do and do not go to college. Studies of this sort are familiar, though still in an early stage of development and hampered by inadequate data. Recent examples of noteworthy work include books by Jencks and Riesman (1968), Jaffe and Adams (1969), and Folger and Nam (1967). The analysis undertaken here takes a different and complementary tack by focusing on the availability of educational resources rather than the outcome of the admissions process. The general question is how accessible is higher education? More specifically, how many and what sort of people live within commuting distance of a free-access (inexpensive and relatively nonselective) college?

Answering these questions means first identifying all the free-access colleges among the 2,600 undergraduate institutions in the country. Second, it requires an analysis of the characteristics of the populations living near those free-access colleges. The purpose is to develop an empirical description of the accessibility of higher education in each state and to relate that accessibility to the characteristics of local institutions and the statewide organization of higher education.

Naturally, accessibility is a relative term and must be interpreted in the context of recent developments and current values. College admissions doesn't mean what it used to mean. In the past decade there have been numerous dramatic developments that have had a critical impact upon what access to higher education means today. It is both worthwhile and necessary to outline briefly those developments.

Major developments of the 1960s

Each of the five developments outlined in the following paragraphs represents to some extent a shift in public attitudes, but each also includes observable events that have had direct effects upon college admissions. Each development has long roots but, to a marked extent, it is a creature of the past decade.

The move to universal higher education

More than 20 years ago the Truman Commission (1947) declared, "The time has come to make education through the 14th grade available in the same way that high school education is now available." This prophetic statement stirred up enough excitement to require a lengthy rebuttal (McConnell, 1949) to the critics. On the other hand similar sentiments expressed during the past 10 years by such public groups as the Eisenhower Commission (1960), the Educational Policies Commission (1964), and the Carnegie Commission (1968) have been accepted without a ripple. Furthermore, the Higher Education Facilities Act (1963), the Higher Education Act (1965), and the Higher Education Amendments (1968) represent concrete evidence of the political acceptability of substantially broadened opportunity for higher education.

Witnessing the continued underrepresentation of black Americans (Egerton, 1969) and children from low-income families (Creager et al., 1968) even in public institutions, some observers have wondered whether the country was not overly optimistic about the rate at which greatly expanded postsecondary opportunity might be achieved. There is an important distinction between proportional representation of disadvantaged groups and general expansion of higher education. It seems clear by now that inequities in opportunity are so imbedded in the American culture that substantial change will require great effort. But a general and marked expansion of college matriculation in the past decade is easily documented.

Table 1. Three indicators of the expansion of higher education from 1948 to 1968

Year	Number of colleges	First-time enrollment (FTE)	Ratio of FTE to high school graduates
1948	1,808	617,000	.52
1958	1,903 (+5%)	862,000 (+40%)	.57
1968	2,491 (+31%)	1,908,000 (+121%)	.70

Sources: *Opening Fall Enrollment* (1958 and 1968 editions); *Education Directory*, Part 3, 1948; *Digest of Educational Statistics*, 1968; *Projections of Educational Statistics*, 1968.

Educational statistics are subject to so many legitimate variations in definition that "exact" data are often illusory. Nonetheless, Table 1 gives a reasonably accurate picture based upon gross statistics derived from standard sources. Each of the three barometers included shows marked expansion in higher education since World War II, with most of the growth occurring during the past 10 years. To some extent facilities and enrollment increases can be attributed to natural increases in the age group and improved retention in high school, but this is not true in the case of the ratio of first-time enrollment to high school graduates. The ratio of .70 in 1968 is a highly significant figure since it suggests that a much larger percentage of students are continuing their education after secondary school than has been typical for the past 80 years (Jaffe and Adams, 1965).

Recent data from independent sources suggest that the ratio is probably accurate. The Bureau of Labor Statistics reports that 55 percent of youth who graduated from high school in the previous year were enrolled in college in October 1968 (Perrella, 1969). This figure can be increased by at least 10 percent to account for those who enter college more than one year following high school. New breakdowns of census information reported by Johnson and Reed (1969) indicate that there are even more late entrants than a 10 percent adjustment would imply. These somewhat startling data show that 1 out of 3 first-year college students do not matriculate during the fall following high school graduation but wait an additional year or more. This proportion seems certainly inflated by varying understandings of the term "first-year" and by numerous doubly counted first-time students who wander in periodically to take a course or two. On the other hand these estimates do not include the substantial but uncertain number of students in postsecondary vocational schools, proprietary institutions, and other alternatives to college. Even with these various qualifications considered, the age of massive postsecondary education is definitely upon us.

There is no sign of any slacking off in this trend. If anything, the Eisenhower Commission's (1960) goal that "Two-year colleges should be within commuting distance of most high school graduates" has been sought with accelerating vigor. The Carnegie Commission (1968a) has recommended 500 new two-year colleges by 1976, and the development of the community colleges has been described as "one of the highest priorities of the New [Nixon] administration" (*Chronicle,* 1969b). At this writing, implementing legislation is under active consideration in Congress (*Higher Education and National Affairs,* 1969a, 1969b).

A questioning of values

Undoubtedly the most dramatic and important development in higher education, brought about by the civil rights movement and the student rebellion, has been the questioning of fundamental values. The interests of black Americans with respect to access to higher education can be accounted in uncomplicated terms; it is the majority response that is complicated, tense, and otherwise fraught with uncertainty. The demand is clearly to redress injustice and to distribute privilege, power, and dignity in a more socially equitable manner. Since college training is widely regarded as one of the most important routes to social opportunity, considerable attention has been focused upon the admissions process. Resolutions adopted in a "Statewide seminar on race and poverty in higher education" in California (McKendall, 1968) provide a concrete illustration of the basic values involved. A few of the major items were:

"Institutions of higher learning in California should not receive federal funds unless there is proportional representation of minority group persons on every level of institutional activity, including the student body, faculty, administration, and governing boards.

"That upon acceptance of minority/poverty students, the institution make a total commitment to them in nonacademic student-related areas, as well as in academic areas.

"That admission of marginal Mexican American and black students be determined respectively by Mexican American and black student organizations where they are active on campuses, otherwise by minority interest groups.

"That these students not be required to take admission tests.

"That they be given a one-year period in which to adjust to the university environment after which the EOP [Educational Opportunity Program] staff, including minority students, will decide whether students will be allowed to continue."

It is plain that these proposals are in considerable conflict with traditional meritocratic selection designed to channel talent where it is most needed and utilize limited high-level educational resources as efficiently as possible. Few doubt the urgent necessity to democratize higher education—the main question is how and when it will be accomplished. The ironic aspect of proposals that threaten to seriously diminish academic standards in selective institutions is that they may undermine the value of that which is sought. As Whitehead once said in homely language, there's a ditch on both sides of the road.

The student rebellion, which cannot be clearly differentiated from the civil rights movement, shares some of the latter's tone regarding college admissions. In addition to broader national concerns, the main thrust of the student's complaint seems to be a questioning of the social and educational relevance of higher education (see Axelrod et al., 1969; and Willingham, 1970 for recent reviews). This includes increasing criticism of the grading system, the impersonal "punchcard" treatment, the discipline orientation of the curriculum, and the blasé faculty. One result is pressure to stop admitting and educating "by the numbers." More specifically it is a humanistic plea to treat people as individuals with their own special talents, limitations, aspirations, and needs. In a nutshell the disaffected student has come to expect the college to help him understand and relate to a strife-filled world. Many are angry because the college falls short. Serious consideration of educational opportunity must take account of that fact.

Accelerating public expectations

These two trends—the move to universal higher education and the accompanying pressure of shifting values—raise difficult questions subject to reasonable disagreement by informed observers. Has the expansion of higher education really meant expanded opportunity? How much social responsibility can higher education handle? To what extent will student and minority-group pressure actually strengthen the egalitarian function of higher education? Perhaps the answer to all three questions is "not much." If so, higher education is in for a great deal of trouble because these two trends have created a third that is important in its own right—accelerating public expectations. For example, it is increasingly accepted that:

- Some form of postsecondary education for the enhancement of career development and adult responsibility is a right, not merely a privilege.
- Education must be relevant to the talents and interests of individual students, though they may differ considerably from those of traditional college students.
- Inadequate preparation at the secondary level must be rectified, not used as a reason for rejecting the student or not educating him.
- Extraneous barriers such as accidents of birth and the cost of college should not hamper the accessibility of higher education.
- Social inequities in the rate of college admissions among various groups are a public responsibility to identify and alleviate.
- It is insufficient that opportunity simply be available; it must be available in a form and under conditions that are likely to attract students.

These are not sentiments subject to scientific documentation. Rather, they are a part of the zeitgeist and evidence of their influence runs through political statement and foundation action, as well as campus rally. Again, it is noteworthy that these are ideas of the 1960s. It is true that they characterize the community college movement that started in the 1930s, and the GI Bill is often regarded as the first guarantee of higher education. But a generation ago the community college was somewhat on the fringe of higher education in many parts of the country. And the GI Bill was actually intended to pay a debt of gratitude and ease the national transition to peace. (Its original name was the "Servicemen's Readjustment Act of 1944.")

The assumption of public responsibility

The increasing assumption of public responsibility for higher education can be regarded in either of two ways. On the one hand it can be seen as the inevitable result of social demand. It is almost axiomatic that any major social mechanism for individual reward, punishment, or regulation tends to become regarded as a public responsibility. It is particularly true when rights are involved rather than merely privileges. As previously discussed, access to higher education is increasingly associated with social opportunity and, even though there are pockets of dissent, public expectations have accelerated markedly during the 1960s. This public attitude creates the enormously complex task of public supervision of equal opportunity.

As more and more high school graduates and their families regard college attendance as a right, considerable pressure is brought to bear through political channels to see that the public interest is protected. In turn, political action requires sufficient legal control to organize programs in the public interest. Not only are public funds necessary to meet the extremely high costs, it is also necessary to insure that those funds are spent appropriately — all of which moves access to higher education into the public domain. It functions as a major mechanism for the distribution of social power and privilege. As such, its planning and governance entail a host of complex issues.

A complementary view of the public assumption of responsibility for higher education is simply descriptive. During the past decade there has been a notable expansion of federal involvement through the partial funding of new facilities, categorical aid to institutions, student aid programs, research and development, and equal opportunity programs. Other programs in vocational education may ultimately have a considerable effect upon higher institutions. Except for civil rights enforcement, federal programs in education have been remarkably free of strings and pork barrel politics.

Nonetheless, the mere existence of national programs that require monitoring and periodic evaluation does impose some standardization of procedure. In order to avoid similar standardization of programs, federal guidelines for local or state projects have been kept reasonably general. This model of federal funding and state spending has supported another very significant development in the assumption of public responsibility — the growth of state planning mechanisms.

State planning and coordination has a long history, but Mayhew (1969a) documents its recent explosive growth. Until this decade only a few states had master plans. At latest count only 10 states were without master plans or background studies in progress. Mayhew lists the following ideas that, among others, are typically found in most master plans: some assumptions relating the universal opportunity for higher education; dispersed two-year colleges as an efficient way to handle many students; stratification into a multilayer system involving two-year colleges, four-year colleges, and universities that assume most of the research function; coordination as an essential means for budgeting, establishing new programs, carrying out studies, and so forth; attention to continuing education and the training of college teachers.

It is too early to gauge the ultimate effectiveness of state coordinating agencies with respect to access, and they will no doubt continue to vary a great deal from state to state. As Kirp (1969) argues, "Constitutional and statutory provisions, judicial decisions and long standing custom all bear witness to the states' responsibility for public education," and its responsibility to develop schools that will compensate as fully as possible for inequalities of prior training and background. It does seem very likely that there will be continued or even heightened tension between the state bodies and the institution regarding who makes what decisions. Matters in the public interest but not vital concerns of the large powerful institution are naturally the most likely possibilities for asserting central authority. These include equal opportunity programs, student aid, auxiliary guidance and admissions services, and various studies of human resources and educational progress.

It would be an omission not to recognize one additional aspect of public responsibility in college admissions. Public opinion and moral persuasion have done much to alter institutional attitudes regarding admissions. Many public and private colleges now demonstrate a sense of social obligation not common a few years ago. Whether or not these social and governmental influences on college admissions are judged proper or effective, they are nonetheless there and seem unlikely to be easily reversed. Institutional autonomy in admissions has already been diminished and will probably become more so. An important problem that trend creates is how to meet public responsibility and at the same time retain as much institutional initiative and diversity as possible.

The role of research

There has been in the 1960s an unprecedented explosion of social research related to access to higher education. It hasn't gone under that name since access to higher education has not really existed as a recognized field of inquiry or as a primary interest of any particular discipline. There have been several reasons for the expansion of research. An obvious need has existed for certain types of data and studies as background for or evaluations of the federal, state, and private programs initiated in an unusually innovative period. Also, the general climate has fostered intense interest in social problems and the social engineering that might solve those problems. Finally, there is the rather important consideration that federal funds for research and development have been available in quantities not necessarily sufficient but certainly much greater than was true heretofore. This expansion of research has occurred in five important areas.

First, there has been a considerable expansion of work directly concerned with who goes to college. Surveys of the postsecondary plans and outcomes of nationally representative samples of high school students were almost unknown prior to 1960. Whereas such data still leave much to be desired, education has profited greatly from Project TALENT (Flanagan et al., 1964), special study of two census samples (Cowhig and Nam, 1962; Johnson and Zappolo, 1969), and other special follow-up studies (Cole, 1957; Seibel, 1965; Tillery, 1969). Studies of the social and personal dynamics of college admissions have recently become comprehensive and sophisticated (Jencks, 1968; Sewell and Shah, 1967). The state survey of student plans is another type of research in this general category; it has old roots but shows recent signs of much needed vigor (Clear, 1969; Grant, 1968; Martin, 1969; McQuitty and Tully, 1969).

Second, this decade has seen massive research on many aspects of social disadvantage. These efforts are far too numerous even to mention by categories, but the studies of Negro education (McGrath, 1965; Jencks and Riesman, 1968; Jaffe et al., 1968), the Coleman report (1966), and descriptions of Negro college students (Bayer and Boruch, 1969; Blumenfeld, 1966) are noteworthy for their direct bearing upon inequality of educational opportunity.

A third new development in research is the emergence of important new fields of interest. These include the economics of higher education, a new-found interest of economists (Bowman, 1966); human resources, the special province of a new scholarly journal (for example, see Folger, 1967); the development of new models connecting educational planning to manpower needs (Hollister, 1967); and career development, another excursion of psychology into education (Holland and Whitney, 1969). These fields are either quite new or greatly enlarged in scope and intensity. Each has a critical relevance to expanded postsecondary opportunity.

A fourth innovation is the development of information systems. Some are designed primarily to interface with inquiring clients in search of an educational or career identity (Tiedeman, 1965). Most are designed to handle transactions with students and also to provide summary information useful for planning, budgeting, or daily administration (Glover, 1967; Western Interstate Commission on Higher Education [WICHE], 1969). The information system is variously regarded as an absolute necessity, an intellectual menace, or a dehumanizing ogre. In any event it is a child of the 1960s—and a bedfellow of the 1970s.

The fifth development is not substantive but represents the maturation of significant research centers during the past decade. The major ones include American Council on Education, American College Testing Program, Center for Research and Development in Higher Education, National Merit Scholarship Corporation, National Opinion Research Center, Southern Regional Education Board, and Western Interstate Commission on Higher Education. There are a few older agencies like Educational Testing Service and the College Entrance Examination Board but, in large part, organized research on access to higher education has been developed during the past 10 years.

These developments in research have had important effects. In part they have resulted from interest in the problems, but they have also fostered that interest. Research has encouraged an innovative spirit and an objective attitude about complex educational problems. Small successes and occasional light shed on perplexing questions have also dramatized the scope of the social issues involved and the level of effort required for their solution. One might almost say that higher education discovered research in the 1960s. Research will have greater influence because the increasingly complex social responsibilities of educational administrators will require far more and far better data than have been available. Whether survey data and research findings are relevant and accurate will consequently be of special importance.

Implications of developments in the 1960s

This report was described earlier as an examination of the accessibility of higher education. The developments of the past decade are momentous because they have had a decisive bearing on what accessibility and equal opportunity mean. In discussing the concept of equality of educational opportunity, Coleman

(1969) relates the fact that the role of the secondary school and the community has been to provide a set of free, local resources. An important conclusion of the developments of the 1960s is that this concept of equal opportunity has now moved to higher education. An important addition is the expectation that programs shall also be "relevant," though what that term means is still indefinite. There are three major implications—a new interpretation of college admissions, the new importance of proximity, and a new level of commitment.

A new interpretation of college admissions

All the major trends of recent years point in the same direction. They represent a dramatic shift to a societal as distinguished from a scholastic philosophy of college admissions. The scholastic view implies restrictive admissions, traditional curriculums, and close attention to academic standards and preparation (Bowles, 1966). Historically, it has been the dominant philosophy in most institutions. College was for those who could afford to go and had the inclination to study or sit through what was offered. Even in supposedly democratized state colleges, attendance was no doubt heavily dependent upon middle-class values and financial resources.

The 1970 interpretation of the societal view of college admissions does not, strictly speaking, include admissions at all but rather assumes a predictable and continuous relationship between a student and his local college. It emphasizes periodic enrollment to develop and maintain the individual's intellectual awareness, his career skills, and his value to the community. The primary emphasis is upon fitting the college to the characteristics and needs of the student rather than the other way around. This is recognized as the guiding philosophy of the community college—their experience confirms the long and difficult road to effective implementation. What is new is the dramatic extent to which educational and political leaders are now willing to apply this interpretation to all public postsecondary education.

Needless to say, large numbers of students will continue to go to public and private colleges under variously modified versions of the scholastic philosophy for many years to come. The important point is that proper examination of the accessibility of higher education must take account of the main barriers to the increasing number of "new" students making the transition to college within the societal context. These new students will not be involved with the rigmarole of multiple applications a year in advance, sweating out offers of admission, or selecting the "right" college. But they will have to face the familiar barriers of cost and institutional selectivity. Taken together these two can define the accessibility of a given institution, though the societal view of admissions makes it necessary to include proximity as an additional variable.

The new importance of proximity

Proximity has become a key element in the accessibility of higher education for several reasons. The most important considerations are related to the connection between proximity and opportunity. It is reasonably assumed that a nearby college is more likely to prove attractive to a marginal student because of its intangible identity for him, its familiarity, and its relevance to his interests. Added to these "motivating" characteristics is the fact that the student can live at home, work part-time, and attend classes under circumstances that only commuting status permits.

While the direct evidence supporting these assumptions may be sparse, there are several convincing studies which indicate that the existence of a nonselective, inexpensive college does increase the rate of college attendance in the surrounding area. Early work by Koos (1944a) and much more recent research by Bashaw (1965) indicate that a local community college approximately doubles the college attendance rate of local high school graduates. Recent work of Trent and Medsker (1965) confirms this result. The whole matter of the relationship between college location and equal opportunity is so critical that it is discouraging that so little basic research has been put to the question.

There is another group of reasons why proximity is an important element in a societal interpretation of the accessibility of higher education. They relate to the new functions demanded of colleges. For many students not now attracted to postsecondary education, "going away to college" is somewhat incompatible with their primary interest — a rapid, smooth transition into a useful job in the local community. It is even likely that training for many new service jobs will require close proximity to the work location because of practicum requirements. As advancing technology requires an increasing amount of work–study interaction and continuing education, it seems inevitable that colleges must be located where people live and work.

It is true that the new technology can eventually put an "educational terminal" in every bedroom, though this hardly seems a sufficient view of the educational process, let alone a world worth working toward. As new colleges are increasingly regarded as intellectual and cultural resources, it seems all the more necessary that they be accessible to their clientele on a casual basis. Keniston (1965) has described the shattering of traditional communities and its devastating side effects. The local college is one social institution that should have great potential for shoring up the sense of community — much depends upon whether it is developed with that intent.

A new level of commitment

So long as college attendance was the privilege of a limited proportion of the population, it was sufficient that it proceed with relatively little public monitoring. But as access to higher education has become a major social mechanism, a new commitment to examine the process and to make a public accounting of the outcome has developed. Previous discussion of developments of the 1960s dramatize how little is known and how much more must be known about admission to college if there is to be any hope of moving toward the societal objectives now gaining public acceptance.

The most obvious reason is that institutional, state, and federal planners must have factual details if the public insists they be accountable for equal opportunity in a sound educational system. The types of necessary information include current data on characteristics, aspirations, and postsecondary experiences of high school graduates; resources of and barriers to higher education; problems of particular groups of students; need for special programs and legislation to expand access. Gathering such information, interpreting it in the public interest, and acting on the implications represent a new level of commitment and accountability.

Another type of new commitment is dictated by the fact that accessibility is by no means equivalent to opportunity. An accessible institution provides opportunity only if it offers programs of appropriate quality, serves the community, attracts students, and effectively meets their needs. Meeting student and community needs raises a wide variety of questions concerning the relevance of higher education—questions that are imbedded in major social issues and carry far-reaching implications for students, faculty, and institutions. Thus, accessibility is a necessary but insufficient condition for the existence of opportunity for higher education. There is increasing commitment to the realization that higher education must also be relevant to a wide diversity of individual students. This report focuses upon accessibility because it is a prior question, but Chapter 7 suggests ways in which relevance must be improved and possible means for doing so.

The nature of this study

In focusing upon the accessibility of higher education, this study is intended to: describe the degree of accessibility of all higher institutions in the country and estimate the proportion of various populations living within commuting distance of those colleges judged easily accessible ("free-access" institutions); describe the accessibility of higher education in each state—including pertinent socio-economic characteristics, educational statistics, and information concerning the organization of public higher institutions; suggest a framework for systematic evaluation of access to higher education and improvement in the relevance of educational opportunity.

The main idea is to put together an analysis of educational resources and demographic characteristics as one additional way to judge how higher education serves the population. The procedure first involves rating the degree of accessibility of all colleges with respect to selectivity and cost, and plotting each free-access college with an appropriate commuting radius on detailed state maps. Estimates of the populations that those colleges cover provide the basic data for the report. Chapter 2 gives a description of this procedure with special emphases upon the definition of accessibility. Chapter 3 is concerned with the colleges themselves—how many and what types there are at each level of accessibility and where they are located. Chapter 4 describes the populations living

2. Accessibility—working definitions

In order to describe various proportions of the population that live in proximity to an accessible higher institution, it is clearly necessary to specify what is meant by accessibility and proximity. These are relative terms, and one therefore seeks not truth but useful working definitions. The following sections proceed in that spirit and end with a brief account of the procedure of the study reported here. Accessibility of an institution was defined earlier as the joint effect of cost and selectivity. For the purposes of this study the cost is defined in fairly narrow terms and selectivity somewhat more broadly than usually conceived.

Tuition

In this study cost is defined as tuition (and fees) for local residents for the academic year 1968–69 as reported in standard references or by the institution. Tuition is obviously only part of the cost of college for a commuting student, but other expenses vary because they depend upon the condition and habits of the individual. Institutions were assigned tuition "scores" from one to five as indicated in Table 2.

Selectivity

In defining the accessibility of an institution, selectivity may take one of several forms. In general the purpose is to characterize the institution with respect to how open and appropriate it might appear to a random high school graduate. Thus a college may be inaccessible either because it sets high academic standards or because it has a very narrow purpose, of interest to only a few students (for example, heavy religious emphasis). But by far the most common mode of selectivity is some measure of academic performance.

Basically, there are three types of selectivity measures. These are a national standard such as a test score average for the freshman class; the proportion of applicants rejected; and a measure of selectivity in relation to the high school population from which the college draws. The national standard may give quite a distorted picture of how difficult it is to gain admission to an institution. For

Table 2. Tuition scores assigned to colleges

Tuition score	Number of colleges	Tuition and fees (1968–69)	Percent of median U.S. family income (1967)
1	404	$ 0–160	0.0–2.0%
2	685	161–400	2.1–5.0
3	250	401–800	5.1–10.0
4	466	801–1,600	10.1–20.0
5	241	1,601 and higher	20.1 and higher

Table 3. Selectivity scores assigned to colleges

Selectivity score	Number of colleges	Percent in top half of high school class (primary criterion)	Admissions policy (secondary criterion)
1—Open door	530	0–49%	Accepts all high school graduates
2—Nonselective	429	50–69	Accepts top 75%, C average
3—Selective	420	70–84	Accepts top 50%, C+ average
4—Very selective	268	85–94	Accepts top third, B average
5—Most selective	234	95+	Very competitive

example, there are more than a few institutions in the South with average Scholastic Aptitude Test scores of 350, which would indicate a very accessible college. The fact is many of these institutions admit only those students from the top half or quarter of their high school class.

The proportion of applicants rejected is even more ambiguous. If students chose colleges carefully, all institutions would have a relatively small number of rejected applicants, that quantity being unrelated to the academic quality of the students admitted. This is not exactly what happens, but the number of rejects is apparently not highly related to other measures of selectivity (Nash, 1969).

The most desirable measure for this study is an index of the competition an applicant faces from those students who apply to his college. At accessible institutions most of these would be local students. One measure of this type of selectivity is the formal admissions policy of the institution, for example, "We accept students with a 'C' average." The advantage of using policy statements to define selectivity is that practically all colleges make some such public statement, which can be roughly categorized. The disadvantage is the discrepancy that sometimes creeps in between statement and fact.

The most objective and generally satisfactory measure is the percentage of the freshman class who ranked in the top half of their high school class. This measure provides the best indication of whether applicants with average records from feeder high schools are or are not typically admitted—either by explicit policy or de facto circumstances. The measure is available for most four-year colleges and some two-year colleges. Consequently, "percent in top half of class in high school" was used as the primary criterion to define selectivity, and an equivalent statement of admissions policy was used as a secondary criterion[1] wherever

1. Equivalent selectivity scores based upon admissions policy or percentage of freshmen in top half of high school class were determined empirically by plotting equi-percentile "scores" for a representative group of colleges for which both types of information were available.

class rank was not available. On this basis institutions were assigned a selectivity score from one to five as indicated in Table 3.

Neither this table nor the one preceding includes two types of colleges rated very selective. These are special purpose institutions and colleges with heavy religious emphasis. Heavily religious institutions include those that train religious personnel or have publicly stated restrictive policies regarding admissions or student behavior that are religious in character. For example, institutions that require students to attend chapel at least three times a week were classified as religious.

Specialized institutions are those which normally require some special talent or qualification (for example, musical ability, physical handicap) or have a curriculum restricted to one trade or discipline. Thus a photography school would be classed as specialized while an institute with varied technical curriculums would not. The essential question in adding these qualifications to the notion of selectivity is: how many students from the local high school would regard the institution as a likely place to continue their education? If the answer is "very few," then the institution is, in that sense, very selective. It should be mentioned that sex was treated as another form of special selectivity, but very few colleges were classed as selective for that reason alone.

What is a free-access college?

Accessibility of individual colleges was determined by joint consideration of tuition and selectivity. Since these two compensate for one another to only a minor extent (money not typically making up for poor high school grades in gaining admission to a specific college), a five-point accessibility scale was determined through a procedure referred to technically as multiple cutoff. This means simply that the college was automatically assigned an accessibility score equal to the higher of the two five-point scores — selectivity or tuition. Aside from the religious and special purpose institutions, selectivity or tuition data or both were not available from standard sources for about 7 percent of the colleges. In many cases these were new public institutions and reliable estimates could be based upon conditions typical of the parent system. In some 50 doubtful cases information was obtained by direct calls to the admissions office of the college.

Free-access colleges were defined as those institutions with accessibility scores of one or two. Roughly speaking, a free-access college admits at least one-third of its freshmen from the bottom half of their high school class and charges no more than $400 in annual tuition and fees. This definition is not restricted to free, open-door institutions, but is one notch above it. The college rated "two" may frequently reject students who graduated in the bottom quarter of their class.

It can now be said, with less confusion than would have ensued earlier, that the five-point scales for tuition and selectivity were determined in anticipation of defining a free-access college as described here. Thus in both cases the cut between a score of two and three was the primary reference point in establishing the scale. In the case of selectivity that point seems to best represent the level that includes all colleges that practice only mild forms of selection and are typically willing to make an effort to educate all but the most ill-prepared. In the case of tuition, $400 includes almost all community colleges and almost no private four-year institutions — seemingly a useful empirical dividing point between two divergent types of institutions.[2]

How proximity was defined

As previously outlined, proximity of institutions to people has special relevance to a societal model of access to higher education. It would be helpful to be able to turn to a body of data and writings that would clarify the role of proximity to accessibility, but little is available. Most of the attention given to location and proximity of colleges has been spurred by state master plans, but these have typically contributed more rules of thumb than substantive analysis. Many states carefully examine the educational and political implications of alternative locations, but such analysis usually applies to specific situations. Consequently, there is no concensus on the definition or significant aspects of proximity, much less useful information on how it affects students and their aspirations.

The practical need here is to find a method of identifying what populations are in proximity to a particular college. Such a method would make it possible to link demography to educational resources. Obviously, there are no pat answers or methods — it is a matter of reaching useful and reasonable working definitions of the limits of proximity that can be applied systematically to hundreds of colleges across the country. There are several approaches. One is to examine present patterns of commuting. Another is to seek evidence of the "pull" of an institution as proximity is decreased. Finally we can refer to judgments reached as a basis for the development of state systems, or judgments based upon assumptions concerning the future social role of higher education.

Recent survey data indicate that some 70 percent of junior college students live within 10 miles of their college (Comparative Guidance and Placement Program, 1968). Of course, these colleges exist in congested as well as sparsely settled communities, but other data show that 70 percent of junior college students are also within 30 minutes' commuting time of their institutions (Baird et al., 1969). In a study of an urban system, it was found that typically 60 percent of the students in Chicago City Junior College lived within 2½ miles of the college (Willis, 1958).

The work of Koos (1944b) is well known and often cited. His study of 65 com-

---

2. It can be argued that the tuition limit of a free-access college should vary with the per capita income of a state. In actual fact it doesn't make much difference because the principal effect of setting the tuition limit is to separate the public colleges, almost all of which charged less than $400 in 1968, from the private colleges, virtually all of which charged well above $400. For example, adjusting the tuition limit in the South and Midwest in accordance with per capita income does alter the percentage of the population covered by free-access colleges in the expected directions — but much less than 1 percent in each case.

munities showed that 44 percent of graduates from local high schools entered the local junior college, while the percentage dropped to 12 percent for those schools only 7–15 miles away. This was the classic study of the attractive pull, associated with the proximity of a college. This study has been extended by recent work in Chicago (Willis, 1964). Those results showed a dramatic drop in student residential density beyond a one-mile radius from the college; students within one mile were three times as likely to enroll as were students who lived 2½ miles distant.

The Chicago work on proximity over the past decade forms the basis for an important implication not always fully recognized. The attractive pull of a local college is effective in a much smaller radius than the area from which the college enrolls students. Often it seems that geographical guidelines of state planning groups reflect what is possible with respect to commuting distance, not the close proximity that is really likely to encourage students to attend.

Commuting guidelines for master plans vary from state to state. Illinois assumes 30 minutes and New York uses 60 minutes as reasonable commuting times. Some states apply a uniform mileage assumption regardless of the urbanization of the area (for example, Florida bases its estimates of state coverage on 30-mile radii around junior colleges).

These various lines of evidence would indicate using small radii if proximity is to mean that distance which is definitely associated with heightened student enrollment—or larger radii if proximity means the distance from which a student can make the trip given sufficient motivation. For the purposes of this study a compromise of 45 minutes' door-to-door commuting time was used.

Naturally, 45 minutes can be translated into widely varying distances, depending upon the specific location and type of community. Precise estimates of the number of people living within that commuting time of a college would require detailed study of housing and transportation patterns around hundreds of colleges. Since such an undertaking is neither practical nor sensible for a national survey of this sort, some rough approximations must suffice.

The most important determinant of feasible distance in a 45-minute period is

Table 4. Commuting distances assumed for areas of different populations

One-way commuting mileage	Type of area (population)
2½	Large central city, metropolitan area more than 1 million
5	Suburban area, metropolitan area more than 1 million
5	Metropolitan area, 500,000–1,000,000
10	Metropolitan area, 250,000–499,000
15	Metropolitan area, 50,000–249,000
20	Town, 10,000–49,000
25	Rural area and town, less than 10,000

congestion or population density. Furthermore, the Standard Metropolitan Statistical Areas of the Census Bureau are preferred for measuring density in populous areas since they are designed to reflect areas that are economically and socially integrated though politically separate. On the bases of all the foregoing considerations the commuting radii shown in Table 4 were used for the analyses of this study.[3] Naturally, interpretation of these data must take into account the fact that such a national yardstick cannot always reflect accurately the commuting reality of individual locations.

Procedure

What is a college?

In defining the accessibility of higher education, the troublesome first task is to decide what shall be included in higher education. Including only accredited institutions would omit many colleges that provide significant educational opportunity. Including everything that calls itself a college is also not reasonable. The U.S. Office of Education provides the most widely accepted compromise in its publication, *Opening Fall Enrollment* (OFE) (Chandler, 1968). It includes all institutions that are either accredited, approved by the state education agency, or have their credits accepted by three accredited institutions. The population of colleges included in OFE was used as the population for this study with two qualifications.

Since we are concerned here with access to higher education, all those 220-odd institutions without first-time freshman enrollment were omitted. The omitted institutions include some that are primarily identified as professional schools, but may have a few first-time students in some technician programs, e.g., medical schools.

A more complicated situation arises in the case of branch institutions. In recent years a number of branches have been listed separately in OFE.[4] A branch is typically listed in OFE when it offers at least two years of study in full curriculums (rather than assorted courses) and has an administrative structure at least comparable to that of a small college. It is particularly appropriate that such branches be included for the purpose of this study, since they serve as alternate locations for students and thereby affect the accessibility of a system. A complication arises because of the fact that some such branches are not listed separately in OFE, while others are listed one year and not the next.

This state of affairs results from the inconsistent action of the parent institutions in exercising their prerogative to list or not list a branch. Consequently an

---

3. As an exception to Table 4, five-mile radii were used in the central cities of Anaheim, Miami, and San Bernardino because these cities are not densely populated enough to justify a distinction between city and fringe.

4. In this study a branch is an institution listed in OFE under a parent institution. Institutions listed as equal-rank components of a system were treated as independent colleges. For this reason some states such as Indiana and New Mexico may appear to be short of branches in the data reported here.

extensive search was made of standard directories to identify all branches of junior or senior institutions that would qualify on the criteria mentioned above. As a result 60 additional branches were treated as separate institutions. In practically all cases located, the existence of such branches was recognized in OFE by an "all campuses" listing. Thus the data in this report are based upon 2,596 colleges — all the recognized undergraduate institutions in the 50 states and the District of Columbia that admit undergraduates.

Identifying the free-access colleges

Rating the accessibility of 2,596 colleges and identifying the free-access colleges among them entailed locating the necessary tuition and selectivity information for fall 1968 and applying the guidelines discussed earlier. A problem results from the fact that no published source includes either type of information for more than half of those 2,596 colleges. Also, different sources sometimes disagree — often because the data change from year to year.

Several sources were used to locate both tuition and selectivity data.[5] Conflicting information was resolved by referring to additional sources. Nonetheless it seems highly likely that information on a few colleges is out of date. Primary emphasis was placed upon determining whether a college was at or above the accessibility level (one and two) defining "free-access" colleges. The free-access colleges so identified were then located on maps of the individual states.

Plotting the colleges

Each free-access college was located on a state or urban tract map at its most recent address, available from the U.S. Office of Education. Those located in metropolitan areas of 500,000 or more people were placed at exact street addresses. The central city of such a metropolitan area would typically have a population of about 250,000. The commuting distance of smaller cities is large enough to make small errors of location unimportant, so in these cases colleges were arbitrarily located in the center of the city.

Circles of the prescribed radii were drawn around each college as an indication of the commuting area. Two types of adjustments were made in these commuting areas. They were not extended across state boundaries on the supposition that such colleges are not typically accessible to out-of-state students — either because of higher tuition or a natural institutional preference for state residents.

A second type of adjustment was necessary when the commuting area of a

---

5. Sources of tuition information were used in the following order: *Junior College Directory* (AAJC, 1968), *College Costs* (Life Insurance Agency Management Association, 1968), *Student Expense Budgets of American Colleges and Universities for the 1968–69 Academic Year* (Warga, 1968), *Lovejoy's College Guide* (Lovejoy, 1968), *Colleges and Universities* (Singletary, 1968), *The College Blue Book* (Burckel, 1968).

Information concerning selectivity was obtained from sources in the following order: *Colleges and Universities* (Singletary, 1968), *Comparative Guide to American Colleges* (Cass and Birnbaum, 1968), *American Junior Colleges* (Gleazer, 1967), *Barron's Guide to Two-Year Colleges* (Eskow, 1967), *The New American Guide to Colleges* (Hawes, 1966), *The College Blue Book* (Burckel, 1968).

college extended into a geographical area with a different population density and consequently a different prescribed commuting radius. In such instances that portion of the arc in the area of different density was altered proportionally in order to approximate a reasonable commuting area.

Estimating population coverage

The populations covered by free-access colleges in each state were estimated by political subdivisions—typically counties, but also census tracts or occasionally congressional districts in all those metropolitan areas larger than 1 million. In counties, estimates of the number of people within commuting areas were obtained mainly by examining the population of individual small towns that lay inside or outside commuting arcs.[6] In the case of census tracts, and for congressional districts that were used for Philadelphia, Detroit, and New York only, it was typically a question of whether the area was within a commuting arc or not.

This procedure produced estimates of the proportion of the population in proximity to a free-access college for every county in the country, plus much more detailed subdivisions for the 29 major metropolitan areas. In turn, these proportions were applied to racial groups within those subdivisions and the subdivisions were grouped according to type of community and geographical location. It is these summary estimates by state, city, race, and so forth, that provide the primary data of this report.

Several additional analyses were undertaken in order to elaborate the interpretation of the data. For example, the number of additional colleges that would be required to increase the proportion of the population covered to 50, 60, 70 percent, and so forth, was estimated for each state. Also, several rough approximations were made in order to examine the effects of changing the working definitions adopted here. These various estimates were carried out along similar lines to the procedures already described. In general, however, these secondary analyses produced approximations that were less precise than the primary estimates.

There are several qualifications to these procedures that should be recognized. Perhaps the most important is the point already made in Chapter 1. Because higher education is accessible does not mean that it is relevant, of good quality, or utilized. It is also important to recognize that systematic discrimination distorts any estimate of accessibility, and there appears to be no completely satisfactory way to adjust for this form of selectivity.

Finally, the reader should realize that estimates given here are in no case precise and may, in limited geographical areas, be quite unreliable. An effort has been made in the state profiles of Chapter 5 to note instances where slight changes in definition would cause substantial changes in estimates. Those data

---

6. Estimates were based upon 1960 census data. Although it would have been preferable to have more recent information, changes in population patterns over this period seem, with few exceptions, to be a trivial source of variation in accessibility estimates.

are based upon the most recent available information that may in some instances fail to correspond with a more intimate understanding of local conditions in the fall of 1968. In sum, the data are as accurate as available information and reasonable care can make them, but for those with special responsibility for local educational planning these estimates should serve mainly to provide some national benchmarks and to encourage further study.

3. How accessible are American colleges?

The previous chapter defined five levels of accessibility of higher education on the basis of cost and admissions standards. The two lowest levels were designated "free-access." Having applied these definitions to some 2,600 recognized colleges and universities in the country, we now turn to the question of how many and what sort of institutions there are at different levels of accessibility. How does the accessibility of colleges vary among types of institutions and geographical areas? The answers contain a few surprises, but they also reflect the educational philosophies and territorial styles that have determined the character and development of higher institutions across the country.

Levels of accessibility

Since colleges were assigned to the five levels of accessibility on the basis of cost or selectivity—whichever was higher—the institutions at a given level cover a range of admissions standards and college costs. Obviously, colleges within levels also vary greatly in other ways. Despite these qualifications, the specified sorting process does generate five groups of institutions with characteristic differences.

Level 1. This level is appropriately regarded as purposefully open door. Tuition is free or quite low; all high school graduates are accepted for admission. Public two-year colleges constitute 90 percent of this group of some 280 institutions. They have increased rapidly in the past decade, particularly in the West where almost half of the colleges at level *1* are located. Nationally about 1 out of 5 first-time freshmen enter an institution at this level. The open-door junior college might be erroneously regarded as a small institution because it has only two classes, but the average entering class is largest at this level of accessibility by a considerable margin (1,400 versus 900 at level 2). These numbers reflect the fact that a strong open-door philosophy in such states as California and Florida is frequently associated with rapid expansion of facilities at individual community colleges.

Level 2. There are about 500 colleges at the almost-open-door level. We are speaking here of institutions that accept most high school graduates. What little selecting they practice is usually directed to screening students in the bottom quarter of the high school class—often because of lack of space rather than a specific policy of selective admissions. Tuition is still within reach of most students not clearly in a poverty condition. This level of accessibility is still dominated primarily by the public two-year college, though there is a substantial number of four-year public institutions included. There are practically no private colleges at level 2 and surprisingly few public branches. About 25 percent of all first-time freshmen enter one of the colleges at this almost-open-door level.

Level 3. This is the lowest level to which a substantial number of high school graduates may experience difficulty in gaining access. If the scholastic requirement (top half of class) is not a barrier, then the higher tuition ($401 to $800) may be. Of roughly 400 institutions at this level, the most typical is the public four-year institution or one of its branches. A few public junior colleges have strayed to this level of inaccessibility, and this is the first level at which private colleges appear in noticeable quantity (118). It is an oversimplification to speak of this group as erstwhile free-access colleges; but of the colleges at level 3 that existed in the 1950s, many were less costly and less selective then. From another standpoint this level corresponds to an earlier social definition of opportunity for higher education: comprehensive, regionally located institutions designed to train and serve the well-motivated middle class.

Level 4. This level is dominated by private colleges — partly because many undergraduate special-purpose and heavily religious colleges were assigned here, but also because there just are a great many fairly costly ($800 to $1,600) or selective private institutions. Most private colleges are small, so the average first-time enrollment at this level is quite low. Even though this group includes more than 1,000 colleges, they enroll only some 20 percent of all new students. The 1 college out of 10 at this level that is not private is typically a selective, public four-year institution.

Level 5. The country's major universities, both public and private, and the elite private liberal arts colleges make up the bulk of this group at the highest level of accessibility. There are quite a few of these institutions (some 400) considering that they are either highly selective or charge more than $1,600 a year — frequently both. Roughly 4 out of 5 are private, but public institutions enroll about the same total number of new students as private ones. Most of these are prestige institutions; they range from the largest to the smallest in the nation and collectively enroll about one-sixth of all new freshmen.

Free-access colleges

Free-access colleges were defined earlier as those institutions at the first and

Table 5. Colleges disqualified as free-access for various reasons

Type of inaccessibility	Percent of total group		Total number of colleges
	Public	Private	
Special purpose	0.4%	3.6%	104
Religious emphasis	0.0	15.2	395
Costly — not selective	1.9	10.1	312
Selective — not costly	13.1	0.6	356
Costly and selective	2.2	22.1	632
Non-coed (not already excluded)	0.1	0.2	8
Free-access	**29.7**	**0.7**	**789**
Total	47.5%	52.5%	2,596*

* Does not include some 220 independent post-baccalaureate institutions.

second levels of accessibility. Furthermore, in defining accessibility, special attention was given to the distinction between levels 2 and 3 because most of the analysis reported in subsequent chapters is based upon the location of free-access colleges. Consequently, the winnowing process whereby one sets aside various groups of inaccessible colleges, finally ending with the free-access group, is of particular interest.

There is no simple means of enumerating the different categories of inaccessible colleges because many are inaccessible for more than one reason. Table 5 provides a reasonably useful and uncomplicated compromise. From the total of 2,596 colleges in the country, the table shows first the removal of some 100 special-purpose institutions and an additional 400 or so that incorporate a heavy religious emphasis. Both groups are almost exclusively private and are, therefore, typically expensive as well.

Some 1,300 colleges are inaccessible because they are either too costly, or too selective, or both. The two factors — cost and selectivity — make roughly equal contributions as barriers to higher education purely from the standpoint of admissions practices. It is not surprising that practically all private colleges are costly — as the term is used here; it is less expected that some 4 out of 5 are also selective on some other grounds. Roughly 1 percent qualify as free-access institutions. Naturally, there are large numbers of students in college who wouldn't be there were it not for private higher education, but the free-access institutional function defined for this analysis is almost exclusively a public phenomenon. In the public sector about 3 out of 5 are free-access colleges, and very few are disqualified because of high tuition.

Variations by type of institution

Tables 6 and 7 give additional information concerning the relationship between level of accessibility and type of institution. There are four main observations to make about these data.

1. The vast majority of the public two-year colleges are free-access, and they represent a substantial number of institutions. In 1968 these institutions enrolled almost 40 percent of all new students in higher education.

2. There are fewer public four-year colleges than public junior colleges, and only 3 in 10 of the four-year institutions are free-access. Those that are free-access are not particularly large, so the total group enrolls only about 10 percent of all matriculating freshmen. Another 25+ percent of freshmen matriculate in public four-year colleges that are not free-access.

3. The branches of public four-year institutions are neither very numerous nor very large. Consequently, they enroll a relatively small proportion of new freshmen. Their primary interest here is the comparison they afford with the community college. These data provide clear evidence that, on the whole, branches are no more accessible than their parent institutions and considerably less so than public junior colleges. Roughly 3 out of 10 public senior institutions are free-access; the same ratio holds for their branches. As we shall see later, most of

Table 6. Number of various types of institutions at each accessibility level*

	Number at each accessibility level					Total colleges
	1	2	3	4	5	
Public two-year	262	332	34	13	1	642
Public four-year	8	127	134	90	74	433
Branches	10	33	104	7	5	159
All private	2	15	117	914	314	1,362
Total	282	507	389	1,024	394	2,596

* Includes 50 states and District of Columbia.

Table 7. Total first-time enrollment in various types of institutions at different levels of accessibility (in thousands)

	Level of accessibility					Total
	1	2	3	4	5	
Public two-year	375	308	34	7	2	728
Public four-year	7	148	216	138	146	655
Branches	6	9	34	2	1	50
All private	1	5	34	254	155	449
Total	389	470	318	401	304	1,882

the branches that are free-access fall in an unusual category.

4. The private sector includes a large number of colleges, although those colleges enroll considerably fewer first-time students than do the two-year or four-year public counterparts. The vast majority of students enter private colleges at the two most inaccessible levels.

Regional variations in accessibility[1]

In considering geographic variations in the accessibility of higher education across the country, one immediately prominent fact is discovered: the regional differences are striking. There is an orderly trend of few free-access colleges in the Northeast, a somewhat larger proportion in the Midwest, and the largest number in the West. As Table 8 indicates, this pattern is even more pronounced when one bases the comparison on the percentage of new freshmen who are enrolled in a free-access college in a particular region. That comparison runs: Northeast 22 percent, Midwest 34, South 50, and West 71.

The West is far ahead of other regions with respect to the number of free-access institutions and the proportion of all entering students enrolled in them. But this is well known and need not be lingered over. The special problems of

---

1. In this study the four regions of the United States as defined by the Census Bureau are used. The states included in each region are listed in Table A of Chapter 5.

the Northeast are no secret either, but the data underscore how difficult the situation actually is. While there is an abundance of colleges in the Northeast, access is limited in 6 institutions out of 7. There are very few completely open-door colleges in this region, and 6 matriculating students out of 10 enter relatively inaccessible colleges (levels *4* and *5*). By comparison, only 3 matriculating students out of 10 enter correspondingly inaccessible colleges in the rest of the country. These conditions feed the time-honored admissions panic in the Northeast each year — a seasonal event not fully appreciated by families in other sections of the country.

There are suggestions that higher education in the Midwest is becoming less accessible than it has been in the past. Traditionally the land of nonselective state institutions, the Midwest appears in Table 8 much more like the Northeast than does either the South or the West. The situation is further clarified in Table 9, which shows that relatively few four-year public institutions in the Midwest and practically none of their branches are free-access. For many observers this state of affairs will be not so much a surprise as a suspicion confirmed. The South

Table 8. Percentage of colleges and percentage of first-time enrollment (in parentheses) at each level of accessibility within each region

Region	Level of accessibility				
	1	*2*	*3*	*4*	*5*
Northeast	1	12	13	46	27
	(1)	(21)	(17)	(31)	(31)
Midwest	8	18	17	45	11
	(11)	(23)	(23)	(28)	(15)
South	11	27	19	34	9
	(14)	(36)	(21)	(19)	(10)
West	31	18	7	29	15
	(54)	(17)	(9)	(8)	(12)
Entire U.S.	11	19	15	39	15
	(21)	(24)	(18)	(21)	(16)

Table 9. Percentage of different types of institutions that are free-access within each region

	Northeast	*Midwest*	*South*	*West*	*Entire U.S.*
Public two-year	83	90	95	98	90
Public four-year	7	26	46	31	31
Branches	0	3	54	88	30
All private	0	0	3	2	1
All types of colleges	14	26	38	49	30

is now the principal home of the free-access state college. By region they number: Northwest 6, Midwest 29, South 77, and West 24.

Table 9 also clarifies the problem in the Northeast. The majority of the limited number of public two-year colleges in that region have maintained a free-access status (many are new), but the public senior institutions and their branches have been under severe pressure because of the general lack of college space in the Northeast. As a result, practically none are free-access, and in that sense they are almost comparable to the private institutions of the region.

This state of affairs makes an interesting comparison with California, where it is also true that practically none of the public four-year institutions are free-access. The more important fact is that almost three times as many students are enrolled in free-access colleges in California as in the entire northeastern quarter of the country. The access insurance provided by the California junior college no doubt ameliorates the public anxiety over college admissions so common in the Northeast, despite the fact that public senior institutions are relatively inaccessible in both areas.

Variations by type of community

The population of individual communities provides quite a different perspective of geographic variation in the location of free-access colleges. Table 10 indicates a progressive increase in the likelihood that a college will be free-access as one moves from highly populated to less populated areas. Doubtless there are numerous reasons for this trend including a political structure that fosters more colleges in smaller communities and less admissions pressure in those communities to induce selective admissions.

The suburbs of major metropolitan areas, where about 3 colleges in 10 are free-access, constitute a slight exaggeration of the general trend and provide an interesting contrast to the central city. Suburban colleges are almost twice as likely to be free-access despite the pressing social problems in the central cities and the fact that urban populations are less likely to be educationally mobile. To what extent this represents a real imbalance between educational resources and

**Table 10. Percentage of colleges that are
free-access in different types of communities**

Type of community	Percent free-access	Percent not free-access	Total number of colleges
Metropolitan areas of 1,000,000+			
Central city	15%	85%	402
Fringe	29	71	337
Metropolitan areas of 500,000 to 1,000,000	20	80	259
Metropolitan areas of 50,000 to 500,000	30	70	507
Other counties*	39	61	1,091

* Not in Standard Metropolitan Statistical Areas.

social need can be determined more accurately in subsequent chapters that deal directly with the demography of free-access colleges. But on an absolute basis, there is no question concerning the inaccessibility of higher education in most major cities. There are six metropolitan areas in the country with populations larger than 1 million which have no free-access institution in their central city.

4. Colleges and people

This report is principally concerned with the implication that universal and equal opportunity must be based first upon readily accessible higher education and must therefore include the idea of proximity. The previous chapter described the accessibility of higher institutions by type and geographic location. Through a winnowing process 789 low-cost and relatively nonselective institutions were defined as "free-access" colleges. In this chapter we put colleges and people together and describe what proportions of what populations live within commuting distance of a free-access college. We are concerned here with national data organized to reveal community, racial, and regional variations. Chapter 5 deals with state variations. The map of the United States found in the back of this book gives the overall picture of free-access colleges.

When the 789 free-access colleges are plotted throughout the country, it turns out that slightly more than two-fifths of the population live within commuting distance of them. In a sense it is remarkable that the country has developed accessible higher education facilities to this extent. On the other hand it is sobering to realize that the educational opportunity of three-fifths of the population is inhibited by the simple fact that they do not live near an accessible college. This ratio is one of the less complicated indices of how far the country has to go in equalizing educational opportunity.

It should be clear that the absolute level of this and other estimates reported here are fallible in the sense that different definitions of accessibility yield different estimates of population "covered" by (within commuting distance of) a free-access college. For example, if the tuition limit for free-access colleges were $600 rather than $400, the national proportion of the population covered would be 46 percent instead of 42 percent; if free-access were redefined to include moderately selective in addition to open-door and slightly selective institutions, the national estimate of population covered would go from 42 to 49 percent.

The primary value of these estimates lies in the fact that they are more or less comparable from one area to another. They provide a set of benchmarks and general impressions that can be useful to educational planners when they consider priorities and objectives. The following paragraphs describe a variety of national imbalances—illustrated here and there with local examples.

Inequities among communities

There are characteristic differences in the proportion of people living near free-access colleges in different types of communities. As Table 11 shows, a small metropolitan area is the most favorable location for a poor, marginal student to find accessible higher education. Moving from sparsely to heavily populated areas, the proportion of people having ready access to college first increases—24 percent in rural areas to 63 percent in small metropolitan areas—and then decreases to 38 percent in the major cities.

Even though it may be unfair, it is nonetheless largely unavoidable that students in sparsely populated areas are less likely to live near an accessible college. On the other hand the orderly differences in accessibility among different sized metropolitan areas make little sense. It is true that the more populous metropolitan areas are more likely to have free-access colleges—half of the small metropolitan areas have an accessible college, whereas 4 out of 5 of the largest do. But the number of accessible colleges doesn't compensate for the large numbers of people in the more populous areas. Metropolitan areas of one-half million or more are frequently short-changed when it comes to accessible higher education.

From the traditional pattern of the city as the seat of learning, one might assume that college is more available in the central city than in the urban fringe of the major metropolitan areas. Across the nation this is evidently not true. Considering that median family income is about one-quarter higher in the fringe than in the city (U.S. Bureau of the Census, 1969), it can be argued that there should be more free-access colleges in the heart of the metropolitan area. Equally important, however, are the marked variations that occur among the major cities with reference to the scarcity of accessible higher education.

Of the 29 metropolitan areas that have a population of more than 1 million, Atlanta, Boston, Buffalo, Cincinnati, Detroit, and Paterson-Clifton-Passaic do not have one free-access college located within their city limits. In eight additional metropolitan areas, less than one-third of the central city population lives within commuting distance of a free-access college. In another nine metropolitan

Table 11. Percentage of different populations within commuting distance of a free-access college in the 50 states

Area	Total population (millions)	Percent within commuting distance			
		White	Black	Mexican-American	Entire U.S.
Metropolitan areas (SMSA): *					
1,000,000 +					
Central cities	32.6	36%	42%	42%	38%
Fringes	33.2	37	31	68	37
500,000 to 1,000,000	20.0	36	46	66	38
250,000 to 500,000	16.0	47	61	37	48
50,000 to 250,000	16.2	62	70	56	63
Counties not in SMSA:					
Over 20,000	45.0	48	52	42	48
Under 20,000	16.2	24	27	13	24
Entire U.S.	179.3 (million)	42%	47%	47%†	42%

* Standard Metropolitan Statistical Areas.
† Mexican Americans in five Southwestern states; also includes Puerto Ricans in New York City and Chicago.

areas, less than a third of the fringe population is covered. Since any one of these conditions must be regarded as a serious urban problem, it is reasonable to conclude that 23 of the 29 largest cities of the country have a major deficiency in the accessibility of higher education. Equally disturbing is the number of metropolitan areas that have no free-access college at all (as of 1968). The Census Bureau defined 228 Standard Metropolitan Statistical Areas, most of which had a population of 100,000 or greater. In 102 metropolitan areas the principal city had no free-access colleges.

Racial imbalances

Across the country a slightly larger proportion (47 percent) of blacks live within commuting distance of a free-access college than whites. At first thought this seems inconsistent with the fact that rural areas and large central cities are less likely to have accessible colleges, and these areas are where most blacks are generally presumed to live. In actual fact, blacks are almost proportionally present in communities of all sizes with an important exception—there are more blacks in the central core and fewer in the outer fringe of the largest cities. As Table 11 indicates, blacks are somewhat more likely than whites to live near a free-access college in all types of communities except the fringes of the largest cities (where they are least numerous).

Mexican Americans (in the five Southwestern states) and Puerto Ricans (in New York City and Chicago) are also somewhat more likely to live near an accessible college than are whites. This was a fairly consistent finding in the various areas where demographic data for these groups were examined.

While it is also true that the overall analysis indicated no marked regional variations in the percentage of blacks living near free-access colleges, there are obviously some very important exceptions and qualifications. First, there are states and metropolitan areas where these generalizations do not hold. In California, Maryland, Massachusetts, Nebraska, and New York, substantially fewer blacks than whites live near accessible institutions. The same is true of Atlanta, Boston, Buffalo, and Los Angeles. On the other hand, there are states and metropolitan areas where blacks are much more likely than whites to live within commuting distance of a free-access college. The best statewide examples are Missouri, New Jersey, and Pennsylvania; a similar trend exists in Kansas City, Milwaukee, and Newark. Data on all states and Standard Metropolitan Statistical Areas with more than 1 million people are given in Tables A and B in Chapter 5.

Another general exception to the data on minority groups cited in Table 11 is the problem of discrimination. Of course, discrimination is another form of selectivity that can make an institution inaccessible just as surely as cost or academic requirements can. It would have been useful to include discrimination in this analysis as a form of selectivity were it not for the impossible task of deciding which colleges discriminate against which students to what extent. Through much of the country one must simply introduce a subjective "correction" for the obvious fact that much of higher education is, for many reasons, less accessible to blacks and other sociocultural minorities than to middle-class whites. The situation in the Deep South, however, is even more complicated by a long tradition of formally segregated institutions including many that serve blacks almost exclusively.

Since the predominantly Negro colleges of the South cannot be construed as free-access for whites, it is possible and necessary to partially correct the estimates of white populations covered by accessible institutions in the Southern states. This can be done simply by excluding the predominantly Negro free-access institutions and repeating the individual state estimates. The results are shown in Table 12. Alabama, Arkansas, and Mississippi are the only states where the difference is very noticeable. This is because relatively few colleges are involved in most states. Among all recognized colleges that are more than 85 percent black (*Chronicle,* 1969a) or listed by McGrath (1965) as predominantly Negro, only 1 in 5 can be classified here as free-access. Excluding the Negro institutions reduces the percentage of whites covered in the South from 50 percent to 47 percent.

Table 12 clearly underestimates the effect of segregation upon accessibility in the South because it does not reflect the limited access of blacks. It seems doubtful that it is possible to make realistic and defensible estimates of the pro-

Table 12. Percentage of whites within commuting distance of a free-access college in the Southern census region

		Percent of whites within commuting distance	
State	Number of free-access Negro colleges	All free-access colleges	Excluding Negro free-access colleges
Alabama	5	57%	48%
Arkansas	2	43	30
Delaware	0	21	21
Florida	1	62	62
Georgia	0	33	33
Kentucky	0	51	51
Louisiana	0	49	49
Maryland	2	59	55
Mississippi	5	67	57
North Carolina	2	69	66
Oklahoma	0	31	31
South Carolina	1	58	58
Tennessee	2	39	35
Texas	2	37	36
Virginia	0	52	52
West Virginia	0	53	53
Entire South	22	50%	47%

portion of blacks living within commuting distance of an accessible institution in some of the Southern states. It is clear from available statistics that blacks do not have ready access to many public higher institutions (Egerton, 1969). On the other hand the predominantly white free-access colleges do serve substantial numbers of blacks — obviously estimates for blacks could not be based upon the Negro colleges alone. It would appear that the only safe working assumption is that the various estimates for minority populations are generally inflated and, in some states, substantially so.

The regions vary

The accessibility of higher education varies markedly among the four main census regions of the country but not always in expected ways. The Northeast, for example, has never been a region known for accessible colleges. Private education has been dominant to such an extent that some states — particularly New York and more recently Pennsylvania — have purposefully allocated substantial student aid resources in order to use the private sector for public purposes. Furthermore, the Northeast has been slow to develop the egalitarian interpretations of higher education represented by the community college and comprehensive postsecondary educational opportunity.

Despite these facts the Northeast is only slightly below the national average with respect to the proportion of people living within commuting distance of a free-access college. As Table 13 indicates, this region falls behind the South and West only in metropolitan areas of one-half million or more people. However, such areas contain two-thirds of the population in the Northeast. In addition to its urban problem, the Northeast has frequently not developed and supported its free-access institutions. As we shall see in the state-by-state analyses in Chapter 5, public higher education in the Northeast often receives niggardly appro-

Table 13. Percentage of the population within commuting distance of a free-access college in different types of communities for each region

Area	Northeast	Midwest	South	West
Metropolitan areas (SMSA):				
1,000,000+				
Central cities	29	44	38	44
Fringes	27	30	38	62
500,000 to 1,000,000	38	12	53	55
250,000 to 500,000	49	39	53	48
50,000 to 250,000	71	47	71	61
Counties not in SMSA:				
Over 20,000	51	35	55	50
Under 20,000	24	23	28	17
Overall percentage for each region	38	33	50	51

priations and enrolls very small proportions of some states' high school graduates.

The Midwest is the surprise of the four regions. Traditionally it has assumed a view of higher education in contrast to that of the Northeast. Its state institutions, long a source of national pride, have been identified historically with inexpensive, nonselective admissions. The data of Table 13 seem inconsistent with this tradition. The proportion of people living near an accessible college is substantially lower in the Midwest than in other regions. It is lower in every type of community except the largest and the smallest. In overall coverage, two Midwestern states are well above the national average while six are considerably below it (see Table A in Chapter 5).

The coverage of free-access colleges in Midwestern cities of one-half to one million people is extremely low, although the largest cities hold their own with cities of other regions. The principal reason the largest cities appear better off than the Midwest generally is the existence of the community college systems of Chicago and St. Louis. These systems serve a great many people and seem attributable to unusual leadership—but they are not typical of the region. Of all moderately large metropolitan areas in the country without any free-access colleges, more than half are in the Midwest. Thus, there seem to be special (and outstanding) exceptions to the general finding that the Midwestern region provides accessible higher education to a smaller proportion of the population than the rest of the country. Of course, local conditions vary and most states have peculiar characteristics that make any generalization conditional.

It should be recognized further that many state universities have nonselective colleges or divisions. Also, a number of public institutions are officially open door but de facto selective. That is, they enroll most of their students from the top half of the high school class. Both of these circumstances may be more common in the Midwest than in other regions. Such institutions are not classified here as free-access because the definition depends not upon whether *some* less apt students are admitted, but whether the total institution is likely to be regarded by perspective students as truly accessible. The best generally available measure of that accessibility would seem to be the proportion of high school graduates in the bottom half of their class who are enrolled.

The situation in the South is interesting for several reasons. Despite very limited resources and a decentralized population, the region has managed to place free-access colleges within almost as large a proportion of its people as is true in the wealthier and more centralized West. This accomplishment has come about through the use of widely different models; the comprehensive junior colleges of Florida, the technical education centers of South Carolina, the open-door senior institutions of Louisiana, and the university two-year system of Kentucky are good examples of the diversity described in the state profiles in the next chapter.

Concerning the accessibility of higher education, the Southern region has two large problems—too well known to belabor and too critical to dismiss. Racial segregation of institutions will necessarily hinder educational opportunity as long as it drains attention and resources from the development of relevant educational opportunity for high school graduates. And it is the limited resources and opportunities that constitute a second difficult problem. In spite of considerable progress in making higher education available to their youth, some Southern states still have a very low rate of college attendance.

Roughly half of the population in the Western United States lives near an accessible institution. This proportion is somehow lower than one might have expected, considering that 1 Westerner out of 2 lives in California, the state that is known for accessible higher education. The proportions indicated for different types of communities in Table 13 are not unusual except in the case of central cities versus the fringes of major metropolitan areas in the West.

In a region usually associated with statewide planning of higher education facilities, it is ironic to find that suburban areas are better provided with free-access colleges than are the central cities. This result is largely attributable to imbalances that exist in the three major metropolitan areas of California — Los Angeles, San Francisco, and San Diego. In each, residents of the fringe areas are much more likely to live near a free-access college than are residents of the central city. This condition — not typical of the country — may relate to the tendency in California to locate junior colleges where fairly large tracts of land are available. Of course, one can argue that the commuting radii should be larger in these cities because of the emphasis upon personal transportation on expressways, but it seems doubtful that this consideration changes the general result described.

Who is not served?

A complementary way of looking at the accessibility of higher education is to examine who is *not* served. There are two main questions: What kinds of people do not live near an accessible institution? And what sort of locations are not covered? It is these interpretations of the data that lead most easily to implications concerning the need for new institutions or new arrangements. Data based upon individual states are the most useful for practical purposes, and these appear in the state profiles in the following chapter. Summary information does provide an overview, however, that affords a better national perspective.

Table 14 summarizes the nature of the total population that does not live near a free-access college. The largest group is easily the whites living in the large metropolitan areas of the Northeast. Other very large groups of people not having ready access to higher education are whites in the nonmetropolitan areas of the South and whites in each of the three demographic divisions of the Midwest. All other categories of whites plus blacks in the rural South account for smaller but still substantial numbers of people not living in proximity to accessible colleges.

With respect to location, there are several states that are far below the norm in the availability of accessible colleges. For example, there are 14 states in which less than one-third of the population is covered. Preceding paragraphs contain several references to the numerous urban areas that are either deficient or lacking in free-access colleges. This circumstance has an important bearing upon the strategy of improving accessibility — first, because accessibility is deficient in urban areas generally, and also because the congested areas are where additional colleges can most efficiently cover large numbers of people.

Location of the new colleges

Unfortunately, there is little sign that recent emphasis upon expanding educational opportunity has had much effect upon the overall efficiency of college location. In the fall of 1968 a large number of new free-access colleges opened (76 in fact). These colleges increased the proportion of the nation's population living near such a college from 38 to 42 percent. On the average each of these new colleges serves some 100,000 people. This is essentially the same average number of people living within commuting distance of those free-access colleges in existence prior to 1968.

As a matter of theoretical interest, these new colleges were plotted in 76 hypothetical locations throughout the country where they could cover the maximum number of people. The results were not surprising; those 76 colleges in ideal locations could have covered an average of 300,000 people and raised the national proportion so covered by 14 percent instead of the 4 percent increase that actually resulted. Putting it another way, 28 states added one or more free-access colleges in 1968; in only 8 of those states was any college opened in the general location where it could serve the largest number of people.

Naturally, the location of a college is determined by a number of factors, many of which may be quite valid and have little to do with accessibility. The data do

Table 14. Number of whites and minorities not living within commuting distance of a free-access college in different communities in each region (in millions)

	Northeast	Midwest	South	West	Total for U.S.
Whites:					
Large metropolitan areas	15.3	10.4	4.6	5.4	35.7
Medium-sized metropolitan areas	5.7	9.0	6.1	3.2	24.0
Other counties	4.4	12.8	10.7	3.8	31.7
Minorities:＊					
Large metropolitan areas	2.2	1.5	1.2	0.8	5.6
Medium-sized metropolitan areas	0.1	0.6	1.6	0.3	2.7
Other counties†	—	0.2	3.4	0.3	4.0
Total for U.S.	27.7	34.5	27.6	13.8	103.7

＊Blacks, Mexican Americans, and Puerto Ricans.
† That is, counties not in Standard Metropolitan Statistical Areas.

illustrate, however, that estimates of the number of colleges that might be required to achieve various goals with respect to educational opportunity are subject to considerable uncertainty. Furthermore, the various forces that determine college location are not likely to result in new institutions always being placed in convenient juxtaposition to populations they might serve.

How many colleges are needed?

The preceding comments provide a useful introduction to Table 15, which estimates the resources required to increase the proportion of the population within commuting distance of a free-access college. Entries in this table show the present number of free-access colleges in each region and the number of colleges (new or redefined) that would be required to increase the percentage of the population covered to various levels in all states in the region; that is, 16 additional colleges would increase the percentage to 50 percent for each state in the West. A systematic qualification is the assumption that no state would add a college that did not cover at least 25,000 people within its commuting area.

The data in Table 15 were developed by plotting hypothetical new free-access colleges in optimal locations in each of the 50 states and estimating the populations that would be covered. It is evident that accessibility could be greatly improved in the Northeast with a limited number of colleges. It could also be improved greatly in the West, but the gross population involved there is much smaller. The South and Midwest have a large and widely distributed population. A high degree of coverage in these regions would require more than twice as many additional colleges as in the West or Northeast.

Roughly speaking, this analysis indicates that some 375 additional colleges in optimal locations would put two-thirds of the population of most states near an accessible institution. Considering that locations cannot be expected to be optimal, it would appear from recent experience cited above that the 550 new colleges recommended by the Carnegie Commission would have the approximate effect of raising the national proportion of population covered from 4 in 10

**Table 15. Estimate of additional colleges
required to put specified percentages of the population within
commuting distance of a free-access college**

Region	Present free-access colleges	Additional free-access colleges required to cover: *				
		50%	60%	70%	80%	90%
Northeast	92	20	14	21	32	56
Midwest	193	56	41	43	80	138
South	312	20	33	65	103	153
West	192	16	13	45	37	63
National total	789	112	101	174	252	410

* These figures refer to additional colleges required and should be added to find the total required at any percentage level.

to 7 in 10. It should be emphasized, however, that this rough estimate assumes that the 550 colleges would be opened immediately. In the 5 to 10 years that might be required to develop that many institutions, the accessibility of existing colleges would likely erode to an unknown extent due to urbanization, increasing costs, and increasing selectivity.[1]

In some areas it may be quite unrealistic to consider a new college as the only or even the preferred answer to a lack of accessible higher education. For political or financial reasons, it may be more reasonable to change the admissions characteristics and fees of an existing college. It should be recognized, however, that some senior institutions have little interest in serving the free-access function and will do so only under considerable pressure—and even then perhaps halfheartedly. In any event the foregoing discussion assumes that state planning groups will consider local conditions and weigh the advantages of new institutions versus alterations in existing ones in future development of free-access higher education.

---

1. A systematic study of the status of free-access higher education in 1958 and the underlying changes that have occurred during the past decade is being undertaken by Richard Ferrin of the College Board's Access Research Office.

5. State profiles

The summary data of the previous two chapters are instructive and useful as a frame of reference for considering college location, but most of the action is at the state level. States have had the formal responsibility for providing education, and there is every reason to assume that extensions of that responsibility in the form of equal opportunity for higher education will also be organized at the state level. Coordinating groups in many states have given close attention to college location, though needs and alternatives have typically been interpreted in a local context where politics have a heavy bearing.

It is in the analysis of individual state situations that one senses the considerable variety of resources, circumstances, and organization. This variety not only facilitates better understanding of the national scene but clarifies the problems and programmatic possibilities at the level where change actually occurs. One function of the state profiles, then, is to describe accessibility as it exists across the country. Another is to sense the different models of organization and restraints on accessibility that programs to expand opportunity will have to cope with.

Types of information included

Information in these profiles is based partly on data generated in the course of this study and partly on various other types of data collected from a number of sources. In order to make the text more readable, those references have not been cited repeatedly. Instead, the different types of information are listed in the paragraphs below; summarized in the tables indicated, and also identified in "Reference notes to Tables A to G," at the end of this chapter.

Demographic information such as population characteristics, employment, and income are given in Tables C and D.

Access characteristics of each state (Tables E and F) include the following:

a. The ratio of high school graduates to 18-year-olds.
b. The ratio of college entrants to 18-year-olds.
c. The ratio of college entrants to high school graduates for 1963 and 1968.
d. A breakdown of the proportion of 1968 high school graduates attending college into three components—those remaining in public institutions in the state, those in private colleges in the state, and those migrating out of the state.

Characteristics of higher education such as state appropriations, free-access two-year colleges opened between 1958 and 1968, and proportion of first-time enrollment in free-access colleges are given in Table G.

Planning and coordination of higher education in each state has been examined recently in two extensive studies of governance (Mayhew, 1969b; Palola et al., 1970).[1] Information in the profiles about planning and coordination is

---

1. I am indebted to these authors for making this material available prior to formal publication of their own work. Other studies of state coordination have recently been completed by Berdahl (1970) and Yarrington (1969).

based on these two studies as amended by more recent personal communications with individuals in various states.

Accessibility of colleges is indicated in Table 1 of each profile. It should be noted that status is defined as of fall 1968, and according to the specifications given in Chapter 2.

Populations covered by a free-access college are described in Table 2 of each profile; data for states and major metropolitan areas are summarized in Tables A and B. Absence of accessible higher education is indicated by a zero; a dash indicates that no estimate was made because the population base was below 10,000.

Effect of new colleges is indicated in Table 3 of each profile. Estimates of accumulated population covered assume that successive additional colleges (or redefined existing institutions) are placed in optimal locations to cover the maximum number of people.

What do the maps represent?

In each profile there is an outline map of the state showing all metropolitan areas of 50,000 population or more. The orange circles indicate the location and a schematic commuting area for each free-access college in the state. These vary in size according to the population of the area in which the college is located: the commuting area is assumed to be smaller in more congested areas.

There is not an orange circle for every college in the state — only for free-access colleges. A free-access college is (1) one that in fall 1968 charged no more than $400 annual tuition and (2) one where at least one-third of all entering freshmen in fall 1968 ranked below average as high school graduates. See Chapter 2 for more detailed definitions and descriptions of procedure.

Alabama

In many respects Alabama is typical of the Deep South states. Almost one-third of the population is black, and a relatively small proportion of the work force is white-collar. The per capita income is among the lowest in the nation. As is often the case, these conditions are associated with a relatively low proportion of high school graduates, almost half of whom go on to college. This college access rate is below the national average but considerably higher than it was a few years earlier, when there were virtually no junior colleges in the state. State appropriations for higher education in Alabama are among the lowest in the nation, though close to average in relation to state resources. In 1969 Alabama authorized an advisory board called the Higher Education Commission.

The 24 free-access colleges in Alabama are fairly well distributed throughout the state, and they enroll 2 out of 3 first-time students. Since the rate of college attendance is limited, these are, on the average, relatively small institutions, even though some are four-year colleges. The senior institutions that are not free-access are only slightly too selective or expensive.

There is a free-access college within commuting distance of 56 percent of the population of Alabama (48 percent if Negro colleges are excluded). These colleges are somewhat more accessible to students living in urban areas, but this is true in most states. Alabama would be a difficult state to cover with proximal institutions because much of the population is evenly distributed and not urbanized. Twenty additional colleges would raise the coverage to 80 percent, though such a goal should not necessarily represent a high priority. The overall picture indicates a need to organize the limited resources of the state to strengthen the capability of the existing institutions to serve larger numbers of Alabama youth than now go on to college.

Table 1. Number of recognized colleges at different levels of accessibility in Alabama (fall 1968)

| | Level of accessibility | | | | | |
| | Free-access | | Less accessible | | | Total |
Type of college	1	2	3	4	5	colleges
Public two-year	14	0	1	0	0	15
Public four-year	0	6	3	0	1	10
Branches	0	2	2	1	0	5
All private	0	2	4	13	1	20
Total colleges	14	10	10	14	2	50

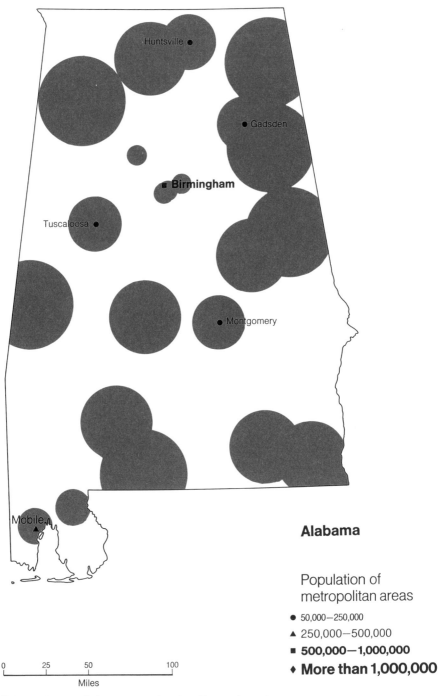

Alabama

Population of
metropolitan areas

● 50,000−250,000
▲ 250,000−500,000
■ **500,000−1,000,000**
♦ **More than 1,000,000**

| 0 | 25 | 50 | | 100 |

Miles

● Commuting area of a free-access college (see Chapter 5 for explanation)

Table 2. Percentage of different populations within commuting distance of a free-access college in Alabama (fall 1968)

Type of community	Population in thousands	Percent within commuting distance		
		White	Black	Total
Metropolitan areas (over 1 million)				
Central city	0	—*	—	—
Fringe	0	—	—	—
Other metropolitan areas.	1,690	66	66	66
Counties over 20,000.	1,272	49	44	48
Counties under 20,000.	306	42	31	37
Total state	3,268	57	54	56

*Dash (—) = base too small for reliable estimate.

Table 3. Estimate of additional colleges required to put specified percentages of the population of Alabama within commuting distance of a free-access college

	As of fall 1968	Hypothetical additional colleges			
Number of free-access colleges	24	2†	8	11	17
Cumulative percent of population within commuting distance.	56%	60%	71%	80%	90%
Average population within commuting distance of each college (in thousands)	76	70†	44	27	19

† Figures in this line are not cumulative. Each refers to an independent set of additional colleges.

Alaska

Despite the fact that Alaska is one of the fastest-growing states in the nation, it is still among the smallest in population. The population density is almost too slight to even register. The natural wealth of the state is by now legend; the relatively high proportion of white-collar workers in the labor force is perhaps less well known. A very low incidence of high school graduation (42 percent of the age group) is one indication of the developmental challenge in Alaska. Almost half of those graduates do continue their education, but some 50 percent attend college outside the state.

Alaska has one public university and, in a somewhat unusual arrangement, seven community colleges as branches. A single Board of Regents coordinates and governs all higher education in the state. The system is well supported by state funds, though only limited studies of resources and needs have been undertaken.

The community colleges are open door and inexpensive. The state university is also quite accessible, and since there are only two private institutions in the state, 9 out of 10 first-time students are enrolled in free-access colleges. It should be understood, however, that most of the community colleges are relatively new and extremely small.

Whereas only 31 percent of the population of Alaska resides within commuting distance of a free-access institution, those institutions are well located in relation to the population. Because of the unusually sparse settlement of Alaska, there are few other centers that seem to be good candidates for additional institutions in the near future. Thus, the state has unique problems in developing its higher education resources in order to serve its many high school graduates now attending college in the coterminous United States and to reach somehow that large proportion of Alaskan students who may never live near an institution of higher education.

Table 1. Number of recognized colleges at different levels of accessibility in Alaska (fall 1968)

| | Level of accessibility | | | | | |
| | Free-access | | Less accessible | | | Total |
Type of college	1	2	3	4	5	colleges
Public two-year	0	0	0	0	0	0
Public four-year	0	1	0	0	0	1
Branches	2	5	0	0	0	7
All private	0	0	1	1	0	2
Total colleges	2	6	1	1	0	10

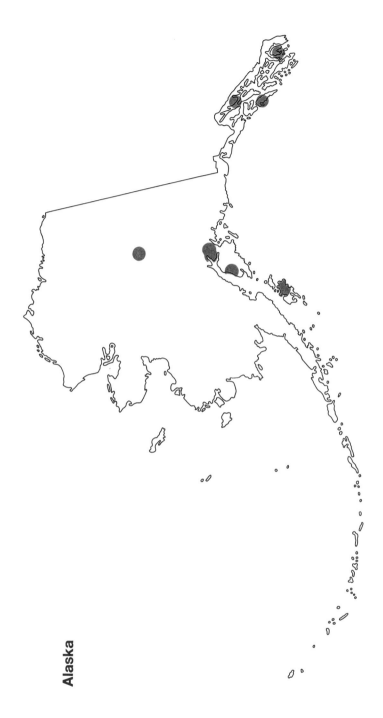

Alaska

0 50 100   200   300   400   500
         Miles

● Commuting area of a free-access college (see Chapter 5 for explanation)

Table 2. Percentage of different populations within commuting distance of a free-access college in Alaska (fall 1968)

Type of community	Population in thousands	Percent within commuting distance
Metropolitan areas (over 1 million)		
Central city	0	—*
Fringe	0	—
Other metropolitan areas.	0	—
Counties over 20,000.	126	44
Counties under 20,000.	101	14
Total state	227	31

°Dash (—) = base too small for reliable estimate.

Table 3. Estimate of additional colleges required to put specified percentages of the population of Alaska within commuting distance of a free-access college

	As of fall 1968	Hypothetical additional colleges
Number of free-access colleges	8†	6
Cumulative percent of population within commuting distance.	31%	52%
Average population within commuting distance of each college (in thousands)	9†	8

† Figures in this line are not cumulative. Each refers to an independent set of additional colleges.

Arizona

Like most Western states Arizona is not heavily populated. It is also not a rich state, but its climate and topography have generated a certain glamour, which has made Arizona one of the fastest-growing states in the union. Despite this growth, somewhat below-average financial resources must be spread thin in meeting the needs of substantial Indian and Mexican American minorities.

The most recent data indicate that first-time college students from Arizona are almost as numerous as Arizona high school graduates. This anomalous situation is hard to accept at face value. It may be that the recent surge of in-migration has included many first-time students who are adults living near a community college for the first time (see note 6 to Tables A to G, on page 206). Consistent with this hypothesis is the fact that the percentage of Arizona college students attending public institutions in the state is the highest in the nation (91 percent).

Half of the 14 colleges in Arizona are public two-year institutions coordinated by a separate board. The state university system with its three components has been governed by a single board since 1945. In 1966 a report on long-range planning assessed present and future facility needs in the state in relation to employment opportunities and manpower requirements, but there were no specific proposals for changing the organization of the present system. State appropriations for higher education in Arizona are somewhat above the national average in an absolute sense and also relative to state income.

The eight free-access institutions in Arizona consist of the seven community colleges and one component of the university system. The two major state institutions enroll somewhat too few students from the lower half of their high school class to qualify as free-access. Most of the accessible colleges are large institutions; they enroll two-thirds of the first-time students in the state.

These data indicate that the accessibility of higher education in Arizona is slightly below the national average, but the picture they give is incomplete. Since the population of the state is highly concentrated in only a few areas, only two or three additional colleges properly placed could substantially increase accessibility. A community college is scheduled soon to open in Tucson, the principal area not now covered by a free-access institution. If one regards a moderate degree of selectivity as an adequate public response to educational opportunity, almost two-thirds of the state's population is already covered. In any event, it is important to recognize that Arizona has a highly developed community college system and an extremely high rate of college attendance.

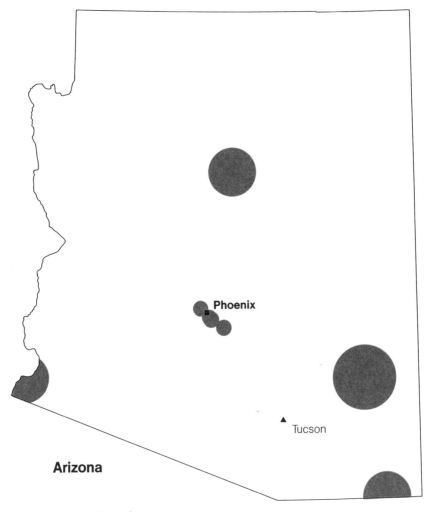

Phoenix

▲ Tucson

Arizona

Population of
metropolitan areas

● 50,000—250,000
▲ 250,000—500,000
■ **500,000—1,000,000**
♦ **More than 1,000,000**

| 0 | 25 | 50 | 100 | 200 |

Miles

● Commuting area of a free-access college (see Chapter 5 for explanation)

**Table 1. Number of recognized colleges at different levels
of accessibility in Arizona (fall 1968)**

| | Level of accessibility | | | | | |
| Type of college | Free-access | | Less accessible | | | Total colleges |
	1	2	3	4	5	
Public two-year	6	1	0	0	0	7
Public four-year	0	1	2	0	0	3
Branches	0	0	0	0	0	0
All private	0	0	0	4	0	4
Total colleges	6	2	2	4	0	14

**Table 2. Percentage of different populations within commuting distance
of a free-access college in Arizona (fall 1968)**

| | | Percent within commuting distance | | | |
Type of community	Population in thousands	White	Black	Mexican American	Total
Metropolitan areas (over 1 million)					
Central city	0	—*	—	—	—
Fringe	0	—	—	—	—
Other metropolitan areas	930	51	—	45	50
Counties over 20,000	329	5	—	4	5
Counties under 20,000	45	32	—	7	24
Total state	1,304	39	42	30	38

*Dash (—) = base too small for reliable estimate.

**Table 3. Estimate of additional colleges
required to put specified percentages of the population of Arizona
within commuting distance of a free-access college**

	As of fall 1968	Hypothetical additional colleges		
Number of free-access colleges	8	1†	1	9
Cumulative percent of population within commuting distance	38%	54%	60%	70%
Average population within commuting distance of each college (in thousands)	61	218†	73	15

† Figures in this line are not cumulative. Each refers to an independent set of additional colleges.

Arkansas

Though one-fifth of Arkansas' labor force is in manufacturing, it is largely an agricultural and rural state. There are very few white-collar workers and a substantial black population, though not as large as most of the other Deep South states. A very low per capita income is an important fact of life in Arkansas. A relatively low proportion of students graduate from secondary school, though more than 1 in 2 continue on to college. The distribution of Arkansas youth to higher education conforms roughly with national proportions: for every six high school graduates, four go to public institutions in the state, one attends a private institution within the state, and one migrates outside the state. A substantial number of students attend postsecondary vocational schools.

Half the institutions in Arkansas are public, and these are primarily four-year colleges. In 1961 the Commission on Coordination of Higher Educational Finance was created to coordinate all public colleges in the state. The state has no master plan, but one is under development. Appropriations for higher education in Arkansas are low in an absolute sense and only slightly above average with respect to the resources of the state.

Arkansas is unusual in that all public four-year colleges are readily accessible, and these constitute most of the free-access colleges in the state. Three-fourths of the matriculating college students in Arkansas enter one of its 12 free-access colleges.

The proportions of the population within commuting distance of a free-access college in Arkansas do not differ greatly from that of the nation at large. Slightly more than four-tenths of the population is covered. There is also a characteristic tendency for a somewhat larger proportion of urban populations to live near a free-access college. The population of the state is fairly evenly distributed, and the colleges are reasonably well placed.

These generalizations are conditioned by the fact that historically two of the colleges here classified as free-access have been predominately Negro institutions—one of these a small denominational college in North Little Rock. Consequently it may be more reasonable to estimate the coverage of the state at something like 30 percent, with a deficiency in the urban areas.

Whereas there are a number of population centers in the state without a free-access college, none are really large except Little Rock, with its problematical situation. Ten new free-access colleges would be required to raise the proportion of the population covered to about 2 out of 3. Additional colleges beyond that number would be hard to rationalize on the basis of present population patterns.

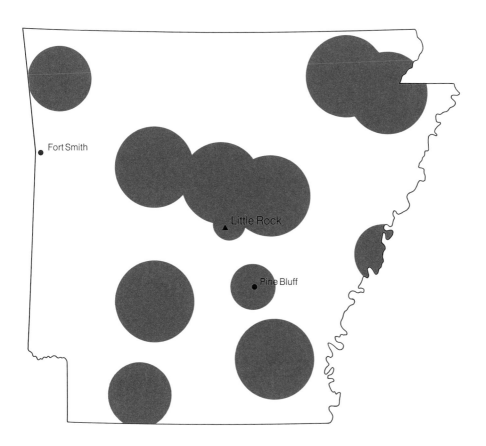

Arkansas

Population of
metropolitan areas

- 50,000—250,000
- ▲ 250,000—500,000
- ■ **500,000—1,000,000**
- ♦ **More than 1,000,000**

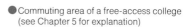 Commuting area of a free-access college
(see Chapter 5 for explanation)

0	25	50	100

Miles

Table 1. Number of recognized colleges at different levels of accessibility in Arkansas (fall 1968)

	Level of accessibility					
	Free-access		Less accessible			Total
Type of college	1	2	3	4	5	colleges
Public two-year	1	0	1	0	0	2
Public four-year	0	8	0	0	0	8
Branches	1	0	0	0	0	1
All private	0	2	3	7	0	12
Total colleges	2	10	4	7	0	23

Table 2. Percentage of different populations within commuting distance of a free-access college in Arkansas (fall 1968)

	Population in thousands	Percent within commuting distance		
Type of community		White	Black	Total
Metropolitan areas (over 1 million)				
Central city	0	—*	—	—
Fringe	0	—	—	—
Other metropolitan areas	521	50	56	51
Counties over 20,000	836	49	36	46
Counties under 20,000	428	26	31	27
Total state	1,785	43	42	43

*Dash (—) = base too small for reliable estimate.

Table 3. Estimate of additional colleges required to put specified percentages of the population of Arkansas within commuting distance of a free-access college

	As of fall 1968	Hypothetical additional colleges			
Number of free-access colleges	12	2†	4	5	9
Cumulative percent of population within commuting distance	43%	49%	61%	70%	80%
Average population within commuting distance of each college (in thousands)	64	59†	50	34	20

† Figures in this line are not cumulative. Each refers to an independent set of additional colleges.

California

California is an important state because it is often regarded as a progressive bellwether for the future shape of higher education in the rest of the nation. Not only is it a large state; heavy in-migration since World War II has also made it the most populous. Per capita income is very high, and white-collar workers constitute a relatively high proportion of the labor force. California's minority communities are well known. Blacks are underrepresented but numerous; Mexican Americans also constitute a very sizable disadvantaged group.

The proportion of 18-year-olds in California who graduate from secondary schools is only slightly above the national average, but the rate of college attendance is among the highest in the nation. The most recent state-by-state data indicate that 3 out of 4 California graduates attend college—a slightly lower proportion than in 1963, when some suspected that estimated access rates were inflated by inadvertent "double counting" of adult students or transfers. As would be expected, the vast majority of California students remain in the state and attend California public colleges.

There are 187 colleges in California—the largest number in any state in the nation except New York. These include 86 public community colleges; 31 of which have opened in the past decade. This host of public two-year colleges rightly astonishes at first blush, though it is well to remember that this number is only a small overrepresentation for the state considering that 1 United States citizen in 10 lives in California. The state is also well known for the showplace units of its single state university and the numerous large state colleges.

The junior colleges are governed by local boards and a statewide Board of Governors; the state colleges by a Board of Trustees; and the university by a Board of Regents. The Coordinating Council on Higher Education and its active professional staff undertake a variety of special studies. A primary function of the Council is to implement the state master plan, but it is an advisory body with limited powers. The California Master Plan for Higher Education published in 1960 is perhaps the best-known state planning document in the country. The plan has a critical relationship to access to higher education in the state in two respects. First, it set specific admissions standards making the university and the state colleges fairly selective and the community colleges completely open door. Second, it called for community-oriented two-year institutions within commuting distance of most prospective students. The plan has often worked well but has not been without problems, both political and fiscal. The community colleges are heavily dependent on local tax support, which is not always completely reliable. State appropriations to higher education in California are well above average in absolute dollars, but actually represent an average effort in relation to the financial resources and appropriations for higher education in other states. In recent years the level of appropriations has been the subject of a good deal of debate and acrimony.

The free-access higher institutions in California are almost exclusively the

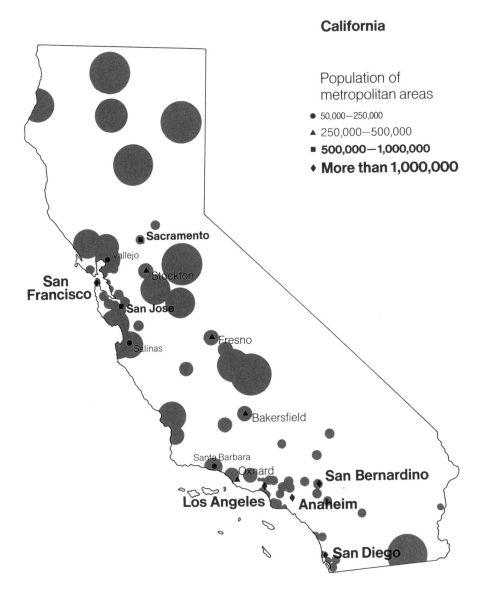

California

Population of metropolitan areas

- 50,000—250,000
- ▲ 250,000—500,000
- ■ **500,000—1,000,000**
- ◆ **More than 1,000,000**

Sacramento

Vallejo

Stockton

San Francisco

San Jose

Fresno

Salinas

Bakersfield

Santa Barbara

Oxnard

San Bernardino

Los Angeles

Anaheim

San Diego

0   25   50   100   200

Miles

● Commuting area of a free-access college (see Chapter 5 for explanation)

public community colleges, because only those students in the top third of their high school class are admitted to the state colleges. Since the public junior colleges are large and numerous, they account for 80 percent of all first-time enrollment in the state. This figure, as much as any other, illustrates the radically different shape higher education will take if it follows the California model.

Throughout the state 60 percent of the population lives within commuting distance of a free-access college. This figure is high, though some observers might have guessed it would be higher or might be surprised that the percentage is greater in four other states (Connecticut, Florida, Mississippi, and North Carolina). A somewhat larger proportion of Mexican Americans and a somewhat smaller proportion of blacks live within commuting distance of a California community college. The main racial imbalance in the state lies in the fact that substantially fewer blacks than whites live near a community college in the Los Angeles area.

Free-access higher education is available to a noticeably smaller proportion of residents in the large central cities than to state residents in general. This is because of inadequate coverage in Los Angeles, San Francisco, and San Diego. Of course, California has placed great emphasis on private transportation, and its cities tend not to be highly centralized. Consequently, the accessibility of higher education in the major central cities may be somewhat better than these data would indicate (see page 35). It is important to recognize, however, the distinction between the commuting distance that can be traversed and the proximity that actually attracts marginal college students. In the major population areas of the state, college is accessible more in the former that in the latter sense.

If we include the central city and the fringe, there is considerable variation among the major metropolitan areas of the state. The proportion of residents who live within commuting distance of a free-access college in the principal metropolitan areas are as follows: Anaheim, 89 percent; Los Angeles, 58 percent; San Bernardino, 45 percent; San Diego, 39 percent; San Francisco, 55 percent.

All major population centers have some accessible higher education, though Table 3 suggests that the junior colleges in the state are not always located optimally in relation to where people live. It would be possible to add 15 to 20 new colleges, each of which would cover more people than does the average present junior college. This increase of about one-sixth in the number of junior colleges would increase the number of people covered from 60 to 75 percent.

But, ironically, the critical current problem in California is inadequate space in the senior institutions to handle new students and junior college transfers. At the close of the sixties — which many would call California's decade in higher education — some state colleges were rejecting 9 out of 10 applications for admission (*San Francisco Chronicle,* 1969). If California is a bellwether, it is surely to signal problems as well as progress.

Table 1. Number of recognized colleges at different levels of accessibility in California (fall 1968)

Type of college	Free-access		Less accessible			Total colleges
	1	*2*	*3*	*4*	*5*	
Public two-year	**78**	**8**	1	0	0	87
Public four-year	**0**	**0**	1	5	20	26
Branches.	**0**	**0**	0	0	0	0
All private	**0**	**0**	1	52	21	74
Total colleges	**78**	**8**	3	57	41	187

Table 2. Percentage of different populations within commuting distance of a free-access college in California (fall 1968)

Type of community	Population in thousands	Percent within commuting distance			
		White	Black	Mexican American	Total
Metropolitan areas (over 1 million)					
Central city	5,015	46	35	53	45
Fringe	6,217	65	72	75	66
Other metropolitan areas.	2,942	69	65	71	69
Counties over 20,000.	1,362	66	69	68	66
Counties under 20,000	175	24	—*	60	60
Total state	15,711	60	48	66	60

*Dash (—) = base too small for reliable estimate.

Table 3. Estimate of additional colleges required to put specified percentages of the population of California within commuting distance of a free-access college

	As of fall 1968	Hypothetical additional colleges		
Number of free-access colleges	86	11†	15	54
Cumulative percent of population within commuting distance.	60%	71%	81%	90%
Average population within commuting distance of each college (in thousands)	110	158†	108	26

† Figures in this line are not cumulative. Each refers to an independent set of additional colleges.

Colorado

Like many of the Western states, the relatively sparse population of Colorado is largely collected in a few urban areas. White-collar workers constitute a higher proportion of the labor force in Colorado than in most states, though the per capita income is about average. The proportion of students graduating from high school is a little low in Colorado, while the proportion of those graduates going on to college is somewhat higher than in most other states. Consequently, the proportion of the age group attending college is close to the national average. Five out of six attend public institutions, which are well supported by state appropriations.

The colleges of Colorado are fairly evenly divided between public two-year, public four-year, and private institutions. A Commission on Higher Education coordinates all public and private higher institutions in the state, but that body must deal with a number of governing boards. In 1966 the Commission completed a master plan basically similar to the California model. Its main characteristics were division of responsibility among different types of institutions and provision of accessible higher education by two-year community colleges insofar as the geography of Colorado permits.

At present all of the two-year public institutions are free-access, as are about half of the four-year colleges. The master plan anticipates that these four-year colleges will become somewhat more selective, as the major senior institutions already have. The 15 free-access colleges now enroll about half of the first-time students in the state.

Colorado is at the national average with respect to the proportion of its population that lives within commuting distance of a free-access college. With the exception of Denver, the metropolitan areas and most smaller cities are covered very well. However, Denver is an important exception, since more than half of all Coloradans live in the greater Denver area. Six to eight new colleges, largely in this urban area, would increase to 70 percent the proportion of the population residing near a free-access college. It seems unlikely that many more institutions could be justified purely on grounds of proximity.

Table 1. Number of recognized colleges at different levels of accessibility in Colorado (fall 1968)

	Level of accessibility					
	Free-access		Less accessible			Total
Type of college	1	2	3	4	5	colleges
Public two-year	6	4	0	0	0	10
Public four-year	0	4	2	2	1	9
Branches	0	1	1	0	0	2
All private	0	0	0	5	3	8
Total colleges	6	9	3	7	4	29

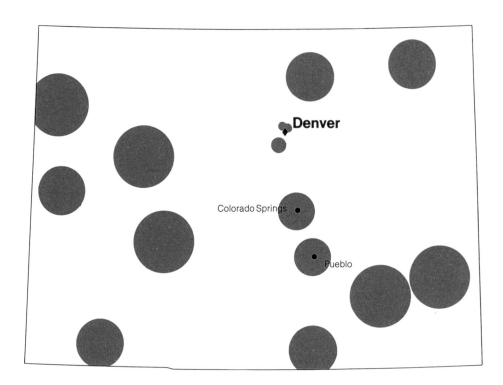

Colorado

Population of
metropolitan areas

● 50,000—250,000
▲ 250,000—500,000
■ **500,000—1,000,000**
♦ **More than 1,000,000**

```
0      25     50          100                    200
|       |      |           |                      |
                        Miles
```

● Commuting area of a free-access college (see Chapter 5 for explanation)

Table 2. Percentage of different populations within commuting distance of a free-access college in Colorado (fall 1968)

Type of community	Population in thousands	Percent within commuting distance			
		White	Black	Mexican American	Total
Metropolitan areas (over 1 million)					
Central city	494	46	53	53	47
Fringe	435	23	—*	11	22
Other metropolitan areas.	263	82	—	84	82
Counties over 20,000.	281	45	—	55	46
Counties under 20,000.	275	22	—	17	21
Total state	1,748	41	58	48	42

*Dash (—) = base too small for reliable estimate.

Table 3. Estimate of additional colleges required to put specified percentages of the population of Colorado within commuting distance of a free-access college

	As of fall 1968	Hypothetical additional colleges			
Number of free-access colleges 15		1†	1	6	9
Cumulative percent of population within commuting distance. 42%		57%	60%	71%	80%
Average population within commuting distance of each college (in thousands) 49		262†	52	33	18

† Figures in this line are not cumulative. Each refers to an independent set of additional colleges.

Connecticut

Even though Connecticut is one of the smallest and most densely populated states in the country, it is actually not highly urbanized. The state's labor force is heavily represented with manufacturing and white-collar workers. In 1967 Connecticut had the highest per capita income in the nation. These are not the only characteristics that make Connecticut a most unusual state.

The proportion of the age group graduating from secondary school and the proportion of high school graduates attending college are both well above the national average, though the distribution of these students is quite atypical. The proportion of Connecticut youth remaining in the state to attend public institutions is low (but has almost doubled in five years). Two students in three either attend private institutions within the state or migrate from Connecticut.

Connecticut is well known for its 25 private institutions, but it is not generally appreciated that the state has 12 community colleges, practically all of which have been opened in the past decade. There are also five public senior institutions with a total of five branches. All of these institutions are coordinated through voluntary representation on a Commission for Higher Education. The state does not have an overall master plan but has been active in undertaking individual studies. State appropriations for higher education are below average and, relative to income, rank among the lowest in the nation.

Free-access higher education in Connecticut is afforded almost exclusively by the community colleges. Only one of the four-year institutions (and none of the branches) is readily accessible. The free-access colleges are not large; together they enroll 1 out of 3 first-time students in the state.

Connecticut lies in the heartland of private education and selective admissions. It is a bit startling that 87 percent of the state's population lives within commuting distance of a free-access college—the highest percentage in the country. Of course, it doesn't take many colleges to cover a state of this size. To add perspective, California has seven times as many free-access colleges as Connecticut but is 30 times as large.

There are only one or two locations in the state where proximity could be much of an argument in favor of a new institution. The various data cited indicate that Connecticut, as much as any other state, needs to strengthen its existing institutions. Ironically, in 1969 the state legislature channeled part of a limited appropriation into the construction of five new community colleges.

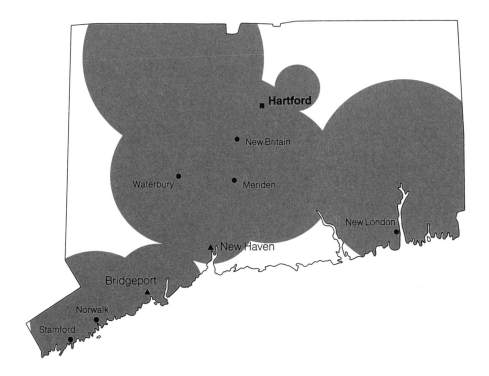

Connecticut

Population of
metropolitan areas

● 50,000–250,000
▲ 250,000–500,000
■ **500,000–1,000,000**
♦ **More than 1,000,000**

Miles

● Commuting area of a free-access college (see Chapter 5 for explanation)

Table 1. Number of recognized colleges at different levels of accessibility in Connecticut (fall 1968)

	Level of accessibility					
	Free-access		Less accessible			Total
Type of college	**1**	**2**	3	4	5	colleges
Public two-year	**6**	**6**	0	0	0	12
Public four-year	**0**	**1**	2	0	2	5
Branches	**0**	**0**	5	0	0	5
All private	**0**	**0**	0	18	7	25
Total colleges	**6**	**7**	7	18	9	47

Table 2. Percentage of different populations within commuting distance of a free-access college in Connecticut (fall 1968)

		Percent within commuting distance		
Type of community	Population in thousands	White	Black	Total
Metropolitan areas (over 1 million)				
Central city	0	—*	—	—
Fringe	0	—	—	—
Other metropolitan areas	2,057	85	96	85
Counties over 20,000	480	97	—	96
Counties under 20,000	0	—	—	—
Total state	2,537	87	90	87

*Dash (—) = base too small for reliable estimate.

Table 3. Estimate of additional colleges required to put specified percentages of the population of Connecticut within commuting distance of a free-access college

	As of fall 1968	Hypothetical additional colleges
Number of free-access colleges	13	2†
Cumulative percent of population within commuting distance	87%	90%
Average population within commuting distance of each college (in thousands)	224	40†

† This figure is not cumulative. It refers to an independent set of additional colleges.

Delaware

The Washington to Boston belt is normally perceived as a solid mass of humanity, though much of Delaware provides a nonurban exception to that rule. The state has a very small population and a very high per capita income. It is somewhat surprising that the proportion of students graduating from secondary school is only average and the percentage going on to college is actually below the national average. A relatively large number of those students migrate to other states.

There are only six colleges in Delaware: three public and three private. The planning and coordination of higher education in Delaware is largely associated with the state university. Its plan for the future, published in 1963, takes a relatively conservative stand with respect to access to higher education, and state support of higher education is about average for the country despite the wealth of Delaware.

Free-access is now provided by one state college and one community college, which has added a northern branch since these data were assembled. These units are small and enroll only 1 out of 6 first-time students in Delaware.

At present roughly one-third of the population of the state is within commuting distance of a free-access college, but that figure will be increased dramatically as the northern branch of the Delaware Technical and Community College becomes established in the main population center of the state. The main question in Delaware is not whether there is a free-access college within commuting distance of all prospective students, but whether the free-access idea will be supported with programs and facilities that will enhance educational opportunity in the state.

Table 1. Number of recognized colleges at different levels of accessibility in Delaware (fall 1968)

| | Level of accessibility | | | | | |
| | Free-access | | Less accessible | | | Total colleges |
Type of college	1	2	3	4	5	
Public two-year	0	1	0	0	0	1
Public four-year	0	1	0	1	0	2
Branches	0	0	0	0	0	0
All private	0	0	0	3	0	3
Total colleges	0	2	0	4	0	6

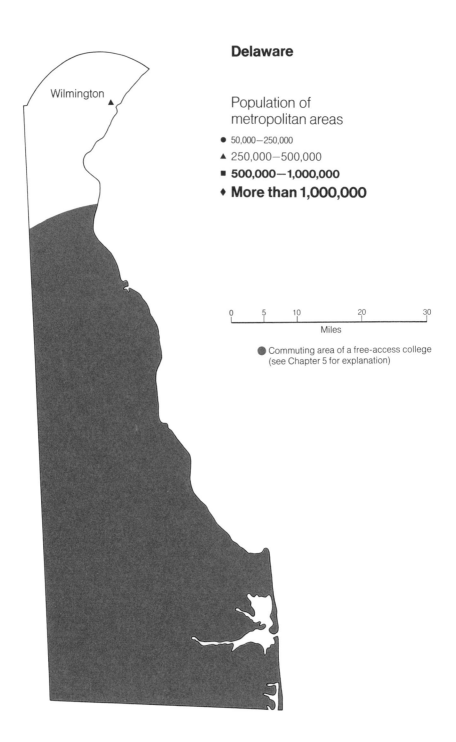

Delaware

Population of metropolitan areas

- ● 50,000–250,000
- ▲ 250,000–500,000
- ■ **500,000–1,000,000**
- ♦ **More than 1,000,000**

Wilmington ▲

0   5   10   20   30
Miles

● Commuting area of a free-access college
(see Chapter 5 for explanation)

Table 2. Percentage of different populations within commuting distance of a free-access college in Delaware (fall 1968)

Type of community	Population in thousands	Percent within commuting distance		
		White	Black	Total
Metropolitan areas (over 1 million)				
Central city	0	—*	—	—
Fringe	0	—	—	—
Other metropolitan areas.	307	4	5	5
Counties over 20,000.	139	100	100	100
Counties under 20,000.	0	—	—	—
Total state	446	35	44	35

*Dash (—) = base too small for reliable estimate.

Table 3. Estimate of additional colleges required to put specified percentages of the population of Delaware within commuting distance of a free-access college

	As of fall 1968	Hypothetical additional colleges		
Number of free-access colleges 2		1†	1	1
Cumulative percent of population within commuting distance. 22%		68%	85%	98%
Average population within commuting distance of each college (in thousands) 38		208†	75	58

† Figures in this line are not cumulative. Each refers to an independent set of additional colleges.

Florida

Florida is a good example of what can be accomplished with aggressive state leadership. In the mid-1950s a Council for the Study of Higher Education was formed. It laid down ambitious plans for expanding educational opportunity in the state, and the legislature enacted most of its recommendations. During the past decade, Florida has been a major center for expansion and innovation.

The state has grown very rapidly in recent years. While agriculture remains important, the labor force contains a very high proportion of white-collar workers. In moving into the technocratic and jet society, the state has had limited resources upon which to call — higher than neighboring states but lower than the national average. Despite this fact, appropriations for higher education have been about average or slightly higher.

The proportion of 18-year-olds completing high school is somewhat low, but the percentage of those students who go on to college is well above the average of other states. The large majority of these students remain in Florida to attend its public institutions. Furthermore, there are probably another 10 to 15 percent of high school graduates attending postsecondary public vocational schools.

Higher institutions in Florida include 26 private colleges, 5 senior institutions that enroll first-time students, and 28 community colleges, two-thirds of which have opened in the past 10 years.

The various studies undertaken in this state resulted in a quasi-master plan in 1956 and a more comprehensive one in 1966. Contrary to the three-level plan of California, Florida has concentrated on two levels. The senior institutions have university status and are organized into a single system governed by a Board of Regents with a sizable staff. There are seven of these, but two, Florida Atlantic University and the University of West Florida, accept only upper-division students. Because of the transfer problems created by the rapid growth of community colleges throughout the nation, this upper-division experiment is being watched closely. The 28 community colleges in the state make up the second level, which is coordinated through the State Department of Education.

As in California, the community colleges in Florida are almost synonymous with free-access higher education in the state. Some of these institutions are quite large (for example, Miami-Dade Junior College has an enrollment of 24,000). In Florida 8 out of 10 students matriculate in a free-access institution.

Almost two-thirds of the population of Florida lives within relatively easy commuting distance of a free-access college. This figure is noticeably lower than estimates provided in the state's own literature, but it may represent more accurately the attractive power of proximity as opposed to theoretically possible commuting, which state estimates often represent. In any event, Florida ranks among the five top states in the country with respect to the accessibility of higher education. In this regard it is one of the success stories of the decade — seemingly accomplished by leadership and a sense of mission despite limited funds.

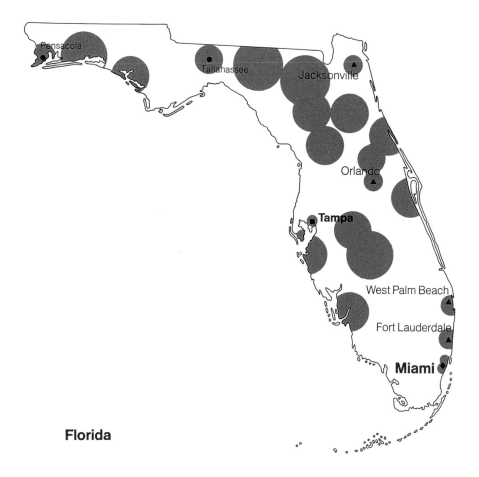

Florida

Population of
metropolitan areas

- ● 50,000–250,000
- ▲ 250,000–500,000
- ■ **500,000–1,000,000**
- ♦ **More than 1,000,000**

0   25   50   100   200

Miles

● Commuting area of a free-access college (see Chapter 5 for explanation)

Table 1. Number of recognized colleges at different levels of accessibility in Florida (fall 1968)

| | Level of accessibility | | | | | |
| | Free-access | | Less accessible | | | Total |
Type of college	1	2	3	4	5	colleges
Public two-year	9	16	3	0	0	28
Public four-year	0	1	1	3	0	5
Branches	0	0	0	0	0	0
All private	0	0	4	17	5	26
Total colleges	9	17	8	20	5	59

Table 2. Percentage of different populations within commuting distance of a free-access college in Florida (fall 1968)

| | Population | Percent within commuting distance | | |
Type of community	in thousands	White	Black	Total
Metropolitan areas (over 1 million)				
Central city	292	94	91	93
Fringe	643	28	51	31
Other metropolitan areas	2,387	73	76	73
Counties over 20,000	1,293	70	67	69
Counties under 20,000	335	19	30	21
Total state	4,950	62	72	64

Table 3. Estimate of additional colleges required to put specified percentages of the population of Florida within commuting distance of a free-access college

	As of fall 1968	Hypothetical additional colleges		
Number of free-access colleges	26	3*	6	10
Cumulative percent of population within commuting distance	64%	72%	81%	90%
Average population within commuting distance of each college (in thousands)	123	152*	73	47

* Figures in this line are not cumulative. Each refers to an independent set of additional colleges.

Georgia

Despite the fact that Atlanta is commonly considered the cultural and commercial metropolis of the Southeast, Georgia does not differ greatly from other Deep South states. It is largely a rural state with a substantial black population. The per capita income is modest at best. Georgia shares with South Carolina the unfortunate dual problem of a very low rate of high school graduation and a very low rate of college attendance among high school graduates. There are, however, substantial numbers of students attending postsecondary area vocational schools.

Georgia does not want for colleges. There are 56, half of which are public. The Board of Regents and its large staff exert strong central governance over all public institutions. It has also been a national leader in collecting admissions and guidance information on all Georgia colleges for the benefit of students and counselors in the state. Otherwise, this body tends to be more conservative than that of neighboring Florida. The junior colleges emphasize the transfer function rather than comprehensive postsecondary programs. There is no comprehensive master plan, and studies of state needs have been limited. State appropriations for the support of higher education in Georgia have been below the average for other states, but at least average in relation to state resources.

The 14 free-access institutions in Georgia are largely the two-year colleges. These are mostly small institutions, and collectively they enroll only 3 out of 10 first-time students in the state. There are nine public four-year institutions, which are inexpensive but somewhat too selective to be classified as free-access. Because of their small size and the fact that many are located in less populous areas, the overall picture of accessibility in the state is not greatly affected by whether or not these nine colleges are regarded as accessible institutions.

About 3 Georgians in 10 live within commuting distance of a nonselective, inexpensive college. Several metropolitan areas in the state lack readily accessible higher education, but Atlanta is the major problem. Even though it is one of the most exuberant and fastest-growing major cities in the country, Atlanta has no free-access institution within its city limits. A relatively small number of additional colleges appropriately placed could substantially increase the proportion of the state's population within commuting distance of a free-access institution. It may well be, however, that more challenging problems lie in the coordination of postsecondary occupational and traditional education in the state. In addition, Georgia shares with most Southern states the serious black-white problems in coordinating higher education.

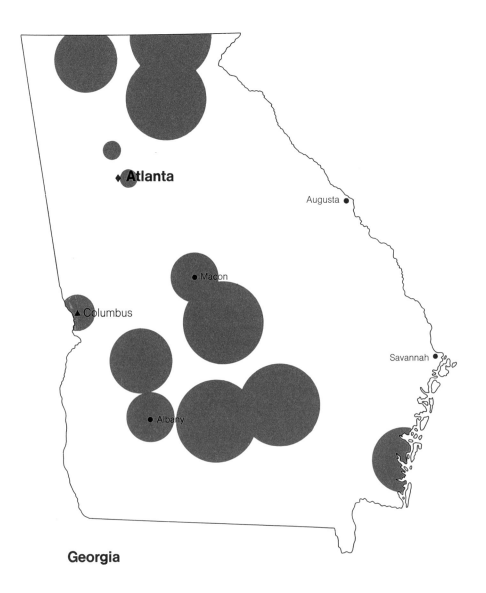

Georgia

Population of
metropolitan areas

● 50,000—250,000
▲ 250,000—500,000
■ 500,000—1,000,000
♦ **More than 1,000,000**

● Commuting area of a free-access college
(see Chapter 5 for explanation)

0   25   50   100

Miles

Table 1. Number of recognized colleges at different levels
of accessibility in Georgia (fall 1968)

	Level of accessibility					
	Free-access		*Less accessible*			*Total colleges*
Type of college	**1**	**2**	*3*	*4*	*5*	
Public two-year	**0**	**11**	0	1	0	12
Public four-year	**0**	**1**	9	2	3	15
Branches	**0**	**1**	0	0	0	1
All private	**0**	**1**	4	17	6	28
Total colleges	**0**	**14**	13	20	9	56

Table 2. Percentage of different populations within commuting distance
of a free-access college in Georgia (fall 1968)

		Percent within commuting distance		
Type of community	*Population in thousands*	*White*	*Black*	*Total*
Metropolitan areas (over 1 million)				
Central city	487	18	4	13
Fringe	530	35	29	34
Other metropolitan areas	797	49	49	49
Counties over 20,000	977	29	21	27
Counties under 20,000	1,144	27	19	24
Total state	3,935	33	24	30

Table 3. Estimate of additional colleges
required to put specified percentages of the population of Georgia
within commuting distance of a free-access college

	As of fall 1968	*Hypothetical additional colleges*				
Number of free-access colleges 14		6*	3	5	9	9
Cumulative percent of population within commuting distance 30%		51%	60%	69%	79%	90%
Average population within commuting distance of each college (in thousands) 84		138*	113	75	45	45

*Figures in this line are not cumulative. Each refers to an independent set of additional colleges.

Hawaii

Except for its rapid growth, Hawaii looks deceptively average with respect to many demographic indexes. Its relatively high per capita income is somewhat offset by the cost of living on the islands. Tourism and agriculture frequently dominate the mainlander's view of Hawaii, though the state university has its own important role in creating a cultural and commercial window to the East. High school graduation rate has been roughly at the national norm, but the new community colleges have evidently brought the college access rate up sharply in recent years so that it is now above the national average.

Of the 11 colleges in the state, 4 are private and the remainder consist of the state university and its 6 branches. These are community colleges similar to the models adopted by Alaska and Kentucky. Public higher education in Hawaii has been under one governing board for more than 50 years. There is no master plan as such, but the university undertook a study of the future of higher education in Hawaii in 1964. The state's appropriations for higher education are the highest in the nation, both on a per capita basis and in relation to income.

Free-access higher education in Hawaii is synonymous with the branches of the state university, except for one branch, which is too selective to qualify under the definitions used here. Almost half of the first-time students in the state matriculate in one of these five free-access community colleges. The commuting area of these institutions covers almost half of the population of Hawaii, and the colleges are well distributed with respect to population centers.

Table 1. Number of recognized colleges at different levels of accessibility in Hawaii (fall 1968)

| | Level of accessibility | | | | | |
| | Free-access | | Less accessible | | | Total |
Type of college	1	2	3	4	5	colleges
Public two-year	0	0	0	0	0	0
Public four-year	0	0	1	0	0	1
Branches	5	0	0	1	0	6
All private	0	0	1	3	0	4
Total colleges	5	0	2	4	0	11

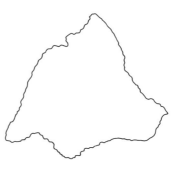

Honolulu

Hawaii

Population of
metropolitan areas

● 50,000–250,000

▲ 250,000–500,000

■ **500,000—1,000,000**

◆ **More than 1,000,000**

● Commuting area of a free-access college (see Chapter 5 for explanation)

| 0 | 25 | 50 | 100 |

Miles

**Table 2. Percentage of different populations within commuting distance
of a free-access college in Hawaii (fall 1968)**

Type of community	Population in thousands	Percent within commuting distance
Metropolitan areas (over 1 million)		
Central city	0	—*
Fringe	0	—
Other metropolitan areas.	500	50
Counties over 20,000.	132	39
Counties under 20,000.	0	—
Total state	632	48

*Dash (—) = base too small for reliable estimate.

**Table 3. Estimate of additional colleges
required to put specified percentages of the population of Hawaii
within commuting distance of a free-access college**

	As of fall 1968	Hypothetical additional colleges		
Number of free-access colleges 5		1†	1	2
Cumulative percent of population within commuting distance. 48%		71%	78%	89%
Average population within commuting distance of each college (in thousands) 60		144†	44	38

† Figures in this line are not cumulative. Each refers to an independent set of additional colleges.

Idaho

Idaho is a land of rugged mountains, but it also ranks high in agricultural production. It is a very sparsely populated state with a lower per capita income than most of its Western neighbors. A somewhat higher proportion of secondary-school students graduates than is true in most states, and the proportion going on to college is also above average. Consequently, the proportion of first-time college students to high school graduates in Idaho is quite high. As in the rest of the country, approximately 4 out of 6 matriculate in public institutions within the state, while the remainder is equally divided between those who migrate out of the state or attend private institutions in Idaho.

The State Board of Education coordinates all public higher education in Idaho. There are the state university, three state colleges, and two community colleges. Some planning studies have been made, though there is no comprehensive master plan for the state. Fiscal support has been generous. In relation to the wealth of the state, Idaho ranks among the top four states in the country in appropriations for higher education.

Except for the state university, which is slightly too selective, all the two-year and four-year public institutions in Idaho are free-access colleges. On the average these are moderately large institutions, and taken together they enroll more than three-fourths of all first-time students in the state. Throughout Idaho 40 percent of the state's population lives within commuting distance of one of these free-access colleges. They are well distributed among the population centers, though there are two or three relatively populous areas without a free-access institution.

Table 1. Number of recognized colleges at different levels of accessibility in Idaho (fall 1968)

| | Level of accessibility | | | | | |
| | Free-access | | Less accessible | | | Total colleges |
Type of college	1	2	3	4	5	
Public two-year	2	0	0	0	0	2
Public four-year	1	2	1	0	0	4
Branches	0	0	0	0	0	0
All private	0	1	1	3	0	5
Total colleges	3	3	2	3	0	11

Idaho

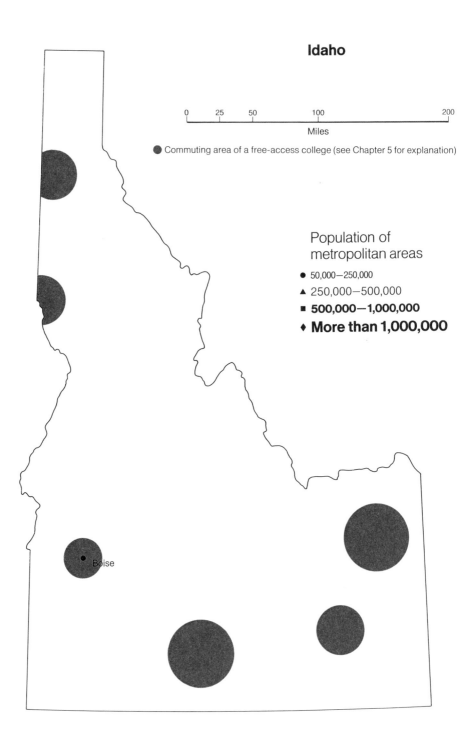

0   25   50   100   200

Miles

● Commuting area of a free-access college (see Chapter 5 for explanation)

Population of metropolitan areas

● 50,000—250,000
▲ 250,000—500,000
■ **500,000—1,000,000**
♦ **More than 1,000,000**

● Boise

Table 2. Percentage of different populations within commuting distance of a free-access college in Idaho (fall 1968)

Type of community	Population in thousands	Percent within commuting distance
Metropolitan areas (over 1 million)		
Central city	0	—*
Fringe	0	—
Other metropolitan areas	93	95
Counties over 20,000	323	44
Counties under 20,000	252	14
Total state	668	40

*Dash (—) = base too small for reliable estimate.

Table 3. Estimate of additional colleges required to put specified percentages of the population of Idaho within commuting distance of a free-access college

	As of fall 1968	Hypothetical additional colleges		
Number of free-access colleges	6	1†	1	4
Cumulative percent of population within commuting distance	40%	51%	59%	71%
Average population within commuting distance of each college (in thousands)	45	75†	53	21

† Figures in this line are not cumulative. Each refers to an independent set of additional colleges.

Illinois

Illinois is somewhat deceptive because it is a diverse state with a variety of resources. The state is very populous and fairly well urbanized; 85 percent of its area is farmland. Chicago, with its institutions and its ghettos, sits in critical balance to those farmlands in the south. Overall, Illinois has a very high per capita income.

The proportion of students graduating from secondary schools in Illinois is no higher than the national average, but the proportion going on to higher education is one of the highest in the country. As in many states these college matriculants are distributed roughly in a 4–1–1 proportion to state institutions, private colleges in the state, and institutions in other states.

Illinois is well known for its many private colleges — only Pennsylvania, Massachusetts, and New York have more. Illinois is also another outstanding example of statewide coordination and leadership in the public sector. While the state has had some form of a central coordinating agency for 25 years, the state legislature established the present Board of Higher Education as the coordinating and planning agency in 1961. This Board serves budgeting, planning, and regulatory functions but is not a governing body.

A master plan was prepared in 1964 and revised in 1966. It is basically similar to the California plan in emphasizing low-cost comprehensive community colleges throughout the state and minimizing duplication of effort. It differs from the California plan in including a fourth system of institutions — the liberal arts universities. Also, Illinois is opening two institutions that will follow Florida's innovative idea of accepting students only at the junior-year level. Some observers consider that establishing upper-division institutions is a critical ingredient in guaranteeing junior college students continued opportunity beyond initial access. The state master plan has been supported and elaborated by numerous statewide surveys and other special studies in Chicago. State appropriations for higher education have been high in absolute dollars and above average in relation to state resources.

Two-thirds of the public junior colleges in Illinois have opened in the past decade. Free-access higher education in Illinois is associated almost exclusively with these institutions. On the average they attract large numbers of students, and as a group they enroll about half of all first-time college students in the state.

Fifty-six percent of the population in Illinois lives within commuting distance of a free-access college, and this is well above the national average. There is no serious bias in the accessibility of such institutions with respect to either race or type of community. There is somewhat of a bias in favor of the central cities as opposed to fringes of metropolitan areas, and this condition stands in contrast to the trend in California. Of the largest cities, Chicago possibly represents the most systematic and successful effort to improve accessibility of higher education through planned locations of colleges.

On the whole, the existing free-access institutions are reasonably well placed

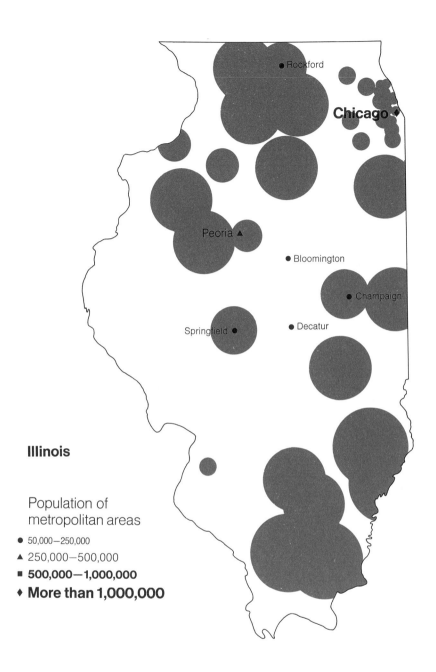

Illinois

Population of
metropolitan areas

● 50,000—250,000

▲ 250,000—500,000

■ **500,000—1,000,000**

♦ **More than 1,000,000**

Rockford

Chicago ♦

Peoria ▲

● Bloomington

● Champaign

Springfield ● ● Decatur

```
0        25        50              100
|--------|---------|---------------|
              Miles
```

● Commuting area of a free-access college (see Chapter 5 for explanation)

in relation to the population of the state, though Table 3 indicates that there are several locations where new colleges could serve considerably larger numbers of people than the average existing free-access college. Since Illinois is a large and populous state, some 30 to 40 additional colleges could probably be justified on grounds of proximity, under conditions of universal postsecondary opportunity.

Table 1. Number of recognized colleges at different levels of accessibility in Illinois (fall 1968)

| | Level of accessibility | | | | | |
| | Free-access | | Less accessible | | | Total |
Type of college	1	2	3	4	5	colleges
Public two-year	24	15	1	0	0	40
Public four-year	0	1	4	3	2	10
Branches	0	0	1	0	0	1
All private	1	0	6	52	15	74
Total colleges	25	16	12	55	17	125

Table 2. Percentage of different populations within commuting distance of a free-access college in Illinois (fall 1968)

| | | Percent within commuting distance | | | |
Type of community	Population in thousands	White	Black	Puerto Rican	Total
Metropolitan areas (over 1 million)					
Central city	3,550	69	63	63	67
Fringe	3,159	41	36	—*	40
Other metropolitan areas	1,225	69	72	—	69
Counties over 20,000	1,595	58	76	—	58
Counties under 20,000	555	38	—	—	37
Total state	10,084	56	59	—	56

*Dash (—) = base too small for reliable estimate.

**Table 3. Estimate of additional colleges
required to put specified percentages of the population of Illinois
within commuting distance of a free-access college**

	As of fall 1968	Hypothetical additional colleges			
Number of free-access colleges	41	2†	3	14	17
Cumulative percent of population within commuting distance	56%	62%	70%	80%	90%
Average population within commuting distance of each college (in thousands)	138	312†	257	76	58

† Figures in this line are not cumulative. Each refers to an independent set of additional colleges.

Indiana

The Midwest is fondly regarded as the great heartland—not only with respect to agriculture and manufacture but also the American ethos. In most respects Indiana is a typical representative of this area, though it is not as populous, urbanized, or as wealthy as its neighbor, Illinois. A below-average rate of college attendance is not really atypical of the region and provides no anticipation of a somewhat anomalous situation in the state.

In addition to 36 private colleges, the state has 16 public institutions, largely consisting of four-year colleges and their branches. A master plan was prepared in 1968, but there is no legally sanctioned coordinating agency. Enacting legislation has been delayed, but some observers feel that the state is moving toward closer coordination. Others are not so optimistic. As Mayhew (1969b) characterizes the situation, "The state prides itself on the success with which voluntary coordination has seemingly met the state's higher educational needs. The Indiana Conference on Higher Education serves as a forum for discussion of higher educational issues, and the public institutions themselves coordinate budgetary requests and long-range program planning. This voluntary characteristic has become almost an item of faith within the state, and it is difficult to see any major change coming about." State appropriations in support of higher education in Indiana are close to the national per capita average with respect to absolute dollars and when considered in relation to the financial resources available.

The startling fact is that there is not a single free-access institution in the state of Indiana. Tuition in the public institutions is not high and admissions policy is not restrictive, but the public institutions tend to admit students in the top half of their high school class. Some units have become fairly selective, though many no doubt still admit substantial numbers of students only slightly above average in secondary school. Thus, moderately selective higher education is available to many Indiana youth.

The lack of more accessible colleges is particularly anomalous in light of the historic leadership the Midwestern state institutions have provided with respect to an egalitarian philosophy of access to higher education. It will no doubt require aggressive action at the state level to alter substantially the present degree of accessibility, but there is no reason to doubt that this can be accomplished if the state chooses to do it. Indiana ranks second in the nation in net migration of college students into the state (Grossman et al., 1968). One wonders, however, whether a careful cost–benefit analysis would support continuing the present, moderately selective system, as opposed to emphasis on more accessible higher education for Indiana residents.

Indiana

Population of
metropolitan areas

● 50,000–250,000
▲ 250,000–500,000
■ **500,000–1,000,000**
♦ **More than 1,000,000**

0   25   50   100

Miles

Table 1. Number of recognized colleges at different levels of accessibility in Indiana (fall 1968)

| | Level of accessibility | | | | | |
| | Free-access | | Less accessible | | | Total colleges |
Type of college	1	2	3	4	5	
Public two-year	0	0	1	0	0	1
Public four-year	0	0	8	1	1	10
Branches	0	0	5	0	0	5
All private	0	0	4	26	6	36
Total colleges	0	0	18	27	7	52

Table 2. Percentage of different populations within commuting distance of a free-access college in Indiana (fall 1968)

| | Population in thousands | Percent within commuting distance | | |
Type of community		White	Black	Total
Metropolitan areas (over 1 million)				
Central city	0	—*	—	—
Fringe	29	0	—	0
Other metropolitan areas	2,824	0	0	0
Counties over 20,000	1,376	0	0	0
Counties under 20,000	438	0	—	0
Total state	4,667	0	0	0

*Dash (—) = base too small for reliable estimate.

Table 3. Estimate of additional colleges required to put specified percentages of the population of Indiana within commuting distance of a free-access college

	As of fall 1968	Hypothetical additional colleges				
Number of free-access colleges	0	9†	4	4	9	18
Cumulative percent of population within commuting distance	0%	50%	61%	70%	80%	90%
Average population within commuting distance of each college (in thousands)	0	258†	126	109	52	38

† Figures in this line are not cumulative. Each refers to an independent set of additional colleges.

Iowa

With 94 percent of its total area in farmlands, Iowa is rightly regarded as an agricultural state. Few appreciate, however, that the state produces three times as much wealth in manufacturing as in farming. Iowa is an average state with respect to population density and per capita income. The state has one of the highest high school retention rates in the country, but is slightly below average with respect to the proportion of those graduates attending college. Of those who do, more than half enroll in public institutions within the state.

Iowa has a number of private colleges (34) in addition to its 3 senior and 21 public junior colleges. Separate boards govern the two- and four-year institutions, but the relatively new and voluntary Iowa Coordinating Council is intended as a public planning forum for all higher institutions. State support for higher education is above average in Iowa, but there are no long-range objectives stated as a formal master plan.

Free-access higher education in Iowa is synonymous with the public junior colleges, though a few are too selective to qualify. The two-year institutions are typically small, and, as a group, they enroll only 1 out of 4 first-time college students in the state.

The proportion of Iowa's population living within commuting distance of a free-access institution is only slightly below the national average, but the locations of those colleges are not as good as they might be. Several cluster near one another in the central portion of the state, and three of the most prominent cities in Iowa (Des Moines, Sioux City, and Dubuque) do not have a free-access institution. As Table 3 indicates, there are six or eight locations where new institutions could serve substantially larger numbers of potential students than does the average existing free-access institution in Iowa. It would take some 20 additional colleges to put 9 out of 10 Iowa youth within easy commuting distance of an accessible college.

Table 1. Number of recognized colleges at different levels of accessibility in Iowa (fall 1968)

| | Level of accessibility | | | | | |
| | Free-access | | Less accessible | | | Total |
Type of college	1	2	3	4	5	colleges
Public two-year	0	18	2	1	0	21
Public four-year	0	0	0	2	1	3
Branches	0	0	0	0	0	0
All private	0	0	3	27	4	34
Total colleges	0	18	5	30	5	58

Iowa

Population of metropolitan areas

- ● 50,000–250,000
- ▲ 250,000–500,000
- ■ **500,000–1,000,000**
- ♦ **More than 1,000,000**

```
0      25    50         100              200
|      |     |          |                |
           Miles
```

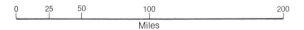 Commuting area of a free-access college (see Chapter 5 for explanation)

Table 2. Percentage of different populations within commuting distance of a free-access college in Iowa (fall 1968)

Type of community	Population in thousands	Percent within commuting distance		
		White	Black	Total
Metropolitan areas (over 1 million)				
Central city	0	—*	—	—
Fringe	0	—	—	—
Other metropolitan areas	915	47	48	47
Counties over 20,000	1,026	42	—	43
Counties under 20,000	812	27	—	27
Total state	2,753	39	52	39

* Dash (—) = base too small for reliable estimate.

Table 3. Estimate of additional colleges required to put specified percentages of the population of Iowa within commuting distance of a free-access college

	As of fall 1968	Hypothetical additional colleges				
Number of free-access colleges	18	2†	3	4	5	6
Cumulative percent of population within commuting distance	39%	50%	61%	72%	82%	90%
Average population within commuting distance of each college (in thousands)	60	153†	100	71	55	40

† Figures in this line are not cumulative. Each refers to an independent set of additional colleges.

Kansas

Kansas shares many characteristics with Iowa. Agriculture dominates the landscape (96 percent of the state is farmland), though there is also a substantial amount of manufacturing. In per capita income and other gross demographic indexes, Kansas is close enough to the national average to serve as an appropriate geographical center of the nation. As in the other Plains states, an unusually large proportion of students graduate from secondary school. Since college attendance is also above average in Kansas, this state has one of the highest proportions of 18-year-olds in college of all states in the union.

About half of the 50 colleges in Kansas are private. All of the seven public senior institutions are governed by the State Board of Regents. The State Board of Education has certain powers of authorization with respect to the 17 public two-year institutions, but these colleges are governed locally. The state doesn't have a comprehensive master plan, but in 1962 a group of outside consultants did prepare a report entitled "Kansas Plans for the Next Generation." Many of their recommendations were adopted, and work on a long-range plan has just been initiated under the sponsorship of the State Legislative Council. State support for higher education is somewhat above average on absolute and relative scales.

All the 17 public two-year colleges and the 4 public senior institutions are free-access. Most of the two-year institutions are fairly small, but the large enrollments of those senior institutions that are still free-access means that about half of the first-time students in Kansas are enrolling in free-access colleges.

In Kansas the proportion of the age group that lives within commuting distance of a free-access institution is about the same as the national average. Most of the smaller cities have a free-access college. The more populous urban areas of the state are less well covered, and, as Table 3 shows, there are several quite populous potential locations for free-access institutions. It would take some 15 additional colleges to cover 80 percent of the state's population. The remaining fifth of the population lives in areas that are at present too sparsely populated to justify additional colleges.

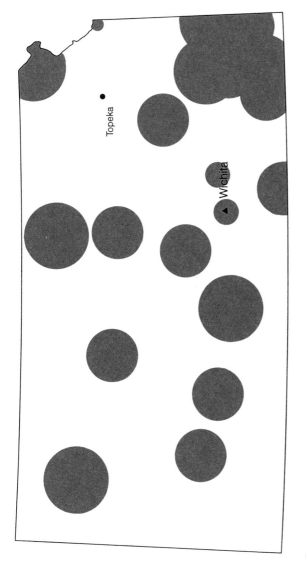

Kansas

Population of
metropolitan areas

- 50,000—250,000
- ▲ 250,000—500,000
- ■ **500,000—1,000,000**
- ◆ **More than 1,000,000**

Topeka

Wichita

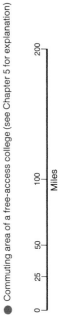

● Commuting area of a free-access college (see Chapter 5 for explanation)

0   25   50   100   200

Miles

Table 1. Number of recognized colleges at different levels of accessibility in Kansas (fall 1968)

| | Free-access | | Less accessible | | | Total |
Type of college	1	2	3	4	5	colleges
Public two-year	11	6	0	0	0	17
Public four-year	0	4	2	1	0	7
Branches	0	0	0	0	0	0
All private	0	0	4	22	0	26
Total colleges	11	10	6	23	0	50

Column group header: Level of accessibility

Table 2. Percentage of different populations within commuting distance of a free-access college in Kansas (fall 1968)

| | Population | Percent within commuting distance | | |
Type of community	in thousands	White	Black	Total
Metropolitan areas (over 1 million)				
Central city	122	59	86	72
Fringe	207	0	—*	0
Other metropolitan areas	522	56	55	56
Counties over 20,000	706	50	42	49
Counties under 20,000	618	32	—	32
Total state	2,175	42	59	43

*Dash (—) = base too small for reliable estimate.

Table 3. Estimate of additional colleges required to put specified percentages of the population of Kansas within commuting distance of a free-access college

	As of fall 1968	Hypothetical additional colleges				
Number of free-access colleges	21	1†	3	3	8	18
Cumulative percent of population within commuting distance	43%	49%	62%	69%	80%	90%
Average population within commuting distance of each college (in thousands)	44	150†	91	56	30	12

† Figures in this line are not cumulative. Each refers to an independent set of additional colleges.

Kentucky

Kentucky is primarily an agricultural state. It resembles the Southern states in its relatively low per capita income and the very small proportion of the labor force in white-collar jobs, but the black population is not large. The proportion of Kentucky youth graduating from high school is one of the smallest in the nation, and the proportion of those graduates going on to college is also below average. They are distributed to higher education in roughly the national 4–1–1 ratio, to in-state public, in-state private, and out-of-state institutions.

There are seven public senior institutions in Kentucky coordinated by a Council on Public Higher Education. The 14 community colleges are organized like those in Alaska and Hawaii; they are branches of the state university. In 1966 the Council on Higher Education published the reports that constitute the master plan for "Higher Education in Kentucky, 1965–1975." Public support for higher education in Kentucky is about average but well above average in relation to the wealth of the state.

Free-access higher education in Kentucky is largely associated with the state university and its various community college branches. Most of these branches are new and quite small, though on the whole roughly one-third of the first-time college students in Kentucky attend a free-access institution.

Slightly more than half the population of Kentucky lives within commuting distance of free-access colleges, which are well distributed in the urban areas of the state. Since the state is fairly densely populated, there are a number of additional locations in the state with sufficient population to justify free-access institutions. Ten additional branches, properly located, could cover as much as 80 percent of the state's population. However the critical question concerning the future of access to higher education in Kentucky revolves on the question of how the community college branches will develop over the next 5 to 10 years. Will they get the support necessary to follow the route of comprehensive, accessible higher education that Florida has taken, or will they become limited arms of the public universities, as is the case in Indiana and Ohio just to the north?

Table 1. Number of recognized colleges at different levels of accessibility in Kentucky (fall 1968)

| | Level of accessibility | | | | | |
| | Free-access | | Less accessible | | | Total colleges |
Type of college	1	2	3	4	5	
Public two-year	0	0	0	0	0	0
Public four-year	0	2	4	1	0	7
Branches	0	14	0	0	0	14
All private	0	1	6	17	2	26
Total colleges	0	17	10	18	2	47

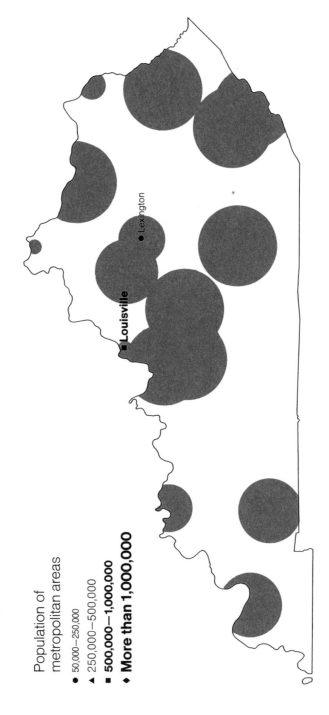

Kentucky

Population of
metropolitan areas

● 50,000—250,000
▲ 250,000—500,000
■ 500,000—1,000,000
◆ **More than 1,000,000**

■**Louisville**

●Lexington

● Commuting area of a free-access college (see Chapter 5 for explanation)

0   25   50   100

Miles

**Table 2. Percentage of different populations within commuting distance
of a free-access college in Kentucky (fall 1968)**

Type of community	Population in thousands	Percent within commuting distance		
		White	Black	Total
Metropolitan areas (over 1 million)				
Central city	0	—*	—	—
Fringe	230	26	—	26
Other metropolitan areas.	829	70	89	73
Counties over 20,000.	1,052	51	56	52
Counties under 20,000.	922	41	45	41
Total state	3,033	51	69	52

*Dash (—) = base too small for reliable estimate.

**Table 3. Estimate of additional colleges
required to put specified percentages of the population of Kentucky
within commuting distance of a free-access college**

	As of fall 1968	Hypothetical additional colleges			
Number of free-access colleges	17	2†	4	4	6
Cumulative percent of population within commuting distance.	52%	60%	71%	80%	90%
Average population within commuting distance of each college (in thousands)	93	117†	85	69	48

† Figures in this line are not cumulative. Each refers to an independent set of additional colleges.

Louisiana

A very high proportion of blacks in the population and a relatively low per capita income make Louisiana similar to other Deep South states, but it is more urbanized and has a greater investment in trade than is typical of the region. The proportion of students graduating from high school, and in turn of those who go on to college is somewhat below average in Louisiana. Of students who go to college, a very high proportion go to public institutions in the state. Louisiana is unusual in having a highly developed system of postsecondary vocational schools, which enroll a substantial proportion of high school graduates.

In the 1930s Louisiana initiated a major development of its state university, which now has five campuses. There are an additional dozen or so state colleges and junior colleges. Despite the traditional emphasis on public higher education, the Louisiana Coordinating Council for Higher Education has been formed only quite recently. State appropriations for higher education are somewhat below the 50-state average but are above average in relation to income.

Louisiana is one of the few states where free-access higher education is provided mainly by senior state institutions (Montana, West Virginia, and Arkansas are others). There are six public two-year institutions, but most of the enrollment is in the four-year colleges. Taken together the free-access institutions in Louisiana enroll three-fourths of the first-time students in the state.

About half of the population in Louisiana lives within commuting distance of a free-access college. These colleges cover practically all the small metropolitan areas in the state. New Orleans is not nearly so well covered, particularly its fringe areas. An additional dozen colleges could put 4 out of 5 Louisiana students within commuting distance of readily accessible higher education. Not many more could be easily justified on grounds of proximity to people.

Table 1. Number of recognized colleges at different levels of accessibility in Louisiana (fall 1968)

| | Free-access | | Less accessible | | | Total |
Type of college	1	2	3	4	5	colleges
Public two-year	1	5	0	0	0	6
Public four-year	1	8	2	0	0	11
Branches	0	0	0	0	0	0
All private	0	0	2	7	1	10
Total colleges	2	13	4	7	1	27

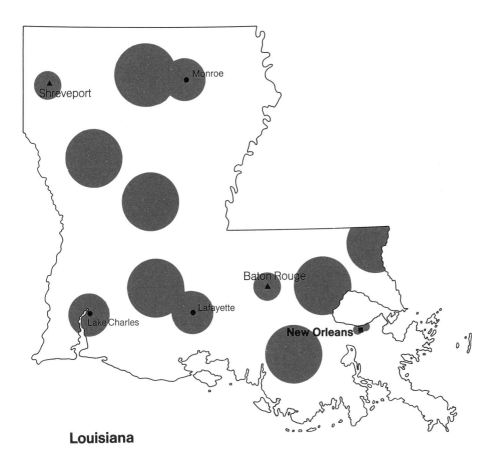

Louisiana

Population of
metropolitan areas

● 50,000–250,000

▲ 250,000–500,000

■ **500,000–1,000,000**

♦ **More than 1,000,000**

● Commuting area of a free-access college (see Chapter 5 for explanation)

Table 2. Percentage of different populations within commuting distance of a free-access college in Louisiana (fall 1968)

Type of community	Population in thousands	Percent within commuting distance		
		White	Black	Total
Metropolitan areas (over 1 million)				
Central city	628	43	40	42
Fringe	280	11	5	10
Other metropolitan areas.	843	85	83	84
Counties over 20,000.	1,154	42	40	41
Counties under 20,000.	352	25	25	25
Total state	3,257	49	47	48

Table 3. Estimate of additional colleges required to put specified percentages of the population of Louisiana within commuting distance of a free-access college

	As of fall 1968	Hypothetical additional colleges			
Number of free-access colleges 15		3†	5	5	11
Cumulative percent of population within commuting distance. 48%		59%	70%	80%	91%
Average population within commuting distance of each college (in thousands) 104		122†	70	62	33

† Figures in this line are not cumulative. Each refers to an independent set of additional colleges.

Maine

No state is typical, but it seems particularly true that Maine is not representative of the Northeast. Of all the states in that region, it has the lowest population density and the lowest per capita income. Maine is also one of the few states in the country that is not gaining population. The proportion of students graduating from secondary school is roughly average for the nation, but the proportion going on to higher education is very low — so low that the ratio of first-time college students to 18-year-olds in Maine is also among the lowest in the nation.

Maine devotes roughly the same proportion of its income to higher education as other states, but that effort is below average in terms of absolute dollars. Financial limitations are exacerbated by the fact that practically all the public institutions in Maine are four-year colleges. Maine has had no master plan. A single board for governance of all public higher education was formed in 1968.

Maine has the dubious distinction of being one of the three states in the country that have not a single free-access institution (Indiana and Nevada are the others). Since most of the population of Maine is "downeast," three free-access colleges could theoretically cover half the population of the state, and it would take only eight or so to cover three-fourths.

To balance the picture it should be recognized that there are a few inexpensive public institutions in Maine that are only slightly too selective to be classified as free-access. About two-fifths of the population lives near one of these partially accessible colleges.

Table 1. Number of recognized colleges at different levels of accessibility in Maine (fall 1968)

| | Level of accessibility | | | | | |
| | Free-access | | Less accessible | | | Total |
Type of college	1	2	3	4	5	colleges
Public two-year	0	0	1	0	0	1
Public four-year	0	0	3	4	1	8
Branches	0	0	0	0	0	0
All private	0	0	1	7	5	13
Total colleges	0	0	5	11	6	22

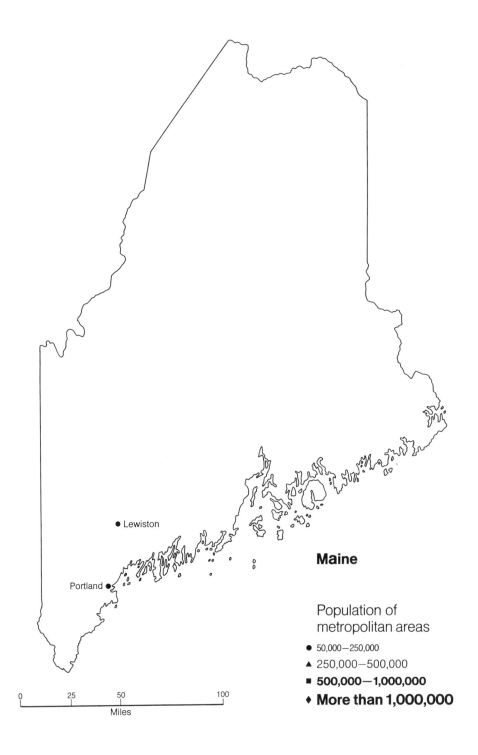

Maine

Population of
metropolitan areas

● 50,000—250,000
▲ 250,000—500,000
■ **500,000—1,000,000**
♦ **More than 1,000,000**

Lewiston

Portland

0   25   50   100
Miles

Table 2. Percentage of different populations within commuting distance of a free-access college in Maine (fall 1968)

Type of community	Population in thousands	Percent within commuting distance
Metropolitan areas (over 1 million)		
Central city	0	—*
Fringe	0	—
Other metropolitan areas.	209	0
Counties over 20,000.	724	0
Counties under 20,000.	35	0
Total state	968	0

*Dash (—) = base too small for reliable estimate.

Table 3. Estimate of additional colleges required to put specified percentages of the population of Maine within commuting distance of a free-access college

	As of fall 1968	Hypothetical additional colleges				
Number of free-access colleges 0		3†	2	2	4	4
Cumulative percent of population within commuting distance. 0%		49%	60%	70%	82%	91%
Average population within commuting distance of each college (in thousands) 0		157†	56	49	29	21

† Figures in this line are not cumulative. Each refers to an independent set of additional colleges.

Maryland

A good portion of the state of Maryland can be identified as the Southern tail of the Northeastern megalopolis. The state has grown rapidly in recent years and now has by far the greatest population density of any state outside the Northeast quadrant. Maryland retains some of its rural Southern flavor and an overrepresentation of blacks, but it also has a very high proportion of white-collar workers compared with other states. Per capita income is above average and much higher than any other state that might be considered Southern. Maryland's statistics concerning educational attainment are grossly similar to national averages.

Of 50 colleges in the state about half are public. These include 14 community colleges, 7 of which have been opened during the past decade. In 1962 the Commission for the Expansion of Public Higher Education published its report calling for an advisory council for higher education. Since that time the council has published annual reports and worked on the development of a comprehensive master plan. One problem has been the very small share of state funds apportioned to higher education in Maryland.

There are 19 free-access colleges in Maryland; a fourth of those are state colleges. A few of these institutions are large, but most are fairly small. Together they enroll about half the first-time college students in Maryland.

Compared with other states, a relatively high proportion (57 percent) of the population of Maryland lives within commuting distance of a free-access college. Baltimore and the suburban Washington area are the primary exceptions. Higher education in the urban fringes is less likely to be accessible to blacks, but no racial discrepancy exists in other areas. A relatively small number of colleges could substantially increase the proportion of population in close proximity to a free-access institution. On the other hand, the rapid urbanization and technocratic development in the metropolitan regions of the state suggest that higher levels of support for existing institutions and increased overall rates of access to college are primary problems.

Table 1. Number of recognized colleges at different levels of accessibility in Maryland (fall 1968)

	Level of accessibility					
	Free-access		Less accessible			Total
Type of college	1	2	3	4	5	colleges
Public two-year	0	14	0	0	0	14
Public four-year	1	4	1	3	0	9
Branches	0	0	1	0	0	1
All private	0	0	4	14	8	26
Total colleges	1	18	6	17	8	50

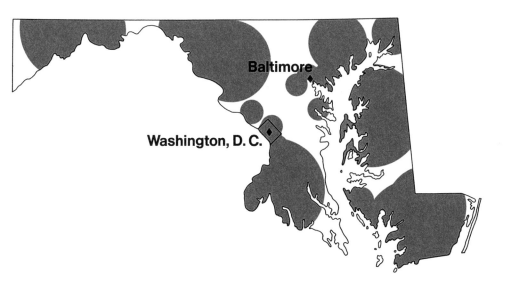

Maryland

Population of
metropolitan areas

● 50,000–250,000
▲ 250,000–500,000
■ **500,000–1,000,000**
♦ **More than 1,000,000**

0   25   50   100

Miles

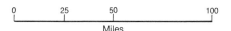 Commuting area of a free-access college (see Chapter 5 for explanation)

Table 2. Percentage of different populations within commuting distance of a free-access college in Maryland (fall 1968)

Type of community	Population in thousands	Percent within commuting distance		
		White	Black	Total
Metropolitan areas (over 1 million)				
Central city	939	36	37	36
Fringe	1,486	57	35	55
Other metropolitan areas.	48	71	67	70
Counties over 20,000.	562	93	89	92
Counties under 20,000.	67	91	90	91
Total state	3,102	59	47	57

**Table 3. Estimate of additional colleges
required to put specified percentages of the population of Maryland
within commuting distance of a free-access college**

	As of fall 1968	Hypothetical additional colleges			
Number of free-access colleges 19		1†	2	4	12
Cumulative percent of population within commuting distance. 57%		62%	71%	80%	90%
Average population within commuting distance of each college (in thousands) 93		141†	127	72	26

† Figures in this line are not cumulative. Each refers to an independent set of additional colleges.

Massachusetts

In many respects Massachusetts is a prototype Northeastern state—industrialized and urbanized, with a high proportion of white-collar workers and a per capita income well above average. The state is also well known as a stronghold of private higher education. The rate of secondary schools' retention and college attendance are both somewhat above average, though very few Massachusetts high school graduates remain in the state to attend public colleges. Massachusetts is the only state in the country in which students remaining in the state are more likely to attend private institutions than public. (Just five years ago this was also true in Connecticut, Pennsylvania, and New York.)

In addition to 75 private institutions, Massachusetts has 15 senior and 15 junior public colleges (two-thirds of the latter have opened in the past decade). A detailed self-study of higher education was completed in 1965, and in that year a Board of Higher Education was created to assume the responsibility as a coordinating agency for all public institutions in the state. Perhaps the most serious problem facing that body is the fact that Massachusetts has, in absolute and relative terms, one of the lowest rates of state support for higher education in the nation.

Of the 13 free-access institutions in Massachusetts, most are colleges in the 12-unit community college system. Some have substantial enrollments, though as a group they enroll only 1 out of 6 first-time students in the state. There are an additional half-dozen inexpensive state colleges, which are somewhat too selective to be called free-access. Because of their size and location, inclusion of these colleges would not greatly alter the general picture presented by the accompanying tables and map.

Slightly more than half the population of Massachusetts lives within commuting distance of a free-access college. The areas not covered lie mostly in metropolitan Boston. Blacks are not as likely to live near an accessible college, but their number is not large. Only three additional institutions could raise the proportion of the total population covered to 75 percent. It would take about 10 colleges to put an accessible institution near 90 percent of the state's residents.

Massachusetts provides an interesting contrast to California. Both are fairly well off financially and are often regarded as east and west focuses of the white-collar technocratic society. The states actually do not differ greatly with respect to some purely demographic aspects of the accessibility of higher education, but they represent different philosophies when it comes to the financial and educational commitment required to attract large numbers of students to local comprehensive education beyond high school.

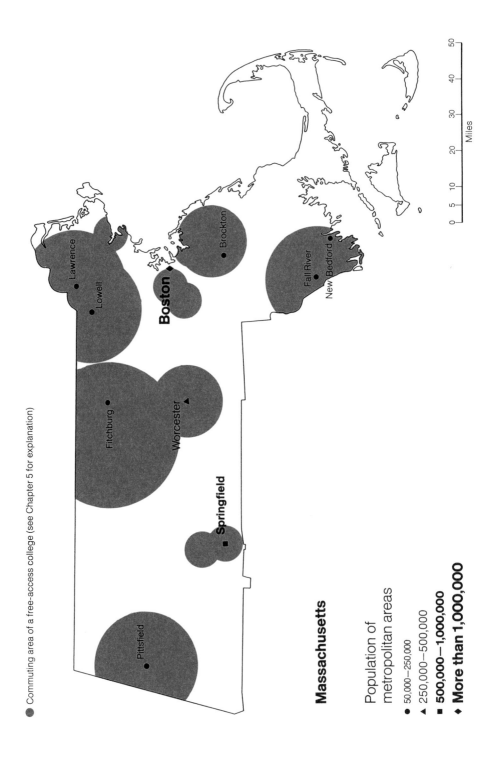

Commuting area of a free-access college (see Chapter 5 for explanation)

Massachusetts

Population of
metropolitan areas

• 50,000—250,000
▲ 250,000—500,000
■ **500,000—1,000,000**
♦ **More than 1,000,000**

Miles
0 5 10 20 30 40 50

Lawrence
Lowell
Brockton
Boston
Fall River
New Bedford
Fitchburg
Worcester
Springfield
Pittsfield

Table 1. Number of recognized colleges at different levels of accessibility in Massachusetts (fall 1968)

| | Level of accessibility | | | | | |
| | Free-access | | Less accessible | | | Total |
Type of college	1	2	3	4	5	colleges
Public two-year	0	12	2	1	0	15
Public four-year	0	1	6	6	2	15
Branches	0	0	0	0	0	0
All private	0	0	1	45	29	75
Total colleges	0	13	9	52	31	105

Table 2. Percentage of different populations within commuting distance of a free-access college in Massachusetts (fall 1968)

| | | Percent within commuting distance | | |
Type of community	Population in thousands	White	Black	Total
Metropolitan areas (over 1 million)				
Central city	697	16	0	15
Fringe	1,898	35	19	35
Other metropolitan areas	1,795	85	81	85
Counties over 20,000	747	52	—*	52
Counties under 20,000	10	0	—	0
Total state	5,147	53	25	52

* Dash (—) = base too small for reliable estimate.

Table 3. Estimate of additional colleges required to put specified percentages of the population of Massachusetts within commuting distance of a free-access college

	As of fall 1968	Hypothetical additional colleges			
Number of free-access colleges	13	1†	2	3	5
Cumulative percent of population within commuting distance	52%	62%	74%	81%	90%
Average population within commuting distance of each college (in thousands)	206	529†	297	124	92

† Figures in this line are not cumulative. Each refers to an independent set of additional colleges.

Michigan

A diversified economy and topography give Michigan a variety of strengths and problems. The southern portion of the state is densely populated and heavily industrialized, while the north leans to agriculture, and is actually quite sparsely settled. The high school retention rate is somewhat above average, but the proportion of students going on to higher education is lower in Michigan than in most states. Those who do attend college tend to remain in public institutions in the state.

There are 88 colleges in Michigan, half of which are private. Two-thirds of the public colleges are two-year institutions; many of these opened in the 1960s. Public higher education in Michigan has been coordinated since 1964 in a limited fashion through the State Board of Education. This agency has very restricted legal responsibility for overall policy and planning and does not govern individual institutions. The state's master plan, calling for an expansion of the junior college system, was formally adopted in 1969. Currently, state financial support for higher education in Michigan is about average considering the state's resources.

Free-access higher education in Michigan is almost synonymous with the public junior colleges. On the average these are fairly large as two-year colleges go. Collectively they enroll about 1 out of every 2 first-time college students in the state.

There is a free-access college within commuting distance for 2 out of 5 Michigan residents—only slightly below the national average. Whites are somewhat more likely to live within commuting distance of such a college than are blacks, but a more serious discrepancy lies in the city of Detroit. Only one-sixth of Detroit's total population is near an accessible institution, and there is actually no such college physically within the limits of the city. There are several locations in and around the Detroit area where accessible institutions could serve very large numbers of potential students, and currently there are efforts to develop community colleges in the city. As Table 3 indicates, even six additional colleges would raise the proportion of population covered in Michigan from 40 to 70 percent. It would probably take some 40 institutions to raise that figure to 90 percent.

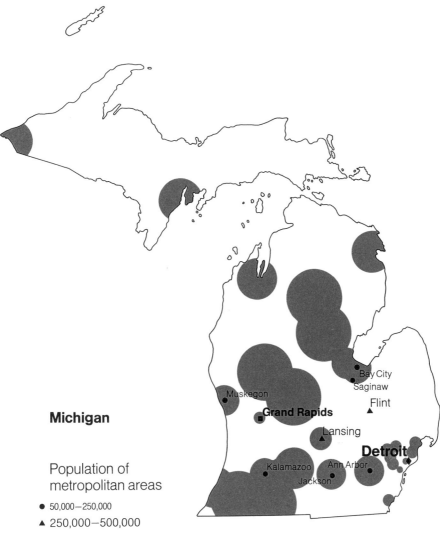

Michigan

Population of
metropolitan areas

● 50,000–250,000
▲ 250,000–500,000
■ **500,000–1,000,000**
♦ **More than 1,000,000**

Muskegon

Grand Rapids

●Bay City
Saginaw
Flint

Lansing

Detroit

Kalamazoo   Ann Arbor
        Jackson

0   25   50   100   200

Miles

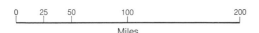

● Commuting area of a free-access college (see Chapter 5 for explanation)

Table 1. Number of recognized colleges at different levels of accessibility in Michigan (fall 1968)

	Level of accessibility					
	Free-access		Less accessible			Total
Type of college	1	2	3	4	5	colleges
Public two-year	3	24	3	0	0	30
Public four-year	0	2	2	6	3	13
Branches.	0	0	1	0	0	1
All private	0	0	2	37	5	44
Total colleges	3	26	8	43	8	88

Table 2. Percentage of different populations within commuting distance of a free-access college in Michigan (fall 1968)

	Population	Percent within commuting distance		
Type of community	in thousands	White	Black	Total
Metropolitan areas (over 1 million)				
Central city	1,670	13	22	16
Fringe	2,092	39	42	39
Other metropolitan areas.	2,200	57	58	57
Counties over 20,000.	1,524	47	78	48
Counties under 20,000	335	23	—*	23
Total state	7,821	41	33	40

*Dash (—) = base too small for reliable estimate.

Table 3. Estimate of additional colleges required to put specified percentages of the population of Michigan within commuting distance of a free-access college

	As of fall 1968	Hypothetical additional colleges				
Number of free-access colleges	29	2†	2	2	7	25
Cumulative percent of population within commuting distance	40%	52%	64%	72%	80%	90%
Average population within commuting distance of each college (in thousands)	108	470†	455	324	87	32

† Figures in this line are not cumulative. Each refers to an independent set of additional colleges.

Minnesota

Minnesota is well known as a farming state, though almost half of its population lives in the industrialized Minneapolis–St. Paul area. It is consequently a diversified though generally not densely populated state. A very high proportion of Minnesota youth graduate from secondary school, though a somewhat below average percentage go on to college. Of those who do, roughly the national proportion of 4–1–1 attend public institutions within the state, private institutions in the state, or colleges outside the state.

Half of Minnesota's 54 colleges are private. In the public sector many are two-year colleges, half of which have been built since 1958. The Higher Education Coordinating Commission was established in 1966 to facilitate planning in all public higher institutions. No comprehensive master plan has yet been completed. Financial support for higher education in Minnesota is somewhat above average compared with other states.

Free-access higher education in Minnesota is largely associated with the two-year colleges, though there are five readily accessible four-year institutions. Furthermore, there is a substantial enrollment in postsecondary area vocational schools, which are not included in this report. The free-access colleges are frequently not large, and as a group they enroll some 43 percent of the first-time college students in Minnesota.

Slightly less than 3/10 of the population of Minnesota live within commuting distance of a free-access institution — noticeably less than the national average. These institutions are fairly equally distributed with respect to type of community. One result is that most of the individual free-access colleges in Minnesota cover a relatively small number of people. As Table 3 indicates, there are six or eight areas — mostly in the densely populated capital area — where additional free-access colleges could serve large numbers of people.

Because of the sparsely populated character of most of the state, it would be difficult to justify putting a college near more than about 80 percent of the population. Even this would require at least 20 new institutions.

Table 1. Number of recognized colleges at different levels of accessibility in Minnesota (fall 1968)

| | Level of accessibility | | | | | |
| | Free-access | | Less accessible | | | Total |
Type of college	1	2	3	4	5	colleges
Public two-year	4	12	2	0	0	18
Public four-year	0	5	1	2	1	9
Branches	0	0	0	0	0	0
All private	0	0	1	20	6	27
Total colleges	4	17	4	22	7	54

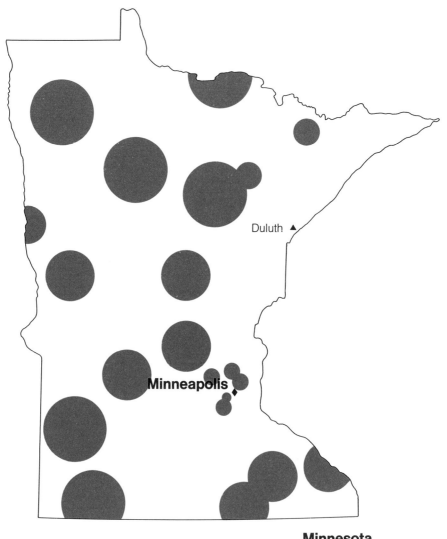

Minnesota

Population of
metropolitan areas

● 50,000–250,000
▲ 250,000–500,000
■ **500,000–1,000,000**
♦ **More than 1,000,000**

0   25   50   100   200
                    Miles

● Commuting area of a free-access college (see Chapter 5 for explanation)

Table 2. Percentage of different populations within commuting distance of a free-access college in Minnesota (fall 1968)

Type of community	Population in thousands	Percent within commuting distance		
		White	Black	Total
Metropolitan areas (over 1 million)				
Central city	796	26	25	26
Fringe	686	24	—*	24
Other metropolitan areas	271	24	—	24
Counties over 20,000	1,079	39	—	39
Counties under 20,000	580	26	—	26
Total state	3,412	30	24	29

*Dash (—) = base too small for reliable estimate.

Table 3. Estimate of additional colleges required to put specified percentages of the population of Minnesota within commuting distance of a free-access college

	As of fall 1968	Hypothetical additional colleges				
Number of free-access colleges	21	5†	3	5	8	17
Cumulative percent of population within commuting distance	29%	50%	60%	70%	80%	90%
Average population within commuting distance of each college (in thousands)	48	142†	108	68	42	20

† Figures in this line are not cumulative. Each refers to an independent set of additional colleges.

Mississippi

To the extent that Massachusetts is a prototype Northeastern industrial state, Mississippi is a prototype of the Deep South. Its economy is primarily agricultural, there is a very low degree of urbanization, and a very small proportion of the labor force is white-collar. It is well known that Mississippi has a higher proportion of blacks than any other state in the country. The proportion of students graduating from high school is among the lowest of all states, but the proportion of those graduates going on to college is above average. Most of these students remain in the state to attend public institutions.

The public institutions of Mississippi outnumber the private 29 to 17. Two-thirds of these public colleges are two-year institutions that operate under the jurisdiction of a junior college commission and the State Board of Education. All the public senior institutions in the state have been governed since 1910 by the Board of Trustees of Institutions of Higher Learning. State appropriations for higher education are very low in Mississippi — a condition that may be influenced by the recently completed master plan for the state. It should be noted, however, that state support in relation to state resources is about average.

There are 26 free-access institutions in Mississippi — an unusually large number considering the population and resources of the state. Most are public junior colleges, though four are public senior institutions and two are private. Most of these institutions are small, though collectively they do enroll 7 out of 10 first-time students in Mississippi.

Roughly two-thirds of the population of Mississippi lives within commuting distance of a free-access college. This is one of the highest rates in the country, though it is inflated by the fact that five of the free-access colleges are predominantly Negro. Not counting those institutions, some 57 percent of whites live near accessible, predominantly white colleges. There are only a few areas in the state where substantial numbers of people have no accessible institution within commuting distance, but the whole matter of accessibility of higher education in this and other Deep South states is, of course, considerably complicated by segregated facilities — de facto and otherwise.

Mississippi

Population of
metropolitan areas

- 50,000–250,000
- ▲ 250,000–500,000
- ■ **500,000–1,000,000**
- ◆ **More than 1,000,000**

Miles

● Commuting area of a free-access college (see Chapter 5 for explanation)

Table 1. Number of recognized colleges at different levels of accessibility in Mississippi (fall 1968)

Type of college	Free-access 1	Free-access 2	Less accessible 3	Less accessible 4	Less accessible 5	Total colleges
Public two-year	10	10	0	0	0	20
Public four-year	0	4	3	0	1	8
Branches	0	0	0	1	0	1
All private	1	1	6	7	2	17
Total colleges	11	15	9	8	3	46

Table 2. Percentage of different populations within commuting distance of a free-access college in Mississippi (fall 1968)

Type of community	Population in thousands	Percent within commuting distance — White	Black	Total
Metropolitan areas (over 1 million)				
Central city	0	—*	—	—
Fringe	0	—	—	—
Other metropolitan areas	221	80	81	80
Counties over 20,000	1,353	74	69	72
Counties under 20,000	605	48	43	46
Total state	2,179	67	63	65

*Dash (—) = base too small for reliable estimate.

Table 3. Estimate of additional colleges required to put specified percentages of the population of Mississippi within commuting distance of a free-access college

	As of fall 1968	Hypothetical additional colleges		
Number of free-access colleges	26	1†	3	5
Cumulative percent of population within commuting distance	65%	70%	80%	90%
Average population within commuting distance of each college (in thousands)	55	110†	67	46

† Figures in this line are not cumulative. Each refers to an independent set of additional colleges.

Missouri

In several respects the demographic characteristics of Missouri confirm its border-state image. It has more manufacturing and white-collar workers than the Southern states but less than the industrialized Midwest. Similarly, the black population and the per capita income rest midway between the two regions. The proportion of high school graduates in Missouri is somewhat above average, but the rate of college attendance is average for the nation. College-going students are distributed approximately as they are in the nation at large: four go to public institutions in the state, one to private institutions in the state, and one migrates outside the state.

There are 42 private and 25 public institutions in Missouri. Half the public colleges are two-year institutions, most of which have been opened since 1958. Public higher institutions in Missouri have received less than average state financial support. In 1963 an advisory board of public representatives was formed to coordinate higher education in the state. This Missouri Commission on Higher Education completed the state's first comprehensive master plan in 1966. It is basically similar to the California plan but does not include a policy of free tuition and colleges are not in close proximity to most residents.

Some 4 out of 10 first-time students in Missouri enroll in one of the 15 free-access institutions. Twelve of these are community colleges, most of which are quite small, though Metropolitan Community College in Kansas City and the Junior College of St. Louis County are very large. (In this report, each of the three campuses of the latter is counted as an institution.)

Some 4 out of 10 Missouri residents live within commuting distance of a free-access college; for blacks the ratio is 6 in 10. There are free-access colleges in a number of the smaller cities in the state, and most of the people not covered by such an institution live in or near the two large metropolitan areas, St. Louis and Kansas City, which together account for more than half the population of Missouri. As Table 3 suggests, several locations in these urban areas are good potential sites for new colleges. Because of the size and population of the state, 20 or more additional colleges are needed to cover four-fifths of the state's residents.

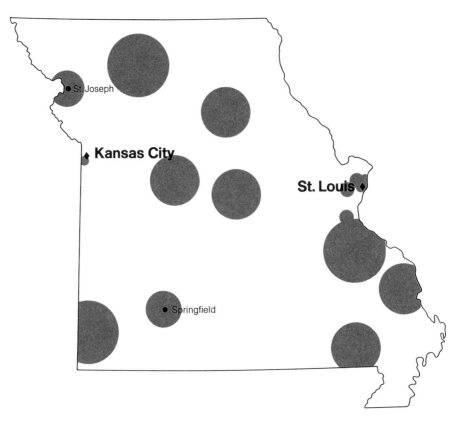

Missouri

Population of
metropolitan areas

● 50,000—250,000

▲ 250,000—500,000

■ **500,000—1,000,000**

◆ **More than 1,000,000**

0	25	50		100		200

Miles

● Commuting area of a free-access college (see Chapter 5 for explanation)

Table 1. Number of recognized colleges at different levels of accessibility in Missouri (fall 1968)

	Level of accessibility					
	Free-access		Less accessible			Total
Type of college	1	2	3	4	5	colleges
Public two-year	6	6	0	0	0	12
Public four-year	0	3	5	4	0	12
Branches................................	0	0	1	0	0	1
All private...............................	0	0	1	31	10	42
Total colleges	6	9	7	35	10	67

Table 2. Percentage of different populations within commuting distance of a free-access college in Missouri (fall 1968)

		Percent within commuting distance		
Type of community	Population in thousands	White	Black	Total
Metropolitan areas (over 1 million)				
Central city	1,225	51	69	55
Fringe	1,156	33	43	33
Other metropolitan areas....................	217	95	100	95
Counties over 20,000.....................	906	40	21	39
Counties under 20,000....................	814	19	—*	19
Total state	4,318	39	60	41

* Dash (—) = base too small for reliable estimate.

Table 3. Estimate of additional colleges required to put specified percentages of the population of Missouri within commuting distance of a free-access college

	As of fall 1968	Hypothetical additional colleges				
Number of free-access colleges 15		3†	5	4	9	15
Cumulative percent of population within commuting distance............... 41%		51%	62%	70%	81%	90%
Average population within commuting distance of each college (in thousands) 118		138†	95	87	52	28

† Figures in this line are not cumulative. Each refers to an independent set of additional colleges.

Montana

The Rocky Mountains cover most of the western half of Montana, and the remainder of the state is devoted to grazing and vast fields of grain. It is one of the least populated states in the nation, and the per capita income is below average. Despite these facts the proportion of students graduating from high school and the percentage going on to college are both above average. Three out of four Montana youths attending college remain in the state and enroll in one of its nine public institutions.

One possible explanation for the relatively high level of educational attainment in Montana is the fact that state appropriations for higher education are above the national average and rank among the highest in the nation in relation to resources available. For 30 years the State Board of Education has coordinated the activities of all public institutions in Montana. In 1962 the Board of Regents of the University of Montana produced a master plan for the state that has been revised periodically.

Eight of the nine public institutions in Montana are free-access as defined here. Montana is one of the few states where most of the free-access colleges are senior institutions. Even though most are quite small, they enroll 3 out of 5 first-time college students in the state.

Only 31 percent of Montana's population live within commuting distance of a free-access institution, but the state is so sparsely populated that very few additional colleges could be easily justified on the basis of proximity to people. The existing free-access institutions are well distributed, except for the minor puzzling fact that Great Falls, the largest city in the state, does not have a free-access college.

Table 1. Number of recognized colleges at different levels of accessibility in Montana (fall 1968)

| | Level of accessibility | | | | | |
| | Free-access | | Less accessible | | | Total |
Type of college	1	2	3	4	5	colleges
Public two-year	2	1	0	0	0	3
Public four-year	0	5	1	0	0	6
Branches	0	0	0	0	0	0
All private	0	0	0	3	0	3
Total colleges	2	6	1	3	0	12

Population of
metropolitan areas

- 50,000–250,000
▲ 250,000–500,000
■ **500,000–1,000,000**
◆ **More than 1,000,000**

● Commuting area of a free-access college (see Chapter 5 for explanation)

Montana

Miles

0   25   50   100   200

Great Falls

Billings

Table 2. Percentage of different populations within commuting distance of a free-access college in Montana (fall 1968)

Type of community	Population in thousands	Percent within commuting distance
Metropolitan areas (over 1 million)		
Central city	0	—*
Fringe	0	—
Other metropolitan areas	152	39
Counties over 20,000	178	49
Counties under 20,000	342	17
Total state	672	31

*Dash (—) = base too small for reliable estimate.

Table 3. Estimate of additional colleges required to put specified percentages of the population of Montana within commuting distance of a free-access college

	As of fall 1968	Hypothetical additional colleges				
Number of free-access colleges	8	6†	8	8	10	14
Cumulative percent of population within commuting distance	31%	50%	60%	70%	81%	90%
Average population within commuting distance of each college (in thousands)	26	22†	9	8	7	5

† Figures in this line are not cumulative. Each refers to an independent set of additional colleges.

Nebraska

Despite the fact that there has been considerable industrial development in eastern Nebraska, the state is still almost a prototype Plains state. Like Kansas and Iowa more than 95 percent of the state is farmlands. Per capita income is somewhat below the 50-state average. The rate of high school graduation is above average, while the rate of college attendance is typical for the country.

There are 16 private colleges in Nebraska. The 12 public institutions are evenly divided between two- and four-year colleges. Most of these institutions are governed by separate boards. State financial support for higher education is somewhat above average in Nebraska, both in absolute terms and relative to resources available. There is evidently relatively little concern for statewide planning. The first voluntary coordinating council was formed as late as 1969.

Free-access education in Nebraska is served by five public junior colleges and three four-year institutions. These are generally quite small and enroll only 3 out of 10 first-time students in the state.

In Nebraska, location of accessible colleges is somewhat unconnected with where the people live. The few free-access colleges are spread throughout the state, but none are in or near the major population centers. As a result only 16 percent of the population of the state live within commuting distance of a free-access institution. A few additional colleges could change this picture considerably. For example, the eight existing free-access colleges serve about 225,000 people; an additional eight colleges appropriately placed could serve about 600,000. An easier and quicker way to increase accessibility in the state would be to make slight adjustments in the tuition and admissions policies in a few of the public institutions that do not now qualify as free-access.

Table 1. Number of recognized colleges at different levels of accessibility in Nebraska (fall 1968)

| | Level of accessibility | | | | | |
| | Free-access | | Less accessible | | | Total |
Type of college	1	2	3	4	5	colleges
Public two-year	3	2	1	0	0	6
Public four-year	0	3	2	0	0	5
Branches	0	0	1	0	0	1
All private	0	0	3	13	0	16
Total colleges	3	5	7	13	0	28

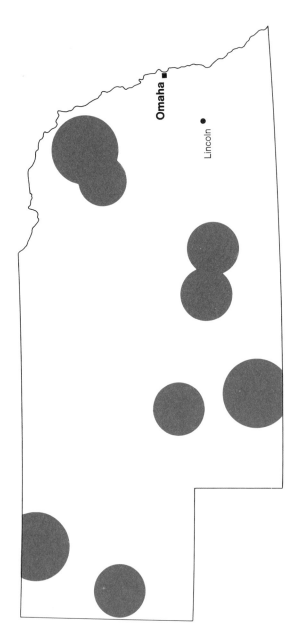

Nebraska

Population of
metropolitan areas

- 50,000—250,000
▲ 250,000—500,000
■ **500,000—1,000,000**
◆ **More than 1,000,000**

● Commuting area of a free-access college (see Chapter 5 for explanation)

Miles

0   25   50   100   200

Omaha ■

Lincoln ●

Table 2. Percentage of different populations within commuting distance of a free-access college in Nebraska (fall 1968)

Type of community	Population in thousands	Percent within commuting distance		
		White	Black	Total
Metropolitan areas (over 1 million)				
Central city	0	—*	—	—
Fringe	0	—	—	—
Other metropolitan areas	541	0	0	0
Counties over 20,000	261	51	—	51
Counties under 20,000	607	14	—	14
Total state	1,409	16	0	16

*Dash (—) = base too small for reliable estimate.

Table 3. Estimate of additional colleges required to put specified percentages of the population of Nebraska within commuting distance of a free-access college

	As of fall 1968	Hypothetical additional colleges				
Number of free-access colleges	8	6†	4	5	6	12
Cumulative percent of population within commuting distance	16%	52%	61%	70%	80%	90%
Average population within commuting distance of each college (in thousands)	28	86†	35	25	25	11

† Figures in this line are not cumulative. Each refers to an independent set of additional colleges.

Nevada

Nevada is a state of interesting extremes. It is one of the most sparsely populated states, but one of the fastest growing. A very small proportion of its work force is in manufacturing, but the per capita income is quite high. The state has no metropolitan area, though most of its population is concentrated in two well-defined localities. The rugged land may have few natural attractions, but the state economy runs largely on the dollars of visitors. A relatively small proportion of Nevada youth graduate from high school but, of those who do, the proportion attending college is about average for the nation. The percentage attending college is considerably below the access rate of five years ago; but that rate may have been temporarily inflated by rapid in-migration and a doubling of public colleges (two instead of one).

The state has only two higher institutions—both public universities. A Board of Regents serves as a single governing board, and several reports have been completed recently concerning the future of higher education in Nevada. The state support for higher education is somewhat above average on a per capita basis, though no better than average in relation to income.

Both of the public universities in Nevada are somewhat too selective to be classified as "free-access" as defined here. Consequently, Nevada is one of the three states in the nation where, as of fall 1968, the proportion of the population living within commuting distance of a readily accessible institution was zero. The unusual demography of the state simplifies the possibilities; one free-access college in Reno and one in Las Vegas would cover 60 percent of the population of the state. Lowering admissions requirements at the two existing institutions could nominally accomplish the same purpose. Actually, one community college has been opened in Elko, Nevada, since these data were collected; another is being actively considered for Las Vegas.

Table 1. Number of recognized colleges at different levels of accessibility in Nevada (fall 1968)

	Free-access		Less accessible			Total
Type of college	1	2	3	4	5	colleges
Public two-year	0	0	0	0	0	0
Public four-year	0	0	2	0	0	2
Branches	0	0	0	0	0	0
All private	0	0	0	0	0	0
Total colleges	0	0	2	0	0	2

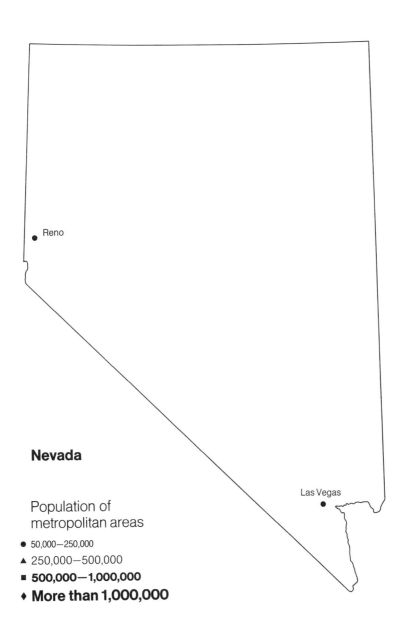

Nevada

Population of
metropolitan areas

● 50,000—250,000
▲ 250,000—500,000
■ **500,000—1,000,000**
♦ **More than 1,000,000**

Reno

Las Vegas

0   25   50   100   200
Miles

Table 2. Percentage of different populations within commuting distance of a free-access college in Nevada (fall 1968)

Type of community	Population in thousands	Percent within commuting distance		
		White	Black	Total
Metropolitan areas (over 1 million)				
Central city	0	—*	—	—
Fringe	0	—	—	—
Other metropolitan areas.	212	0	0	0
Counties over 20,000.	0	—	—	—
Counties under 20,000.	70	0	—	0
Total state	282	0	0	0

*Dash (—) = base too small for reliable estimate.

Table 3. Estimate of additional colleges required to put specified percentages of the population of Nevada within commuting distance of a free-access college

	As of fall 1968	Hypothetical additional colleges		
Number of free-access colleges	0	1†	1	3
Cumulative percent of population within commuting distance.	0	35%	61%	70%
Average population within commuting distance of each college (in thousands)	0	100†	73	8

† Figures in this line are not cumulative. Each refers to an independent set of additional colleges.

New Hampshire

New Hampshire is one of the most attractive states in the nation, but to some extent that beauty has been left to the enjoyment of private colleges. The state maintains its reputation as a relatively conservative New England center of manufacture. Per capita income is about average, as is the proportion of students graduating from secondary school. The rate of college entrance is well below the national average, and students are almost as likely to migrate out of the state as to attend public institutions in New Hampshire.

There are 14 private and 6 public colleges; three public colleges are junior and three senior. In 1963 a Board of Trustees was created to act as a single governing board for the senior institutions. The junior colleges are under the authority of the State Board of Education. No master plan has yet been developed in New Hampshire, though how much could be accomplished without a different public attitude toward the support of higher education in the state seems uncertain. In absolute dollars and in relation to wealth, New Hampshire provides the lowest level of financial support for higher education of all states in the Union.

New Hampshire has two free-access institutions and 44 percent of the state's population lives within commuting distance of one or the other. The state's demography is such that these two plus three additional free-access colleges could cover 85 percent of the state's population.

Such speculation is undermined by noting that the two existing free-access institutions are very small public junior colleges that enroll only 4 percent of the first-time college students in the state. It seems likely that the primary problem in New Hampshire is the development of public sentiment in favor of the support and development of the existing higher institutions and the expansion of opportunity for comprehensive education beyond high school.

Table 1. Number of recognized colleges at different levels of accessibility in New Hampshire (fall 1968)

Type of college	Free-access		Less accessible			Total colleges
	1	2	3	4	5	
Public two-year	0	2	0	1	0	3
Public four-year	0	0	1	2	0	3
Branches	0	0	0	0	0	0
All private	0	0	0	8	6	14
Total colleges	0	2	1	11	6	20

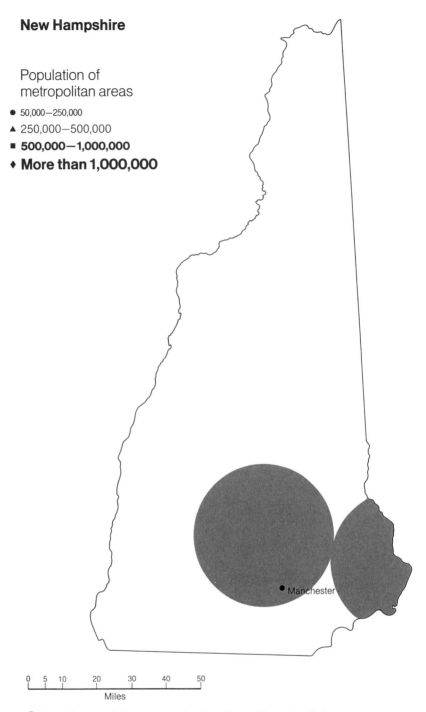

New Hampshire

Population of metropolitan areas

- 50,000—250,000
- ▲ 250,000—500,000
- ■ **500,000—1,000,000**
- ◆ **More than 1,000,000**

● Manchester

```
0   5  10    20    30    40    50
```
Miles

● Commuting area of a free-access college (see Chapter 5 for explanation)

**Table 2. Percentage of different populations within commuting distance
of a free-access college in New Hampshire (fall 1968)**

Type of community	Population in thousands	Percent within commuting distance
Metropolitan areas (over 1 million)		
Central city	0	—*
Fringe	0	—
Other metropolitan areas	108	63
Counties over 20,000	483	42
Counties under 20,000	16	0
Total state	607	44

* Dash (—) = base too small for reliable estimate.

**Table 3. Estimate of additional colleges
required to put specified percentages of the population of New Hampshire
within commuting distance of a free-access college**

	As of fall 1968	Hypothetical additional colleges			
Number of free-access colleges	2	1†	1	1	1
Cumulative percent of population within commuting distance	44%	62%	74%	85%	92%
Average population within commuting distance of each college (in thousands)	134	104†	77	62	48

† Figures in this line are not cumulative. Each refers to an independent set of additional colleges.

New Jersey

Most admissions officers around the country are aware of New Jersey's reputation as a prominent exporter of college students. It is a difficult condition to reconcile with the fact that New Jersey is one of the most densely populated and urbanized states, and has a very high proportion of white-collar workers and a very high per capita income. A larger proportion of students graduate from secondary school than in most states, and a slightly above-average proportion of those graduates go on to college. At the same time, the most recently available data (1968) again confirm that a very low proportion of those students attend public institutions within the state, and the proportion of those who migrate outside the state is the highest of all coterminous states in the country.

There are 33 private and 24 public institutions of higher learning in New Jersey. Half of the public colleges are two-year institutions, most of which have been opened during the past decade. The State Board of Education did govern all educational levels in the state, but recently the Board of Higher Education was created to coordinate the programs of all public and private institutions. The development of a comprehensive master plan in New Jersey has been delayed in part by difficulties in obtaining the requisite state funding to implement proposals based upon state studies. Per capita appropriations for higher education are very low; in relation to wealth, New Jersey ranks with New Hampshire and Massachusetts in providing the least support for higher education of all states.

The free-access colleges in New Jersey consist of 10 community colleges — practically all of which are fairly new. A few are large but many are quite small, particularly considering the dense population of the state. Taken together they enroll 1 out of 4 first-time college students in New Jersey.

Roughly 4 out of 10 students in the state live within commuting distance of a free-access college. The ratio for blacks is 6 in 10. The geographic possibility of locating additional free-access colleges to serve very large numbers of students is greater in New Jersey than in practically any other state. An additional seven such colleges could raise the proportion of the population covered to 80 percent. It seems doubtful, however, whether the New Jersey electorate has fully accepted an egalitarian conception of comprehensive free-access higher education. It is likely that the state's primary problem may be the development and support of existing institutions, but whether this route promises expanding and relevant educational opportunity also depends very much on the institutions themselves.

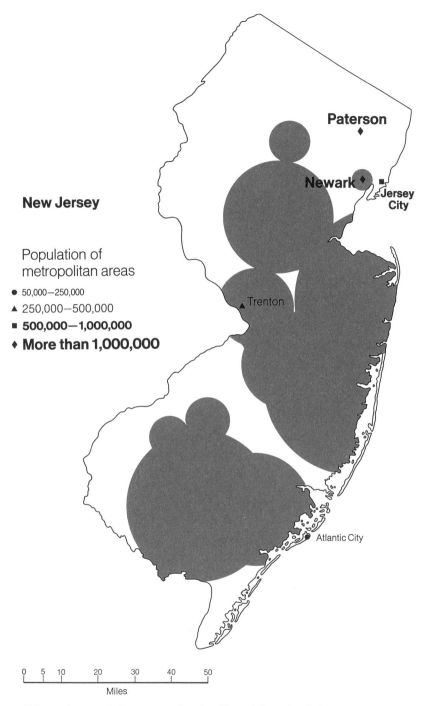

Paterson
♦

New Jersey

Newark ♦ ■
Jersey
City

Population of
metropolitan areas

● 50,000–250,000
▲ 250,000–500,000
■ **500,000–1,000,000**
♦ **More than 1,000,000**

▲ Trenton

● Atlantic City

0   5 10   20   30   40   50
├──┼──┼──────┼──────┼──────┼──────┤
            Miles

● Commuting area of a free-access college (see Chapter 5 for explanation)

Table 1. Number of recognized colleges at different levels of accessibility in New Jersey (fall 1968)

| | Level of accessibility | | | | | |
| | Free-access | | Less accessible | | | Total |
Type of college	1	2	3	4	5	colleges
Public two-year	**0**	**10**	2	0	0	12
Public four-year	**0**	**0**	1	4	3	8
Branches.	**0**	**0**	3	0	1	4
All private	**0**	**0**	0	26	7	33
Total colleges	**0**	**10**	6	30	11	57

Table 2. Percentage of different populations within commuting distance of a free-access college in New Jersey (fall 1968)

| | | Percent within commuting distance | | |
Type of community	Population in thousands	White	Black	Total
Metropolitan areas (over 1 million)				
Central city	685	35	79	45
Fringe	2,943	13	25	14
Other metropolitan areas.	1,160	36	55	38
Counties over 20,000.	1,279	92	13	92
Counties under 20,000.	0	—*	—	—
Total state	6,067	36	59	38

*Dash (—) = base too small for reliable estimate.

Table 3. Estimate of additional colleges required to put specified percentages of the population of New Jersey within commuting distance of a free-access college

	As of fall 1968	Hypothetical additional colleges				
Number of free-access colleges 10		2†	1	2	2	5
Cumulative percent of population within commuting distance. 39%		55%	62%	70%	81%	91%
Average population within commuting distance of each college (in thousands) 237		334†	607	304	304	121

† Figures in this line are not cumulative. Each refers to an independent set of additional colleges.

New Mexico

Like several of the other Western states, much of New Mexico's population is clustered in a few areas. Consequently, it is as urbanized as the nation as a whole, even though it is one of the most sparsely populated states. Per capita income is considerably below the national average. The proportion of students graduating from high school and the proportion of graduates going on to college are both somewhat below the average of other states.

The 16 higher institutions of New Mexico include five two-year and six four-year public institutions. All the public institutions are regulated by the Board of Educational Finance. In 1964 a commission appointed by the Board developed a limited master plan that is similar to that of the neighboring state of Colorado, but is somewhat more conservative with respect to expanding programs and educational opportunity. However, per capita state appropriations for higher education are higher in New Mexico than in most states despite the limited resources available.

Of the eight free-access institutions in New Mexico, half are senior institutions; the state master plan anticipates providing sufficient facilities so that the senior institutions will not have to become more selective than they are at present. Most of these institutions are fairly small; taken together they enroll 4 out of 10 first-time college students in the state.

Only about one-fifth of New Mexico's population lives within commuting distance of a free-access higher institution. The eight existing free-access colleges are spread about the state, but almost all are removed from population centers. Of course, part of the reason is that some of these population centers do have public institutions that are less accessible. For example, Albuquerque has the University of New Mexico, but that institution is somewhat too selective and too expensive to qualify as free-access. Nonetheless, as Table 3 indicates, four additional free-access colleges or adjustments in the admissions standards of some existing institutions could greatly effect the accessibility of higher education for the residents of New Mexico.

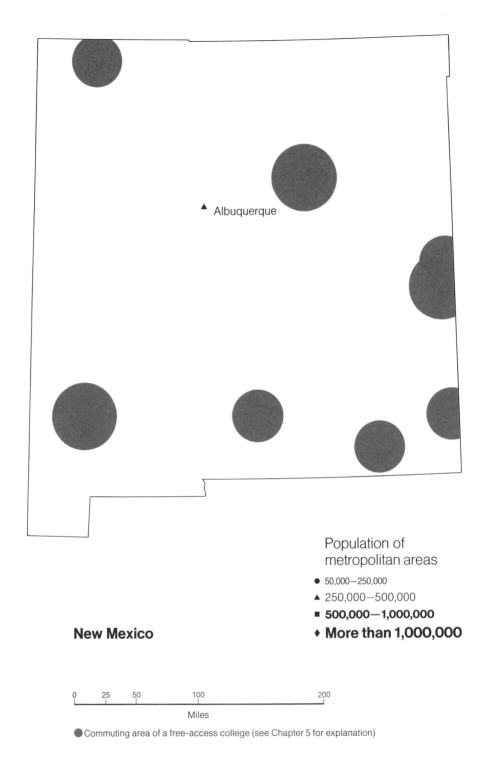

▲ Albuquerque

Population of
metropolitan areas

● 50,000–250,000
▲ 250,000–500,000
■ **500,000–1,000,000**
♦ **More than 1,000,000**

New Mexico

0   25   50   100   200

Miles

● Commuting area of a free-access college (see Chapter 5 for explanation)

Table 1. Number of recognized colleges at different levels of accessibility in New Mexico (fall 1968)

Type of college	Level of accessibility					Total colleges
	Free-access		Less accessible			
	1	2	3	4	5	
Public two-year	1	3	0	1	0	5
Public four-year	1	2	1	1	1	6
Branches*	0	1	0	0	0	1
All private	0	0	3	1	0	4
Total colleges	2	6	4	3	1	16

*See footnote on page 18.

Table 2. Percentage of different populations within commuting distance of a free-access college in New Mexico (fall 1968)

Type of community	Population in thousands	Percent within commuting distance			
		White	Black	Mexican American	Total
Metropolitan areas (over 1 million)					
Central city	0	—*	—	—	—
Fringe	0	—	—	—	—
Other metropolitan areas	262	0	—	0	0
Counties over 20,000	513	37	55	26	35
Counties under 20,000	175	20	—	14	18
Total state	950	24	38	16	22

*Dash (—) = base too small for reliable estimate.

Table 3. Estimate of additional colleges required to put specified percentages of the population of New Mexico within commuting distance of a free-access college

	As of fall 1968	Hypothetical additional colleges		
Number of free-access colleges	8	2†	2	4
Cumulative percent of population within commuting distance	22%	52%	63%	72%
Average population within commuting distance of each college (in thousands)	26	145†	50	21

† Figures in this line are not cumulative. Each refers to an independent set of additional colleges.

New York

Despite the fact that New York State has some of the most sparsely populated areas in the country, it ranks among the top states in overall population density. Because of the unequaled concentration of people, activity, and money in New York City, the state ranks very high in degree of urbanization, proportion of white-collar workers, per capita income, and—one must add—number of minority and poor families.

Despite its wealth and national leadership, New York ranks close to average with respect to the proportion of students graduating from high school. The percentage of those graduates going on to college also had been close to the national average, but recent data (1968) indicate a marked spurt. This increase is evidently spurious; it is caused by the reporting of occupational students to the National Center for Educational Statistics as degree-credit students, a procedural variation from the data of other states and of 1963 New York data. (See footnote 6 on page 206.)

There are more colleges in New York than in any other state. About 2 out of 3 are private, and these institutions as a group have played an unusual role in the history of higher education in the state. Since 1784, the Board of Regents has had broad authority concerning the planning and organization of both public and private higher education. Until fairly recently the state relied heavily on its numerous private institutions to serve its needs in higher education. Public higher education in New York State was largely identified with the city university, plus some vocational and teacher training institutions scattered about the state. The Board of Regents has exerted strong central authority. The Regents examinations and the large Regents scholarship programs provide two examples of its hegemony. The Regents examinations have set academic standards in New York State for many years; the scholarships provide the financial rationale for public utilization of private higher education.

The New York master plan, first produced in 1960 and revised at four-year intervals, provides for the coordination of the three main resources and centers of power in higher education in the state: private institutions, the State University, and the City University. The City University system has an unusually comprehensive master plan of its own. Higher education is financed at a level higher than is typical in most states, though state appropriations in New York represent an average effort if considered in relation to the wealth of the state.

In evaluating the accessibility of higher institutions in New York, the state scholarship program must be taken into account because it automatically makes state aid available to the vast majority of high school graduates (typically about $200 for each student whose family income is at the national median or below). Although this program obviously has some effect on the accessibility of New York institutions, it is to some extent offset by higher tuition fees. Even if the free-access limit of $400 annual tuition is raised to $600 in New York State because of the comprehensive scholarship program, this altered definition has little

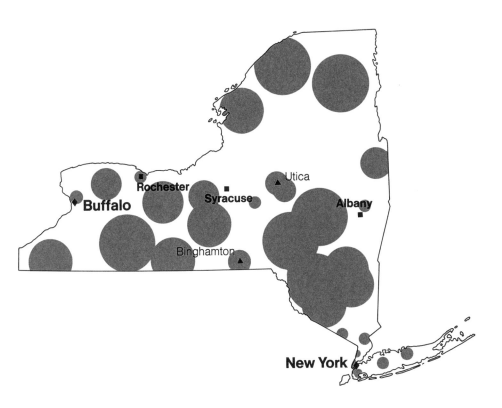

New York

Population of
metropolitan areas

● 50,000–250,000
▲ 250,000–500,000
■ **500,000–1,000,000**
♦ **More than 1,000,000**

0   25   50   100   200
Miles

 Commuting area of a free-access college (see Chapter 5 for explanation)

effect on the actual number of free-access institutions. The effect is small mainly because practically all the public four-year institutions and about a quarter of the public two-year colleges in New York are too selective to qualify as free-access institutions.

The 34 free-access institutions in New York are almost all public two-year colleges. As two-year colleges they are moderately large institutions, but because of their limited number in relation to the population in the state, they enroll only about 1 out of 4 first-time college students.

Slightly more than one-third of the population of the state lives within commuting distance of a free-access college. The proportion is substantially lower for blacks than it is for whites. The principal reason why blacks have less access is that the central cities — particularly New York — either lack free-access colleges or are quite inadequately covered.

New York presents, in fact, a rather startling discrepancy between the non-metropolitan counties and the densely populated urban areas. A number of readily accessible two-year institutions are distributed about the state, often in areas with limited population. As Table 3 indicates, however, there are a number of other locations in New York where free-access institutions could serve massive numbers of people within easy commuting distance. In fact, only 15 additional free-access institutions could raise the proportion of the population covered from 36 to 80 percent. Those areas where free-access higher education is not available are far more densely populated on the average than are areas where free-access colleges are now located.

Table 1. Number of recognized colleges at different levels of accessibility in New York (fall 1968)

| | Level of accessibility | | | | | |
| | Free-access | | Less accessible | | | Total |
Type of college	1	2	3	4	5	colleges
Public two-year	0	32	5	4	0	41
Public four-year	1	0	4	10	11	26
Branches	0	0	4	1	0	5
All private	0	1	2	76	55	134
Total colleges	1	33	15	91	66	206

Table 2. Percentage of different populations within commuting distance of a free-access college in New York (fall 1968)

Type of community	Population in thousands	Percent within commuting distance			
		White	Black	Puerto Rican	Total
Metropolitan areas (over 1 million)					
Central city	8,315	29	19	36	28
Fringe	3,687	32	30	29	32
Other metropolitan areas	2,535	37	39	—*	37
Counties over 20,000	2,206	73	77	—	73
Counties under 20,000	38	76	—	—	76
Total state	16,781	38	23	—	36

*Dash (—) = base too small for reliable estimate.

Table 3. Estimate of additional colleges required to put specified percentages of the population of New York within commuting distance of a free-access college

	As of fall 1968	Hypothetical additional colleges				
Number of free-access colleges	34	3†	2	3	7	21
Cumulative percent of population within commuting distance	36%	53%	60%	70%	80%	90%
Average population within commuting distance of each college (in thousands)	178	906†	630	575	239	78

† Figures in this line are not cumulative. Each refers to an independent set of additional colleges.

North Carolina

As with other Southern states, the basic social topography of North Carolina is heavily influenced by the relatively low per capita income, the very low proportion of white-collar workers in the labor force, and the high proportion of blacks in the population. The state is more heavily engaged in manufacturing than is typical of the region, and it has for some time enjoyed a progressive reputation in education. This reputation is reflected in heavy state support for higher education. Still, the state is below average in the holding power of the secondary schools, and a relatively small proportion of high school graduates go on to college. As a result the proportion of North Carolina college students to 18-year-olds in the state is one of the lowest in the nation.

North Carolina is heavily supplied with colleges — 47 private and 45 public. Of 26 public two-year colleges in the state, 24 have been opened in the past decade. All institutions of higher education in North Carolina are coordinated by the Board of Higher Education established in 1955. A recently completed master plan called for relatively few changes in the organization of higher education, but did result in the governor assuming the chairmanship of the Board of Higher Education.

Practically all the 29 free-access colleges in North Carolina are public two-year institutions. These are typically small institutions and some are technical institutes. Despite their number they enroll only one-third of all the first-time college students in the state.

Two-thirds of the population in North Carolina live within commuting distance of a free-access college. This is one of the largest proportions among all states in the country. Furthermore, these colleges are well placed in relation to population centers. The metropolitan areas are particularly well covered with respect to free-access higher education. There are only a few areas where proximity to people might be a reasonable argument for an additional institution. Increasing the rate of educational attainment, developing existing institutions, and coordinating all forms of postsecondary educational opportunity would now seem to be high priorities for the state.

Table 1. Number of recognized colleges at different levels of accessibility in North Carolina (fall 1968)

| | Level of accessibility | | | | | |
| | Free-access | | Less accessible | | | Total colleges |
Type of college	1	2	3	4	5	
Public two-year	10	15	1	0	0	26
Public four-year	0	4	5	4	3	16
Branches	0	0	3	0	0	3
All private	0	0	10	30	7	47
Total colleges	10	19	19	34	10	92

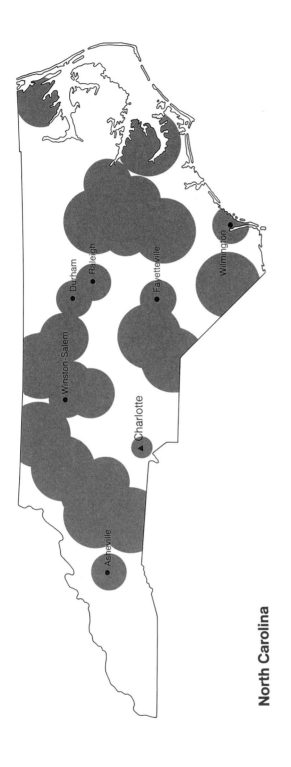

North Carolina

Population of
metropolitan areas

- 50,000–250,000
▲ 250,000–500,000
■ 500,000–1,000,000
◆ **More than 1,000,000**

● Commuting area of a free-access college (see Chapter 5 for explanation)

Miles

0   25   50   100   200

**Table 2. Percentage of different populations within commuting distance
of a free-access college in North Carolina (fall 1968)**

Type of community	Population in thousands	Percent within commuting distance		
		White	Black	Total
Metropolitan areas (over 1 million)				
Central city	0	—*	—	—
Fringe	0	—	—	—
Other metropolitan areas.	1,488	90	93	91
Counties over 20,000.	2,706	62	57	60
Counties under 20,000.	365	34	51	37
Total state	4,559	69	67	68

*Dash (—) = base too small for reliable estimate.

**Table 3. Estimate of additional colleges
required to put specified percentages of the population of North Carolina
within commuting distance of a free-access college**

	As of fall 1968	Hypothetical additional colleges		
Number of free-access colleges 29		1†	4	7
Cumulative percent of population within commuting distance. 68%		72%	81%	90%
Average population within commuting distance of each college (in thousands) 107		153†	104	61

† Figures in this line are not cumulative. Each refers to an independent set of additional colleges.

North Dakota

Vast fields of grain cover most of North Dakota. It is one of the least urbanized and most sparsely populated of the 50 states. Despite its relatively low per capita income, the state appropriations in support of higher education are considerably above average and quite high in relation to resources. Like the other Plains states, high school retention is very high, and the proportion of 18-year-olds going to college is above average. The large majority of North Dakota youth who attend college do so in public institutions within the state.

The 16 colleges of North Dakota include only four private institutions. All the public institutions have been governed by the State Board of Higher Education that was established in 1939. Only recently, however, has the development of a master plan for the state been set in motion.

The eight free-access institutions in North Dakota include four public junior colleges, three senior institutions, and one branch. Although most of these are not large institutions, they enroll more than half of all first-time college students in North Dakota.

Roughly 3 out of 10 people in North Dakota live within commuting distance of a free-access college. These are fairly well spaced, though none is within easy commuting distance of Fargo and Grand Forks, the two largest cities in the state. These cities are the locations of the state's two universities, both of which have relatively low tuition and are only slightly too selective to be considered free-access colleges. It seems doubtful that other potential college locations could be easily rationalized on the basis of the present population.

Table 1. Number of recognized colleges at different levels of accessibility in North Dakota (fall 1968)

| | Level of accessibility | | | | | |
| | Free-access | | Less accessible | | | Total colleges |
Type of college	1	2	3	4	5	
Public two-year	1	3	0	0	0	4
Public four-year	0	3	3	0	0	6
Branches	0	1	1	0	0	2
All private	0	0	2	2	0	4
Total colleges	1	7	6	2	0	16

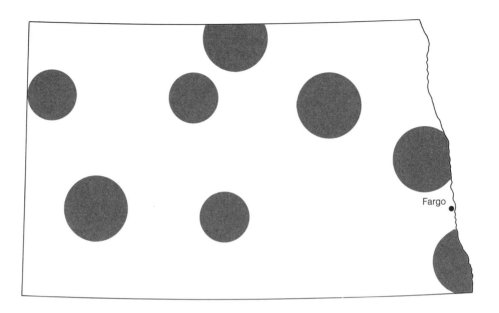

Fargo

North Dakota

Population of
metropolitan areas

● 50,000–250,000
▲ 250,000–500,000
■ **500,000–1,000,000**
♦ **More than 1,000,000**

0   25   50   100   200
Miles

 Commuting area of a free-access college (see Chapter 5 for explanation)

Table 2. Percentage of different populations within commuting distance of a free-access college in North Dakota (fall 1968)

Type of community	Population in thousands	Percent within commuting distance
Metropolitan areas (over 1 million)		
Central city	0	—*
Fringe	0	—
Other metropolitan areas	67	5
Counties over 20,000	198	53
Counties under 20,000	366	23
Total state	631	30

* Dash (—) = base too small for reliable estimate.

Table 3. Estimate of additional colleges required to put specified percentages of the population of North Dakota within commuting distance of a free-access college

	As of fall 1968	Hypothetical additional colleges		
Number of free-access colleges	8	3†	4	5
Cumulative percent of population within commuting distance	30%	52%	62%	70%
Average population within commuting distance of each college (in thousands)	24	44†	16	10

† Figures in this line are not cumulative. Each refers to an independent set of additional colleges.

Ohio

In many respects Ohio is typical of the heavily populated, industrialized Midwest. Even though two-thirds of the state's area is devoted to agriculture, it is one of the top five states with respect to proportion of the labor force in manufacturing. The proportion of Ohio youth graduating from secondary school is typical of the nation, but the proportion going on to college is below average.

The large number of Ohio colleges includes 70 private institutions. In the public sector there are 12 four-year institutions plus 28 branches. The state has only six public junior colleges. There was relatively little coordination among these public institutions until the Board of Regents was created in 1963. A master plan was published in 1966. Per capita state appropriations for higher education in Ohio are below the national average; in relation to resources, the level of state appropriations is one of the lowest in the nation.

The accessibility of higher education in Ohio is somewhat similar to Indiana's, but otherwise it is quite unusual. Ohio is a state that has long been identified with open-door admissions at its state institutions, and, in fact, they are still nominally open door. A number of senior state institutions and numerous branches have been developed in order to extend educational opportunity, but most of these branches are quite small. Furthermore, the very limited financial support of public higher education in Ohio has evidently forced tuition up and also has held back the development of institutional resources, so that space in higher education is not abundant. Thus almost all the public senior institutions and their branches charge $500–600 tuition. Also, they typically report drawing 80 to 90 percent of their first-time students from the top half of high school graduating classes. This admissions restriction may be the result of either the admissions process of the college or self-selection on the part of students; in either event practically none of the public four-year institutions or their branches in Ohio are both nonselective and inexpensive. Most of the few free-access institutions in the state are new junior colleges.

As a result only 12 percent of the population of Ohio live within commuting distance of a free-access college. The small differences by race and by type of community shown in Table 2 are less important than the generally low proportions of the populations covered. Ohio is also unusual because it has a large number of public institutions throughout the state which, though not free-access, are obviously not inaccessible. Thus, if tuition and admissions policies were lowered somewhat in a few senior institutions and their numerous branches, such action could have a pronounced effect on the apparent inaccessibility of higher education in the state. On the whole, however, the principal observation would seem to be that Ohio now follows a fairly conservative policy in state financial support and development of comprehensive educational opportunity beyond high school.

Ohio may be one of the best examples of a state where Table 3 is an oversimplification. Although this table indicates the number of additional free-access

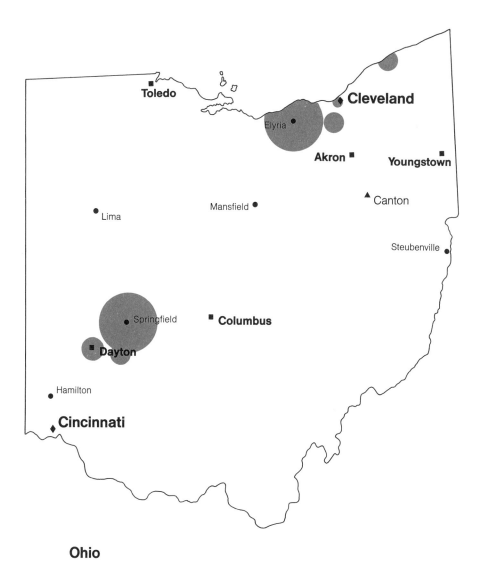

Ohio

Population of
metropolitan areas

- 50,000–250,000
▲ 250,000–500,000
■ **500,000–1,000,000**
♦ **More than 1,000,000**

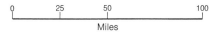 Commuting area of a free-access college
(see Chapter 5 for explanation)

0	25	50	100

Miles

colleges that would be required to make higher education accessible to given proportions of the population, a more basic question would concern the role of branch campuses. With appropriate policies, programs, and financial support, these existing campuses could greatly expand the availability of free-access higher education in Ohio. At this writing, however, there is considerable dispute in the state regarding the governor's proposal to create four-year institutions from branches, which some charge are already underfunded (*Cleveland Plain Dealer,* 1970). Such a move might easily work against the expansion of free-access opportunity. At present, the limited number of high school graduates attending college, the small number of free-access colleges, and the very low level of state appropriations seem to go hand-in-hand.

Table 1. Number of recognized colleges at different levels of accessibility in Ohio (fall 1968)

	Level of accessibility					
	Free-access		Less accessible			Total
Type of college	*1*	*2*	*3*	*4*	*5*	*colleges*
Public two-year	1	5	0	0	0	6
Public four-year	0	1	6	3	2	12
Branches	0	0	26	0	2	28
All private	0	0	1	47	22	70
Total colleges	1	6	33	50	26	116

Table 2. Percentage of different populations within commuting distance of a free-access college in Ohio (fall 1968)

		Percent within commuting distance		
Type of community	*Population in thousands*	*White*	*Black*	*Total*
Metropolitan areas (over 1 million)				
Central city	1,379	15	30	19
Fringe	1,542	15	0	13
Other metropolitan areas	4,433	15	23	16
Counties over 20,000	2,232	1	3	1
Counties under 20,000	122	0	—*	0
Total state	9,708	12	19	12

* Dash (—) = base too small for reliable estimate.

**Table 3. Estimate of additional colleges
required to put specified percentages of the population of Ohio
within commuting distance of a free-access college**

	As of fall 1968	*Hypothetical additional colleges*				
Number of free-access colleges 7		19†	7	8	10	20
Cumulative percent of population within commuting distance. 12%		50%	60%	71%	80%	90%
Average population within commuting distance of each college (in thousands) 166		256†	142	134	84	49

† Figures in this line are not cumulative. Each refers to an independent set of additional colleges.

Oklahoma

Being somewhat of a border state between the Great Plains and the South, Oklahoma evokes images of oil, wheat, and cattle. Even though it is hardly a typical state, it has few outstanding statistical characteristics, either positive or negative. The high school retention rate and the proportion of high school graduates going on to college are average or a little above average in Oklahoma. Most of the youth attending college remain in public institutions within the state.

The 36 colleges in Oklahoma are almost evenly divided among public four-year, public two-year, and private colleges. All the public institutions have been coordinated since 1941 by the State Regents for Higher Education. A number of planning studies have been undertaken in recent years, and a master plan is in preparation. State appropriations for higher education are low but rank close to the national average when compared with state resources.

There are 16 free-access institutions in Oklahoma, 9 of which are public junior colleges. Most of these institutions are fairly small, and taken together they enroll somewhat more than one-third of all first-time college students in the state.

About 3 Oklahoma youth in 10 live within commuting distance of a free-access institution. The discrepancy in coverage between black and white populations is small, but in Table 2 it is clear that there is a bias with respect to type of community. The metropolitan areas of Oklahoma, particularly Tulsa and Oklahoma City, are not well covered by colleges that can be called free-access. As indicated in Table 3, six new colleges, properly placed, could double the population living in proximity to a free-access institution. Furthermore, the additional colleges would cover considerably larger populations than the average free-access college in Oklahoma does now.

Table 1. Number of recognized colleges at different levels of accessibility in Oklahoma (fall 1968)

| | Level of accessibility | | | | | |
| | Free-access | | Less accessible | | | Total |
Type of college	1	2	3	4	5	colleges
Public two-year	2	7	1	0	0	10
Public four-year	0	6	5	0	1	12
Branches	0	0	1	0	0	1
All private	0	1	4	8	0	13
Total colleges	2	14	11	8	1	36

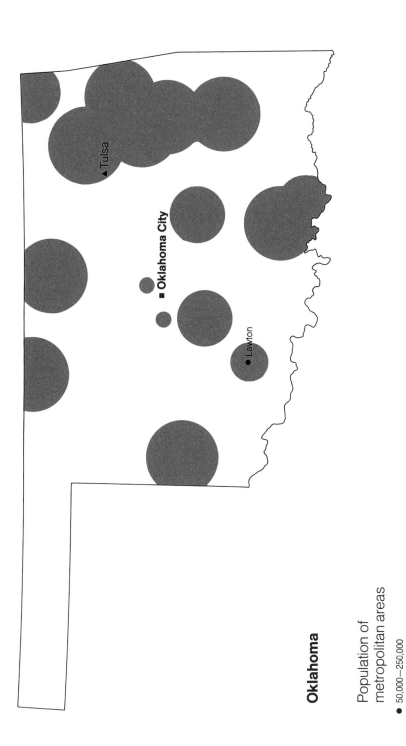

Oklahoma

Population of
metropolitan areas

● 50,000–250,000

▲ 250,000–500,000

■ **500,000–1,000,000**

♦ **More than 1,000,000**

● Commuting area of a free-access college (see Chapter 5 for explanation)

Miles

0   25   50   100   200

Table 2. Percentage of different populations within commuting distance of a free-access college in Oklahoma (fall 1968)

Type of community	Population in thousands	Percent within commuting distance		
		White	Black	Total
Metropolitan areas (over 1 million)				
Central city	0	—*	—	—
Fringe	0	—	—	—
Other metropolitan areas.	1,069	15	16	15
Counties over 20,000.	757	47	48	47
Counties under 20,000.	506	38	17	37
Total state	2,332	31	26	31

*Dash (—) = base too small for reliable estimate.

Table 3. Estimate of additional colleges required to put specified percentages of the population of Oklahoma within commuting distance of a free-access college

	As of fall 1968	Hypothetical additional colleges				
Number of free-access colleges	16	3†	3	4	6	11
Cumulative percent of population within commuting distance.	31%	52%	60%	71%	80%	90%
Average population within commuting distance of each college (in thousands)	45	166†	66	60	37	22

† Figures in this line are not cumulative. Each refers to an independent set of additional colleges.

Oregon

One-half of Oregon's economy is connected in some manner with its lumber resources, though most of the state's population is clustered in those limited areas that are not thickly forested or mountainous. A very high proportion of Oregon youth graduate from secondary school, and an above-average percentage of those graduates goes on to higher education. Consequently, the proportion of the age group attending college in Oregon is one of the highest in the nation. These students are somewhat more likely to attend public institutions within the state than students typically are in other states.

The 38 colleges of Oregon include 20 public institutions, more than half of which are two-year colleges opened within the last 10 years. In 1964 an Education Coordinating Council was created to develop a statewide master plan for all public institutions. The plan was adopted in 1966. Per capita appropriations for higher education in Oregon are among the highest in the nation.

The 13 free-access colleges in the state are almost synonymous with the two-year public institutions. Most of these are fairly large for junior colleges, and taken together they enroll about 1 out of 2 first-time college students in the state. Those public institutions that are not readily accessible are not expensive, though they are moderately to highly selective.

About half of Oregon's population lives within commuting distance of a free-access college. These institutions are well distributed in relation to the population centers of the state. Portland appears to be about the only location in the state where an additional free-access college would cover within its commuting area more people than the average existing free-access college covers. As much as 80 percent of the state's population could be covered by justifiable new colleges or new campuses, though none would be in areas heavily populated at the present time.

Table 1. Number of recognized colleges at different levels of accessibility in Oregon (fall 1968)

	Level of accessibility					
	Free-access		Less accessible			Total
Type of college	*1*	*2*	*3*	*4*	*5*	colleges
Public two-year	6	5	1	0	0	12
Public four-year	0	1	4	2	1	8
Branches	0	0	0	0	0	0
All private	0	1	0	13	4	18
Total colleges	6	7	5	15	5	38

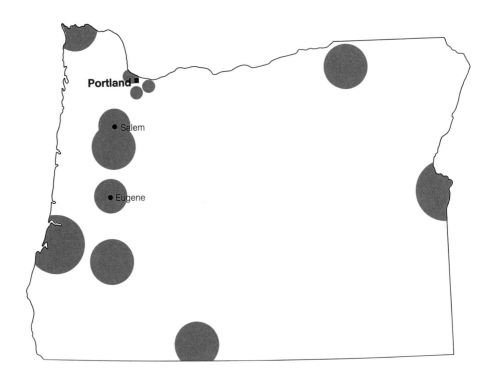

Oregon

Population of
metropolitan areas

● 50,000–250,000
▲ 250,000–500,000
■ **500,000–1,000,000**
♦ **More than 1,000,000**

● Commuting area of a free-access college (see Chapter 5 for explanation)

Table 2. Percentage of different populations within commuting distance of a free-access college in Oregon (fall 1968)

Type of community	Population in thousands	Percent within commuting distance		
		White	Black	Total
Metropolitan areas (over 1 million)				
Central city	0	—*	—	—
Fringe	0	—	—	—
Other metropolitan areas.	1,039	57	75	58
Counties over 20,000.	588	45	—	45
Counties under 20,000.	140	0	—	0
Total state	1,767	49	75	49

* Dash (—) = base too small for reliable estimate.

Table 3. Estimate of additional colleges required to put specified percentages of the population of Oregon within commuting distance of a free-access college

	As of fall 1968	Hypothetical additional colleges				
Number of free-access colleges 13		1†	2	6	7	11
Cumulative percent of population within commuting distance. 49%		55%	61%	70%	80%	90%
Average population within commuting distance of each college (in thousands) 67		100†	55	28	25	16

† Figures in this line are not cumulative. Each refers to an independent set of additional colleges.

Pennsylvania

The population of Pennsylvania is exceeded only by California's and New York's. Like those states, it has a diversified economy, extensive rural areas, and dense urban centers. An important difference is the fact that the per capita income in Pennsylvania is no higher than the national average. The state differs even more with respect to access to higher education.

The proportion of the age group that graduates from secondary school is somewhat above average in Pennsylvania, but the percentage of those graduates going on to higher education is considerably below the average of other states. The distribution of Pennsylvania youth into various higher institutions is similar to that found in other states in the Northeast. Less than half attend public institutions in the state.

As in Ohio, the major state universities have numerous branches, practically all of which are very small. Like New York, the state has a tradition of strong private higher education and has recently developed a massive scholarship program to assist Pennsylvania youth in utilizing the private sector. Unlike New York, Pennsylvania has yet to move decisively in making a broad range of inexpensive postsecondary education available to its population. However, the 15 readily accessible junior colleges (all opened in the past decade) represent a step in this direction. The numerous statewide studies and the comprehensive master plan recently completed by the Council of Higher Education represent additional steps. It is important to recognize, however, the limitations imposed by the fact that state appropriations for higher education in Pennsylvania are, in absolute and relative terms, among the lowest of all states in the nation.

The 16 free-access colleges in Pennsylvania are almost synonymous with the public two-year institutions. The state colleges and the university branches are all relatively inexpensive, though too selective to classify as free-access institutions. The free-access junior colleges have substantial enrollments, but because of their limited number they enroll only about 1 first-time college student in 5.

Roughly one-quarter of the population of Pennsylvania lives within commuting distance of a free-access college. These are fairly well distributed throughout the state. No particular type of community seems heavily favored, though a substantially larger proportion of blacks live in proximity to a free-access college than whites. Because of the relatively light coverage of the state by free-access institutions, there are many locations where free-access institutions could be placed in proximity to substantial numbers of students. As Table 3 indicates, at least 17 colleges could be located to serve larger numbers of students than the average free-access institution now does. About 40 additional colleges (or reoriented existing institutions) would be required to put 4 out of 5 Pennsylvanians within commuting distance of readily accessible higher education. The large number of underdeveloped branches, the limited financial support, and the below average rate of college attendance all indicate that the state has a long way to go just to organize its present resources effectively.

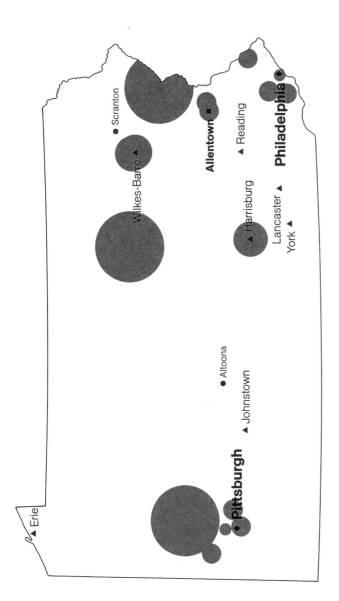

Population of
metropolitan areas

- 50,000–250,000
- ▲ 250,000–500,000
- ■ **500,000–1,000,000**
- ♦ **More than 1,000,000**

● Commuting area of a free-access college
   (see Chapter 5 for explanation)

|0   25   50   100|
          Miles

Pennsylvania

Scranton

Wilkes-Barre ▲

Allentown ■

▲ Reading

Harrisburg ▲

Lancaster ▲

York ▲

Philadelphia ♦

Altoona

▲ Johnstown

Pittsburgh ♦

▲ Erie

Table 1. Number of recognized colleges at different levels of accessibility in Pennsylvania (fall 1968)

| | Level of accessibility | | | | | |
| | Free-access | | Less accessible | | | Total |
Type of college	*1*	*2*	*3*	*4*	*5*	colleges
Public two-year	**0**	**15**	0	1	0	16
Public four-year	**0**	**1**	7	6	3	17
Branches	**0**	**0**	25	0	1	26
All private	**0**	**0**	1	66	29	96
Total colleges	**0**	**16**	33	73	33	155

Table 2. Percentage of different populations within commuting distance of a free-access college in Pennsylvania (fall 1968)

| | | Percent within commuting distance | | |
Type of community	Population in thousands	White	Black	Total
Metropolitan areas (over 1 million)				
Central city	2,607	25	46	30
Fringe	3,391	29	33	29
Other metropolitan areas	2,927	24	31	24
Counties over 20,000	2,291	15	7	15
Counties under 20,000	104	8	—*	8
Total state	11,320	24	41	25

*Dash (—) = base too small for reliable estimate.

Table 3. Estimate of additional colleges required to put specified percentages of the population of Pennsylvania within commuting distance of a free-access college

	As of fall 1968	Hypothetical additional colleges				
Number of free-access colleges	16	11†	6	9	13	17
Cumulative percent of population within commuting distance	25%	50%	60%	70%	80%	90%
Average population within commuting distance of each college (in thousands)	177	260†	192	124	85	66

† Figures in this line are not cumulative. Each refers to an independent set of additional colleges.

Rhode Island

The smallest state in the Union is also the most densely populated. Rhode Island is heavily industrialized, though the per capita income is only slightly above the national average. In the past, high school retention was somewhat below average, as was the proportion of high school graduates going on to college. Recent data indicate that the college access rate in Rhode Island is above average. As is typically true in New England, a relatively small proportion of Rhode Island's youth attend public institutions in their home state.

Most of Rhode Island's colleges are private, though there is one two-year and one four-year public institution in addition to the state university. For a number of years these public institutions have been governed by the Board of Trustees of State Colleges. An act of the legislature in 1969 established a Board of Regents for Education, which has the general responsibility for formulating and implementing a master plan for all levels of public education within the state. At present, state appropriations in support of higher education are slightly above average in comparison with other states.

The state's lone junior college is also its only free-access institution. It is large in comparison with most junior colleges but enrolls only 1 out of 8 first-time college students in the state. Since Rhode Island Junior College is located in Providence, some 4/10 of the population of the state live within commuting distance. There are plans to open two additional junior colleges — one in the Newport area and one north of Providence. These two colleges will substantially improve the accessibility of higher education, assuming they are properly supported. However, numerous clusters of people south of Providence may remain without ready access to higher education.

Table 1. Number of recognized colleges at different levels of accessibility in Rhode Island (fall 1968)

| | Level of accessibility | | | | | |
| | Free-access | | Less accessible | | | Total |
Type of college	1	2	3	4	5	colleges
Public two-year	0	1	0	0	0	1
Public four-year	0	0	2	0	0	2
Branches	0	0	0	1	0	1
All private	0	0	0	8	3	11
Total colleges	0	1	2	9	3	15

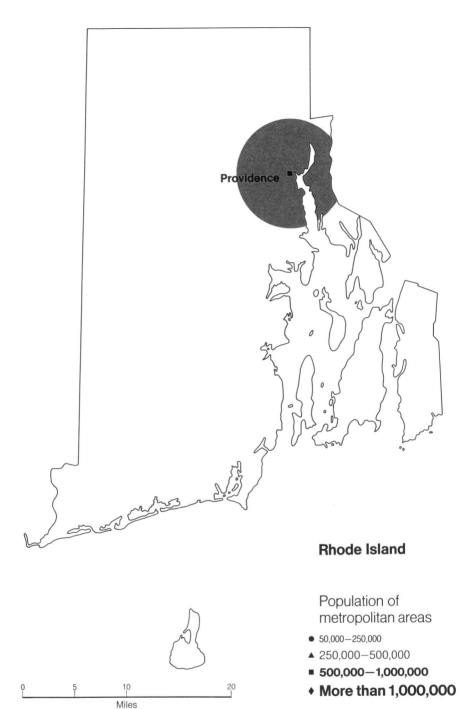

Rhode Island

Population of
metropolitan areas

● 50,000—250,000

▲ 250,000—500,000

■ **500,000—1,000,000**

♦ **More than 1,000,000**

0   5   10   20

Miles

● Commuting area of a free-access college (see Chapter 5 for explanation)

Providence ■

Table 2. Percentage of different populations within commuting distance of a free-access college in Rhode Island (fall 1968)

Type of community	Population in thousands	Percent within commuting distance		
		White	Black	Total
Metropolitan areas (over 1 million)				
Central city	0	—*	—	—
Fringe	0	—	—	—
Other metropolitan areas	850	40	60	40
Counties over 20,000	10	70	—	70
Counties under 20,000	0	—	—	—
Total state	860	40	60	41

*Dash (—) = base too small for reliable estimate.

Table 3. Estimate of additional colleges required to put specified percentages of the population of Rhode Island within commuting distance of a free-access college

	As of fall 1968	Hypothetical additional colleges				
Number of free-access colleges	1	1†	1	1	1	2
Cumulative percent of population within commuting distance	41%	54%	65%	75%	82%	92%
Average population within commuting distance of each college (in thousands)	353	112†	100	82	60	45

† Figures in this line are not cumulative. Each refers to an independent set of additional colleges.

South Carolina

A large black population, a very low per capita income, and a small proportion of white-collar workers give South Carolina the profile of a less advantaged Southern state. The proportion of secondary school students who graduate is very low; the proportion of those graduates who attend college is also very low. As a result South Carolina has the unfortunate distinction, among all 50 states, of having the smallest proportion of 18-year-olds in college. Of those who do go to college a relatively small proportion attend public institutions in South Carolina.

In addition to the 24 private institutions in South Carolina, there are 7 public senior colleges and 10 branches; all the public colleges are quite small. There are also 11 technical education centers, all of which have been opened during the past 10 years. In 1966 a Commission on Higher Education was created to plan and coordinate all higher institutions in the state. A master plan is under development.

In South Carolina free-access higher education, as defined here, is provided almost exclusively by the technical education centers. In some other states of the Deep South—Louisiana and Alabama in particular—there are a number of senior public institutions and their branches that qualify as free-access colleges; but they are not free-access in South Carolina, and the reason is somewhat unusual. In most states the public institutions are not free-access because they are too selective; in South Carolina it's because they are too expensive. Their expense seems to be related to the fact that state appropriations for higher education in South Carolina are, on a per capita basis, among the lowest in the nation.

Somewhat over half of the population of South Carolina lives within commuting distance of a free-access college—which in this instance means a technical education center. These are distributed fairly well throughout the state, though, as Table 3 indicates, there are a few additional locations where free-access colleges could serve substantial numbers of people.

It should be recognized that these data present a somewhat simplistic picture of the accessibility of higher education in South Carolina. Accessibility in the state could be improved by lowering tuition at the public institutions, but it would also be necessary to support adequately their expansion and the development of comprehensive programs. Among the basic problems facing the state are the relatively low level of educational attainment and aspiration, and the need to coordinate all forms of postsecondary educational opportunities.

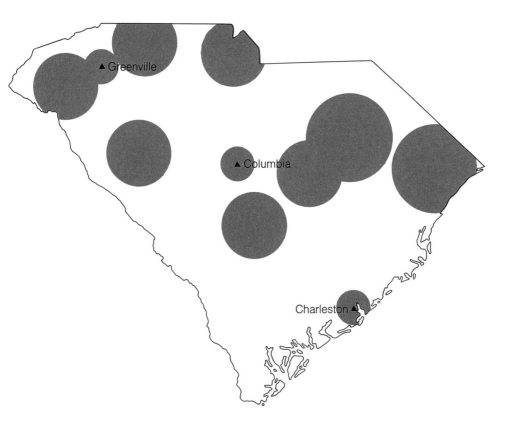

South Carolina

Population of
metropolitan areas

- ● 50,000–250,000
- ▲ 250,000–500,000
- ■ **500,000–1,000,000**
- **◆ More than 1,000,000**

0   25   50   100

Miles

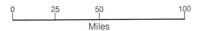 Commuting area of a free-access college (see Chapter 5 for explanation)

Table 1. Number of recognized colleges at different levels of accessibility in South Carolina (fall 1968)

	Level of accessibility					
	Free-access		*Less accessible*			*Total*
Type of college	*1*	*2*	*3*	*4*	*5*	*colleges*
Public two-year	0	11	0	0	0	11
Public four-year	0	1	2	4	0	7
Branches.	0	0	10	0	0	10
All private	0	0	6	16	2	24
Total colleges	0	12	18	20	2	52

Table 2. Percentage of different populations within commuting distance of a free-access college in South Carolina (fall 1968)

		Percent within commuting distance		
Type of community	*Population in thousands*	*White*	*Black*	*Total*
Metropolitan areas (over 1 million)				
Central city	0	—*	—	—
Fringe	0	—	—	—
Other metropolitan areas.	852	49	49	49
Counties over 20,000.	1,404	67	59	64
Counties under 20,000.	126	16	19	17
Total state	2,382	58	53	56

*Dash (—) = base too small for reliable estimate.

Table 3. Estimate of additional colleges required to put specified percentages of the population of South Carolina within commuting distance of a free-access college

	As of fall 1968	*Hypothetical additional colleges*			
Number of free-access colleges	12	1†	3	4	6
Cumulative percent of population within commuting distance.	56%	60%	70%	81%	90%
Average population within commuting distance of each college (in thousands)	111	97†	82	60	38

† Figures in this line are not cumulative. Each refers to an independent set of additional colleges.

South Dakota

The typical characteristics of the Plains states are even somewhat exaggerated in South Dakota. It is a very sparsely populated state that has actually declined slightly in population since 1960. A very small proportion of the labor force is engaged in manufacturing or white-collar occupations. A relatively high proportion of South Dakota youth graduate from high school and an average number of those graduates go on to college. They are distributed to higher education in much the same ratio as is typical across the country: 4 to public institutions within the state, 1 to private institutions within the state, and 1 to colleges outside of South Dakota.

South Dakota is one of only two states in the nation (the other being Nevada) that has no public two-year institutions. Of the state's 16 higher institutions, seven are public and these are all governed by a single Board of Regents. South Dakota does not have a master plan, but a study is under-way to produce one by 1970. Financial support for higher education has been below the per capita average of the 50 states, though somewhat above average in relation to resources available.

Most of the colleges in South Dakota are not free-access because they are too selective. There are three small free-access colleges in the state—two public and one private. Together they enroll only about 1 out of 8 first-time college students in the state.

It also happens that about one-eighth of the population of South Dakota is within commuting distance of one of these free-access colleges. This is very low compared with other states, and none of the major cities have an institution that can be classified as free-access. The sparse population and limited resources may preclude serious consideration of many new institutions in South Dakota. Organization and support of existing institutions may provide the more reasonable route to expanding educational opportunity.

Table 1. Number of recognized colleges at different levels of accessibility in South Dakota (fall 1968)

| | Level of accessibility | | | | | |
| | Free-access | | Less accessible | | | Total |
Type of college	1	2	3	4	5	colleges
Public two-year	0	0	0	0	0	0
Public four-year	0	2	3	2	0	7
Branches	0	0	0	0	0	0
All private	0	1	0	8	0	9
Total colleges	0	3	3	10	0	16

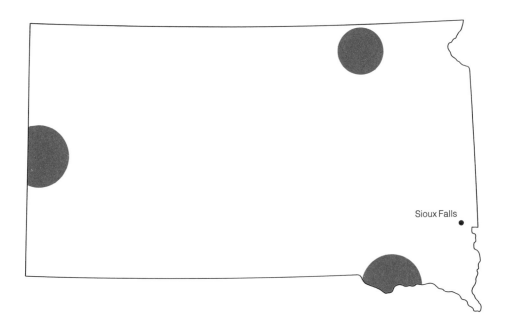

Sioux Falls
●

South Dakota

Population of
metropolitan areas

● 50,000—250,000
▲ 250,000—500,000
■ **500,000—1,000,000**
♦ **More than 1,000,000**

```
0      25    50         100                    200
├──────┴─────┴──────────┴──────────────────────┤
              Miles
```

● Commuting area of a free-access college (see Chapter 5 for explanation)

Table 2. Percentage of different populations within commuting distance of a free-access college in South Dakota (fall 1968)

Type of community	Population in thousands	Percent within commuting distance
Metropolitan areas (over 1 million)		
Central city	0	—*
Fringe	0	—
Other metropolitan areas.	87	0
Counties over 20,000.	154	21
Counties under 20,000.	442	11
Total state	683	12

*Dash (—) = base too small for reliable estimate.

Table 3. Estimate of additional colleges required to put specified percentages of the population of South Dakota within commuting distance of a free-access college

	As of fall 1968	Hypothetical additional colleges			
Number of free-access colleges 3		5†	3	4	5
Cumulative percent of population within commuting distance. 12%		51%	61%	71%	81%
Average population within commuting distance of each college (in thousands) 27		54†	23	16	14

† Figures in this line are not cumulative. Each refers to an independent set of additional colleges.

Tennessee

Tennessee shares many of the border-state characteristics of its neighbor Kentucky. The states have a somewhat similar topography and limited financial resources. They are also similar in that a below-average proportion of students reach high school graduation and a below-average proportion of those graduates go on to higher education. The organization of higher education is, however, rather different in Kentucky and Tennessee.

There are 38 private institutions in Tennessee and until recently all public higher education was offered by senior institutions. The state's five public junior colleges have all opened in the past decade. The state has only recently impaneled a coordinating body. In addition to the traditional lack of coordination and the ascendance of the state university, Tennessee also faces the challenge of increasing state appropriations for higher education — now among the 10 lowest in the nation on a per capita basis.

It may be that the state has subsisted on small appropriations for higher education because of limited educational aspiration. But for whatever reason, most of the public institutions of the state have remained readily accessible. Of the free-access colleges in Tennessee, five are public junior colleges, two are private institutions, and nine are public senior colleges or their branches. Only 3 of the 17 public campuses in the state are not free-access. Nonetheless, the state's numerous private institutions account for roughly half of all the first-time enrollment.

About 4/10 of the population of Tennessee live within commuting distance of one of the free-access colleges. These are fairly well distributed throughout the state with the obvious exception of Knoxville — home of the state university. As Table 3 indicates it would take some 9 or 10 institutions to raise the proportion of population covered from 40 to 70 percent. On the average these colleges would cover substantially more people than the typical existing free-access institutions in the state cover, all of which indicates that there are at least about 10 promising locations for new institutions.

Table 1. Number of recognized colleges at different levels of accessibility in Tennessee (fall 1968)

| | Level of accessibility | | | | | |
| | Free-access | | Less accessible | | | Total |
Type of college	1	2	3	4	5	colleges
Public two-year	3	2	0	0	0	5
Public four-year	1	6	3	0	0	10
Branches	0	2	0	0	0	2
All private	0	2	7	27	2	38
Total colleges	4	12	10	27	2	55

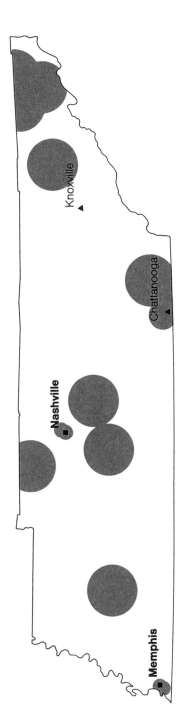

Tennessee

Population of
metropolitan areas

- • 50,000—250,000
- ▲ 250,000—500,000
- ■ **500,000—1,000,000**
- ♦ **More than 1,000,000**

● Commuting area of a free-access college (see Chapter 5 for explanation)

0   25   50   100   200

Miles

Memphis

Nashville

Knoxville

Chattanooga

Table 2. Percentage of different populations within commuting distance of a free-access college in Tennessee (fall 1968)

Type of community	Population in thousands	Percent within commuting distance		
		White	Black	Total
Metropolitan areas (over 1 million)				
Central city	0	—*	—	—
Fringe	0	—	—	—
Other metropolitan areas.	1,697	40	60	45
Counties over 20,000.	1,360	47	38	46
Counties under 20,000.	511	16	15	16
Total state	3,568	39	52	41

*Dash (—) = base too small for reliable estimate.

Table 3. Estimate of additional colleges required to put specified percentages of the population of Tennessee within commuting distance of a free-access college

	As of fall 1968	Hypothetical additional colleges				
Number of free-access colleges	16	2†	3	4	7	9
Cumulative percent of population within commuting distance.	41%	51%	61%	71%	81%	90%
Average population within commuting distance of each college (in thousands)	91	181†	112	90	52	36

† Figures in this line are not cumulative. Each refers to an independent set of additional colleges.

Texas

It is often not appreciated that Texas is now one of the most heavily populated states and is also highly urbanized. Because of its unusual size, the state does have vast areas of sparsely populated land. Similarly, the legendary "wealth" of Texas spreads over its large population to yield a per capita income well below the average for the nation. The state has, however, appropriated funds for higher education at the average level of other states.

The proportion of high school graduates attending college in Texas is above the national average, but high school retention in the state is very low. A very small number of college students migrate out of Texas, and some 5 out of 6 remaining in the state enroll in public institutions.

Texas has 47 private colleges in addition to a large contingent of state institutions. The 66 public colleges of Texas outnumber those of every state in the Union except New York and California. Forty-two of these institutions are public community colleges, over a third of which have been opened in the past decade. In 1955 the Texas Commission on Higher Education was given the responsibility of coordinating these institutions. In 1965 the Commission was reorganized and was given extensive powers under the new name of Coordinating Board, Texas College and University System. A master plan has been under development for several years.

Half of the senior institutions and practically all of the junior colleges of Texas are free-access colleges. These institutions range from very small to very large. Collectively, they enroll almost 2 out of 3 first-time college students in the state.

Despite the very large number of free-access colleges in Texas, less than 4/10 of its population live within commuting distance of one of these institutions. This situation is explained in part by the sheer size of the state, but one imbalance is quite evident. More than a quarter of the population of Texas lives within the two major metropolitan areas of Dallas and Houston. Although both of these areas have free-access colleges, the reasonable commuting perimeters of these institutions cover a much smaller proportion of the population than is typically true of smaller metropolitan areas throughout the state. Furthermore, the only free-access college in the central city of Houston is a predominantly black institution.

Consequently, the state can be imagined in three pieces: sparsely populated counties that almost necessarily have a low degree of coverage by free-access institutions; more populous counties and metropolitan areas that have a fairly high level of coverage compared with most states; and the two major metropolitan areas that are quite deficient with respect to accessible higher education. Additional colleges in the more populous counties and in Dallas and Houston could serve much larger populations than is typically true of the existing free-access colleges. Table 3 indicates it would be necessary to double the present 54 free-access colleges in order to put an accessible institution within commuting distance of 4 out of 5 Texas residents.

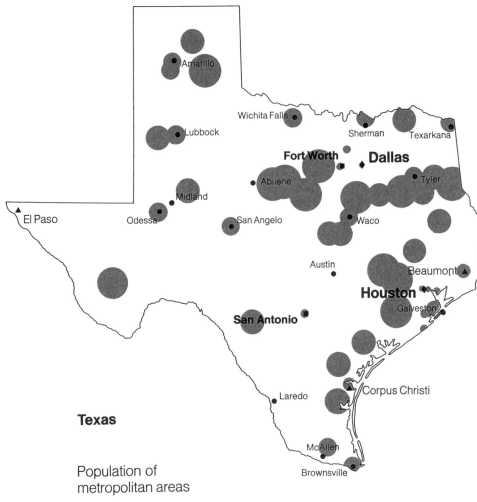

Texas

Population of
metropolitan areas

- ● 50,000–250,000
- ▲ 250,000–500,000
- ■ **500,000–1,000,000**
- ♦ **More than 1,000,000**

0 25 50   100   200   300

Miles

● Commuting area of a free-access college (see Chapter 5 for explanation)

**Table 1. Number of recognized colleges at different levels
of accessibility in Texas (fall 1968)**

	Level of accessibility					
	Free-access		Less accessible			Total
Type of college	1	2	3	4	5	colleges
Public two-year	27	13	2	0	0	42
Public four-year	2	11	7	3	0	23
Branches	0	0	1	0	0	1
All private	0	1	9	32	5	47
Total colleges	29	25	19	35	5	113

**Table 2. Percentage of different populations within commuting distance
of a free-access college in Texas (fall 1968)**

		Percent within commuting distance			
Type of community	Population in thousands	White	Black	Mexican American	Total
Metropolitan areas (over 1 million)					
Central city	1,618	11	32	15	15
Fringe	919	19	8	22	18
Other metropolitan areas	4,074	56	64	50	56
Counties over 20,000	1,513	53	54	46	53
Counties under 20,000	1,452	14	22	10	14
Total state	9,576	37	43	40	38

**Table 3. Estimate of additional colleges
required to put specified percentages of the population of Texas
within commuting distance of a free-access college**

	As of fall 1968	Hypothetical additional colleges				
Number of free-access colleges	54	6*	8	14	25	39
Cumulative percent of population within commuting distance	38%	52%	60%	70%	80%	90%
Average population within commuting distance of each college (in thousands)	68	217*	102	69	37	25

* Figures in this line are not cumulative. Each refers to an independent set of additional colleges.

Utah

Much of Utah is inhospitable land. The state is sparsely populated but quite urbanized. Most of the people of Utah live in the metropolitan area of Salt Lake City or in the area of Ogden or Provo immediately to the north and south. Manufacturing is the principal element in Utah's economy, though it actually accounts for a relatively small proportion of the labor force. Per capita income in the state is below the national average, but per capita state appropriations for higher education are well above average. Consequently, state support for higher education in relation to resources is one of the highest in the nation. The proportion of students completing high school is above average in Utah, while the percentage going on to college is near the national mean. A very large proportion of Utah students who attend college do so in public institutions within the state.

There are only 12 higher institutions in Utah. These include four public senior institutions and two public junior colleges. All the public colleges are governed by the State Board of Higher Education and a master plan is under development.

Five of Utah's colleges are free-access. These include the two public junior colleges, two state colleges, and one branch. With one exception these are fairly small institutions; together they enroll about one-third of the first-time college students in the state.

Four of the five free-access colleges in Utah are located in small towns. There are none in the metropolitan area of Salt Lake City. Consequently, only one-fifth of the population of Utah lives within commuting distance of a free-access college. The University of Utah is located in Salt Lake City, although it does not qualify as a free-access institution, either on the basis of cost or particularly with respect to selectivity. Two or three free-access institutions in the heavily populated area of the state would probably have a very substantial effect on the accessibility of higher education in Utah. Very few colleges beyond that could be justified on the basis of present population patterns.

Table 1. Number of recognized colleges at different levels of accessibility in Utah (fall 1968)

	Level of accessibility					
	Free-access		Less accessible			Total
Type of college	1	2	3	4	5	colleges
Public two-year	1	1	0	0	0	2
Public four-year	0	2	1	0	1	4
Branches	1	0	0	0	0	1
All private	0	0	0	5	0	5
Total colleges	2	3	1	5	1	12

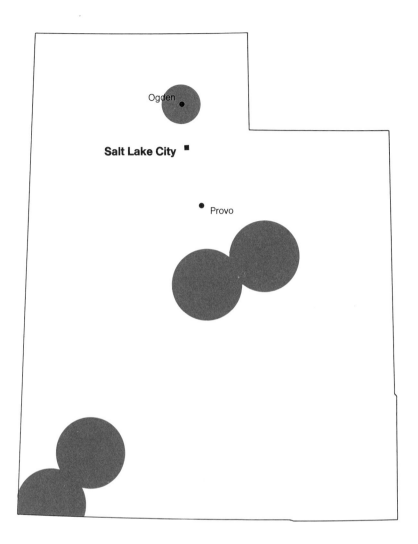

Utah

Population of
metropolitan areas

- 50,000–250,000
- ▲ 250,000–500,000
- ■ **500,000–1,000,000**
- ◆ **More than 1,000,000**

 Commuting area of a free-access college
(see Chapter 5 for explanation)

0	25	50		100

Miles

Table 2. Percentage of different populations within commuting distance of a free-access college in Utah (fall 1968)

Type of community	Population in thousands	Percent within commuting distance
Metropolitan areas (over 1 million)		
Central city	0	—*
Fringe	0	—
Other metropolitan areas	666	16
Counties over 20,000	82	40
Counties under 20,000	146	23
Total state	894	20

*Dash (—) = base too small for reliable estimate.

Table 3. Estimate of additional colleges required to put specified percentages of the population of Utah within commuting distance of a free-access college

	As of fall 1968	Hypothetical additional colleges			
Number of free-access colleges	5	2†	2	3	3
Cumulative percent of population within commuting distance	29%	55%	63%	74%	81%
Average population within commuting distance of each college (in thousands)	36	159†	38	32	22

† Figures in this line are not cumulative. Each refers to an independent set of additional colleges.

Vermont

New England is sometimes associated with large numbers of people crowded together, but Vermont is one of the least populated of all the states and is also one of the least urbanized. Per capita income is somewhat below average, though state support for higher education is higher than is typically true in other Northeastern states. The rate of high school graduation is above average in Vermont, but the proportion of those graduates going on to higher education is substantially below the national average. The pattern of distribution to higher education is basically similar to that of Maine and New Hampshire. Roughly half of Vermont's students remain in state and in public institutions, and relatively few go to private institutions within the state.

There are 15 private institutions in Vermont but only five public colleges: four senior and one junior. The state has no master plan to guide its institutions, nor has it taken steps to develop plans for statewide coordination.

There are three free-access colleges in Vermont—the one public junior and two of the public senior colleges. These are small institutions, and they enroll only 1 out of 6 first-time college students in the state. About two-fifths of the population of Vermont live within commuting distance of one of the three free-access colleges. They are well distributed from the northern to the southern part of the state, though none serves the northwestern quadrant, which is the most heavily populated. One additional college in that area could substantially increase the proportion of Vermont's population living in proximity to readily accessible higher education. It seems likely, however, that the state's educational leadership will have to deal with prior questions first: state planning, coordination, and long-range objectives regarding the possibility of expanded educational opportunity beyond high school.

Table 1. Number of recognized colleges at different levels of accessibility in Vermont (fall 1968)

| | Free-access | | Less accessible | | | Total |
| | 1 | 2 | 3 | 4 | 5 | colleges |
Type of college						
Public two-year	0	1	0	0	0	1
Public four-year	0	2	1	1	0	4
Branches	0	0	0	0	0	0
All private	0	0	1	3	11	15
Total colleges	0	3	2	4	11	20

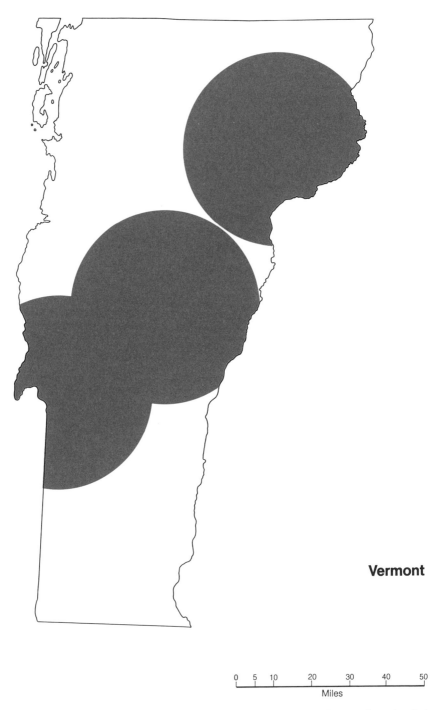

Vermont

0 5 10   20   30   40   50

Miles

● Commuting area of a free-access college (see Chapter 5 for explanation)

Table 2. Percentage of different populations within commuting distance of a free-access college in Vermont (fall 1968)

Type of community	Population in thousands	Percent within commuting distance
Metropolitan areas (over 1 million)		
Central city	0	—*
Fringe	0	—
Other metropolitan areas.	0	—
Counties over 20,000.	353	40
Counties under 20,000.	36	55
Total state	389	41

*Dash (—) = base too small for reliable estimate.

Table 3. Estimate of additional colleges required to put specified percentages of the population of Vermont within commuting distance of a free-access college

	As of fall 1968	Hypothetical additional colleges		
Number of free-access colleges 3		1†	1	1
Cumulative percent of population within commuting distance. 41%		71%	89%	93%
Average population within commuting distance of each college (in thousands) 53		118†	70	13

† Figures in this line are not cumulative. Each refers to an independent set of additional colleges.

Virginia

Providing as it does the southern terminus of the Washington-Boston megalopolis, Virginia blends characteristics of the Appalachian, Southern, and technocratic society — at least to the extent the three are at all compatible. Per capita income is somewhat below average but not nearly so low as most Southern states. A low proportion of Virginia youth completes secondary school, and of these somewhat less than half go on to college. Slightly more than half of the students who attend college do so in public institutions in Virginia.

In addition to 31 private colleges, Virginia has as many public institutions and branches. In 1956 the State Council on Higher Education was created as an advisory body to coordinate all public institutions. A special study commission submitted a report in 1965 and a master plan was published in 1968; one immediate effect was the establishment of a state system of comprehensive community colleges and their own coordinating body. As of fall 1968 there were 13 public two-year colleges, and 11 public senior institutions that have a total of eight branches. Virginia is developing a comprehensive master plan. At present the per capita state appropriations for higher education are somewhat below the national average.

The 15 free-access colleges in Virginia consist largely of public community colleges, though three branches of senior institutions are also readily accessible. The other senior institutions and their branches are typically both too expensive and too selective to qualify. Practically all the free-access colleges are fairly new and of moderate size. Taken together they enroll not quite 1 out of 4 first-time college students in the state.

Half the population of Virginia lives within commuting distance of a free-access higher institution. These are well distributed throughout the state, and there is no marked bias in favor of one type of community or another except for the reasonable condition that few are in sparsely populated areas. As Table 3 indicates, an additional half dozen institutions would raise the proportion of the population covered to 70 percent. Most of these additional institutions would serve as large a population as the average free-access institution in the state does now.

Table 1. Number of recognized colleges at different levels of accessibility in Virginia (fall 1968)

| | Level of accessibility | | | | | |
| | Free-access | | Less accessible | | | Total |
Type of college	1	2	3	4	5	colleges
Public two-year	8	3	0	1	1	13
Public four-year	0	1	1	3	6	11
Branches	1	2	4	0	1	8
All private	0	0	1	20	10	31
Total colleges	9	6	6	24	18	63

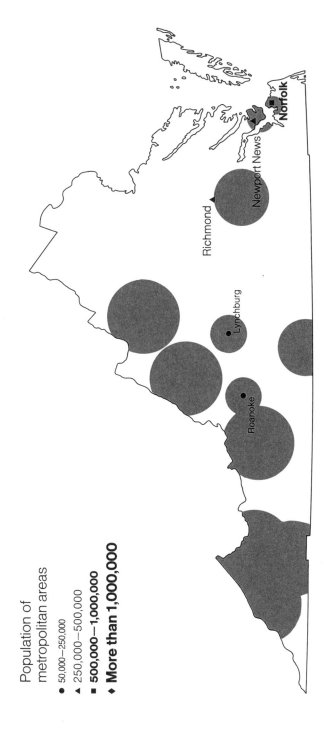

Virginia

Population of
metropolitan areas

• 50,000–250,000

▲ 250,000–500,000

■ **500,000–1,000,000**

◆ **More than 1,000,000**

Norfolk

Newport News

Richmond

Lynchburg

Roanoke

● Commuting area of a free-access college (see Chapter 5 for explanation)

0   25   50   100   200

Miles

Table 2. Percentage of different populations within commuting distance of a free-access college in Virginia (fall 1968)

Type of community	Population in thousands	Percent within commuting distance		
		White	Black	Total
Metropolitan areas (over 1 million)				
Central city	0	—*	—	—
Fringe	614	55	37	53
Other metropolitan areas.	1,520	54	59	55
Counties over 20,000.	1,298	61	42	57
Counties under 20,000.	532	17	9	14
Total state	3,964	52	40	50

*Dash (—) = base too small for reliable estimate.

Table 3. Estimate of additional colleges required to put specified percentages of the population of Virginia within commuting distance of a free-access college

	As of fall 1968	Hypothetical additional colleges			
Number of free-access colleges	15	2†	4	6	11
Cumulative percent of population within commuting distance.	50%	60%	70%	80%	90%
Average population within commuting distance of each college (in thousands)	132	205†	97	68	36

† Figures in this line are not cumulative. Each refers to an independent set of additional colleges.

Washington

Like its sister state, Oregon, Washington has much of its population concentrated in limited areas. The state has a high proportion of white-collar workers, but it is also wealthy in agriculture and manufacturing. Per capita income is high, and state support for higher education is very high in Washington — in absolute terms and in relation to state income.

The proportion of 18-year-olds who finish high school is above the national average, and the proportion of those graduates going on to college is extremely high (3 out of 4). A very high proportion of these students remain in Washington to attend public institutions. In addition, there is a very substantial enrollment in public vocational schools at the postsecondary level.

There are 12 private and 27 public colleges in Washington. The public sector includes 22 junior colleges, over half of which have opened in the past decade. The state has no master plan, and until very recently coordination has been handled by a voluntary organization of institutional representatives. The Washington Council on Higher Education was authorized as an advisory body in 1969. Washington is a particularly interesting state because it provides so many signs of strong state support and aggressive development of comprehensive educational programs beyond secondary school without having had a formal coordinating apparatus. It is, in fact, the only state that presents this picture.

Free-access higher education in Washington is almost synonymous with the public two-year colleges. These are large institutions, and they enroll 3 out of every 4 first-time college students in the state. Half of the population of Washington lives within commuting distance of one of these colleges. They are well distributed, and the only obvious discrepancy is Seattle. Accessible higher education is notably less available in the central city of this major metropolitan area than throughout the rest of the state. As Table 3 indicates, just a few additional colleges could substantially raise the proportion of the population living within commuting distance of a free-access institution in Washington.

Table 1. Number of recognized colleges at different levels of accessibility in Washington (fall 1968)

| | Level of accessibility | | | | | |
| | Free-access | | Less accessible | | | Total colleges |
Type of college	1	2	3	4	5	
Public two-year	7	15	0	0	0	22
Public four-year	0	1	2	0	2	5
Branches	0	0	0	0	0	0
All private	0	0	0	9	3	12
Total colleges	7	16	2	9	5	39

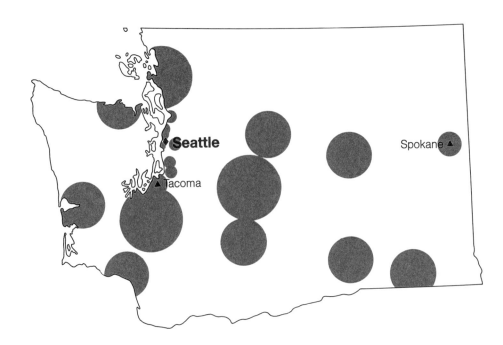

Washington

Population of
metropolitan areas

- ● 50,000–250,000
- ▲ 250,000–500,000
- ■ **500,000–1,000,000**
- ♦ **More than 1,000,000**

```
0    25   50        100                    200
|    |    |          |                      |
              Miles
```

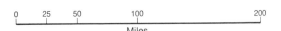 Commuting area of a free-access college (see Chapter 5 for explanation)

**Table 2. Percentage of different populations within commuting distance
of a free-access college in Washington (fall 1968)**

Type of community	Population in thousands	Percent within commuting distance		
		White	Black	Total
Metropolitan areas (over 1 million)				
Central city	557	31	56	32
Fringe	550	57	—*	57
Other metropolitan areas.	694	59	50	59
Counties over 20,000.	900	62	—	62
Counties under 20,000.	151	5	—	5
Total state	2,852	51	53	51

*Dash (—) = base too small for reliable estimate.

**Table 3. Estimate of additional colleges
required to put specified percentages of the population of Washington
within commuting distance of a free-access college**

	As of fall 1968	Hypothetical additional colleges		
Number of free-access colleges 23		2†	5	6
Cumulative percent of population within commuting distance. 51%		61%	74%	80%
Average population within commuting distance of each college (in thousands) 63		138†	56	26

† Figures in this line are not cumulative. Each refers to an independent set of additional colleges.

West Virginia

The fortunes of West Virginians have often turned on the status of the coal industry. It is well known that those fortunes have not been good in recent times. Per capita income is very low, and West Virginia is one of the very few states that has lost population in the last decade. The proportion of young people graduating from high school is only slightly below the national average, but the proportion of those graduates going on to higher education is very low. Most of those who go to college attend public institutions within the state.

These public institutions constitute more than half of West Virginia's 27 colleges. Most of them are four-year institutions; only a few are branches and two-year colleges. In relation to resources, state support for higher education in West Virginia has been considerably above average, but there has been relatively little progress on statewide coordination. The public institutions were placed under a single board in 1969; the state has no master plan.

Most of the public institutions in West Virginia are readily accessible. The 12 free-access institutions consist of seven senior colleges, three branches, and two junior colleges. Most of these are relatively small, but together they enroll almost half of the first-time college students in the state.

There is a free-access institution within commuting distance of somewhat more than half of the population of the state. These colleges are well distributed in relation to the population though, as Table 3 indicates, there are two locations with substantial populations and no free-access colleges. As it happens, these locations correspond exactly to the site of two state institutions— West Virginia Institute of Technology and Fairmont State College—that are slightly too selective to be classified here as free-access colleges. Consequently, higher education in the state is actually more accessible than is generally true in the nation. In West Virginia statewide planning of postsecondary opportunity would seem to have a higher priority than consideration of new colleges.

Table 1. Number of recognized colleges at different levels of accessibility in West Virginia (fall 1968)

| | Level of accessibility | | | | | |
| | Free-access | | Less accessible | | | Total |
Type of college	1	2	3	4	5	colleges
Public two-year	0	1	0	0	0	1
Public four-year	0	7	2	0	1	10
Branches	0	4	0	0	0	4
All private	0	0	2	8	2	12
Total colleges	0	12	4	8	3	27

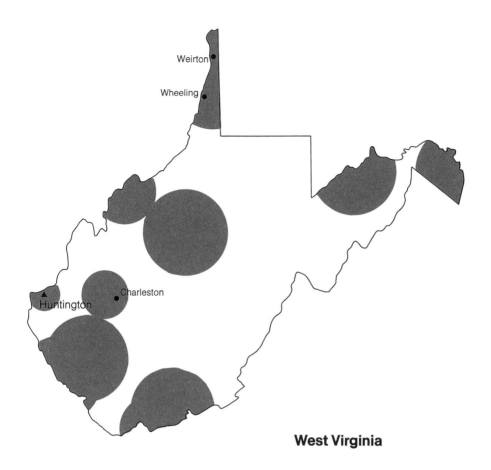

West Virginia

Population of
metropolitan areas

● 50,000–250,000
▲ 250,000–500,000
■ **500,000–1,000,000**
♦ **More than 1,000,000**

0   25   50   100
Miles

 Commuting area of a free-access college (see Chapter 5 for explanation)

Table 2. Percentage of different populations within commuting distance of a free-access college in West Virginia (fall 1968)

Type of community	Population in thousands	Percent within commuting distance		
		White	Black	Total
Metropolitan areas (over 1 million)				
Central city	0	—*	—	—
Fringe	0	—	—	—
Other metropolitan areas.	575	69	70	69
Counties over 20,000.	977	50	52	50
Counties under 20,000.	308	36	100	36
Total state	1,860	53	59	54

*Dash (—) = base too small for reliable estimate.

Table 3. Estimate of additional colleges required to put specified percentages of the population of West Virginia within commuting distance of a free-access college

	As of fall 1968	Hypothetical additional colleges			
Number of free-access colleges	12	1†	1	2	4
Cumulative percent of population within commuting distance.	54%	64%	75%	80%	90%
Average population within commuting distance of each college (in thousands)	84	258†	200	50	47

† Figures in this line are not cumulative. Each refers to an independent set of additional colleges.

Wisconsin

Wisconsin shares a number of general characteristics with her sister state, Minnesota. Manufacturing has developed to a considerable extent in recent years, though the state remains a major agricultural resource. Like Minnesota's, its southern half is moderately well populated, with one major metropolitan area located in the southeastern corner. Wisconsin has also shared with Minnesota the highest rate of high school graduation in the country. On the other hand the proportion of those graduates going on to college is below the national average (but this number doesn't take into account a substantial number of students attending postsecondary vocational schools). Some 3 out of 4 students attending college do so in public institutions within the state.

In addition to 29 private institutions, Wisconsin has a number of public colleges and branches arranged in a somewhat unusual organization. The state university system has 10 components, and the University of Wisconsin now has four campuses. Although the 22 two-year institutions include several technical institutes, they consist mainly of very small county teachers colleges. The planning, budgeting, and programing functions of all public colleges are facilitated by a Coordinating Council for Higher Education, which produced a comprehensive master plan in 1967. State support for higher education is high.

The 22 free-access colleges in Wisconsin consist largely of two very different groups of institutions. Most of the county teachers colleges are readily accessible, though their very small size militates against their effectiveness as free-access colleges. About half of the state university system (formerly the state colleges) can be classified as free-access; the other half has become too selective. Most institutions in the selective group are moderately large. Taken together the free-access colleges in Wisconsin enroll about 1 out of 3 first-time college students in the state.

Almost half of the population of Wisconsin lives within commuting distance of a free-access institution. The smaller metropolitan areas are quite well covered and even the sparsely populated counties are fairly well covered by the numerous county teachers colleges. The principal areas in need of readily accessible higher education are in the heavily populated southeastern portion of the state, particularly the greater Milwaukee area. Milwaukee Technical College is a large two-year institution, but it is the only free-access college in the city. It must necessarily fall short in providing either the proximity or the comprehensive postsecondary opportunities implied by the notion of free-access higher education in one of the nation's major metropolitan areas.

Wisconsin is another state where a number of slightly too selective colleges clouds the picture of accessibility. Those colleges, compounded by the numerous underdeveloped small institutions, make it difficult to draw simple generalizations about the state. An impending revision of the state master plan may create more order.

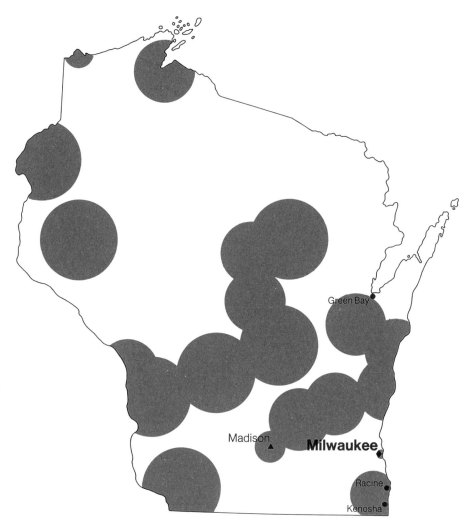

Wisconsin

Population of metropolitan areas

- 50,000—250,000
- ▲ 250,000—500,000
- ■ **500,000—1,000,000**
- ♦ **More than 1,000,000**

 Commuting area of a free-access college (see Chapter 5 for explanation)

```
0        25        50                 100
|         |         |                   |
              Miles
```

Table 1. Number of recognized colleges at different levels of accessibility in Wisconsin (fall 1968)

| | Level of accessibility | | | | | |
| | Free-access | | Less accessible | | | Total |
Type of college	1	2	3	4	5	colleges
Public two-year	7	10	3	2	0	22
Public four-year	0	5	5	1	0	11
Branches.	0	0	8	0	0	8
All private	0	0	3	22	4	29
Total colleges	7	15	19	25	4	70

Table 2. Percentage of different populations within commuting distance of a free-access college in Wisconsin (fall 1968)

| | | Percent within commuting distance | | |
Type of community	Population in thousands	White	Black	Total
Metropolitan areas (over 1 million)				
Central city	741	32	92	37
Fringe	538	2	—*	2
Other metropolitan areas.	635	74	—	74
Counties over 20,000.	1,733	57	—	57
Counties under 20,000.	300	42	—	42
Total state	3,947	47	89	47

* Dash (—) = base too small for reliable estimate.

Table 3. Estimate of additional colleges required to put specified percentages of the population of Wisconsin within commuting distance of a free-access college

	As of fall 1968	Hypothetical additional colleges				
Number of free-access colleges 22		1†	2	3	4	8
Cumulative percent of population within commuting distance. 47%		53%	62%	72%	81%	90%
Average population within commuting distance of each college (in thousands) 84		245†	178	140	85	46

† Figures in this line are not cumulative. Each refers to an independent set of additional colleges.

Wyoming

For several reasons Wyoming is a most unusual state. It is a very sparsely populated state that has actually lost population in the past decade. A very small proportion of the labor force is engaged in manufacturing; mining and grazing dominate the Wyoming economy.

Even though the per capita income in Wyoming is slightly below the national average, the state's appropriations for higher education are among the highest in the nation on a per capita basis. The proportion of young people graduating from secondary school is above average, and the percentage of those graduates going on to higher education ranks among the top four or five states. The large majority of these students remain in Wyoming to attend public institutions.

Wyoming is one of two states in the nation that has no private institutions. (Nevada is the other.) The state does have seven public institutions—the state university and six community colleges. The university's Board of Trustees is in the unique position of governing all higher institutions in the state. There is, however, a separate coordinating commission for the junior colleges.

An even more unusual situation is the fact that every institution in the state is a free-access college. Despite the very low population density in Wyoming, some 43 percent of the state's population live within commuting distance of one of these free-access institutions. This remarkable accomplishment is only slightly diminished by the surprising fact that Cheyenne, the capital and largest city in the state, has no higher institution. Otherwise, every location in the state that under present conditions could defensibly support a college already has one.

Table 1. Number of recognized colleges at different levels of accessibility in Wyoming (fall 1968)

	Level of accessibility					
	Free-access		Less accessible			Total
Type of college	1	2	3	4	5	colleges
Public two-year	2	4	0	0	0	6
Public four-year	0	1	0	0	0	1
Branches	0	0	0	0	0	0
All private	0	0	0	0	0	0
Total colleges	2	5	0	0	0	7

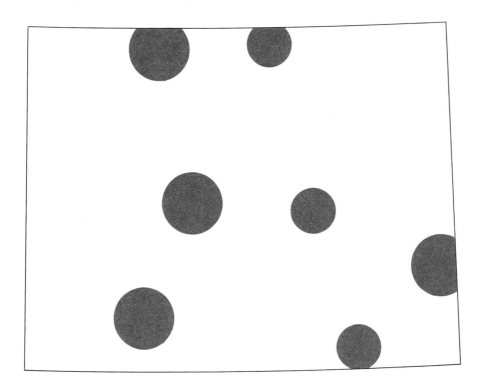

Wyoming

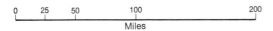

| 0 | 25 | 50 | 100 | | 200 |
Miles

● Commuting area of a free-access college (see Chapter 5 for explanation)

Table 2. Percentage of different populations within commuting distance of a free-access college in Wyoming (fall 1968)

Type of community	Population in thousands	Percent within commuting distance
Metropolitan areas (over 1 million)		
Central city	0	—*
Fringe	0	—
Other metropolitan areas	0	—
Counties over 20,000	157	55
Counties under 20,000	172	31
Total state	329	43

*Dash (—) = base too small for reliable estimate.

Table 3. Estimate of additional colleges required to put specified percentages of the population of Wyoming within commuting distance of a free-access college

	As of fall 1968	Hypothetical additional colleges	
Number of free-access colleges	7	1†	3
Cumulative percent of population within commuting distance	43%	60%	71%
Average population within commuting distance of each college (in thousands)	20	57†	12

† Figures in this line are not cumulative. Each refers to an independent set of additional colleges.

Tables A to G

Information in these tables serves as the basis for the state profiles of Chapter 5. Notes to tables A to G are on page 206.

Table A. Percentage of different populations within commuting distance of a free-access college[1]

| | Population in millions | Percent within commuting distance | | | |
		White	Black	Mexican American[2]	Total
United States	179.3	42	47	47	42
Northeast:	44.7	38	37	—*	38
Connecticut	2.5	87	90	—	87
Maine	1.0	0	—	—	0
Massachusetts	5.1	53	25	—	52
New Hampshire	0.6	44	—	—	44
New Jersey	6.1	36	59	—	38
New York	16.8	38	23	36	36
Pennsylvania	11.3	24	41	—	25
Rhode Island	0.9	40	60	—	41
Vermont	0.4	41	—	—	41
South:	55.0	50	52	—	50
Alabama	3.3	57	54	—	56
Arkansas	1.8	43	42	—	43
Delaware	0.4	35	44	—	35
Florida	5.0	62	72	—	64
Georgia	3.9	33	24	—	30
Kentucky	3.0	51	69	—	52
Louisiana	3.3	49	47	—	48
Maryland	3.1	59	47	—	57
Mississippi	2.2	67	63	—	65
North Carolina	4.6	69	67	—	68
Oklahoma	2.3	31	26	—	31
South Carolina	2.4	58	53	—	56
Tennessee	3.6	39	52	—	41
Texas	9.6	37	43	40	38
Virginia	4.0	52	40	—	50
West Virginia	1.9	53	59	—	54
Midwest:	51.6	33	39	—	33
Illinois	10.1	56	59	57	56
Indiana	4.7	0	0	—	0
Iowa	2.8	39	52	—	39
Kansas	2.2	42	59	—	43
Michigan	7.8	41	33	—	40

*Dash (—) = base too small for reliable estimate.

Table A continued

	Population in millions	Percent within commuting distance			
		White	Black	Mexican American[2]	Total
United States	179.3	42	47	47	42
Minnesota	3.4	30	24	—*	29
Missouri	4.3	39	60	—	41
Nebraska	1.4	16	0	—	16
North Dakota	0.6	30	—	—	30
Ohio	9.7	12	19	—	12
South Dakota	0.7	12	—	—	12
Wisconsin	3.9	47	89	—	47
West:	28.0	51	48	55	51
Alaska	0.2	31	—	—	31
Arizona	1.3	39	42	30	38
California	15.7	60	48	66	60
Colorado	1.7	41	58	48	42
Hawaii	0.6	48	—	—	48
Idaho	0.7	40	—	—	40
Montana	0.7	31	—	—	31
Nevada	0.3	0	0	—	0
New Mexico	1.0	24	38	16	22
Oregon	1.8	49	75	—	49
Utah	0.9	19	—	—	20
Washington	2.9	51	53	—	51
Wyoming	0.3	43	—	—	43

*Dash (—) = base too small for reliable estimate.

Table B. Percentage of different populations within commuting distance of a free-access college in each metropolitan area of 1 million or more[1]

Metropolitan area	Population in millions	Percent within commuting distance			
		White	Black	Mexican American	Total
Anaheim	0.70	89	—*	89	89
City	0.29	100	—	100	100
Fringe	0.42	81	—	81	81
Atlanta	1.02	29	9	—	25
City	0.49	18	4	—	13
Fringe	0.53	36	28	—	34
Baltimore	1.73	38	36	—	37
City	0.94	36	38	—	37
Fringe	0.79	39	25	—	38

*Dash (—) = base too small for reliable estimate.

Table B continued

Metropolitan area	Population in millions	Percent within commuting distance			
		White	Black	Mexican American	Total
Boston	2.60	30	2	—*	21
City	0.70	16	0	—	15
Fringe	1.90	35	16	—	35
Buffalo	1.31	33	10	—	32
City	0.53	19	2	—	17
Fringe	0.77	42	60	—	42
Chicago	6.22	57	63	58	58
City	3.56	69	63	58[2]	67
Fringe	2.67	45	61	—	46
Cincinnati	1.27	5	1	—	5
City	0.50	0	0	—	0
Fringe	0.77	11	8	—	10
Cleveland	1.91	21	42	—	24
City	0.88	24	43	—	30
Fringe	1.03	22	—	—	19
Dallas	1.12	10	34	32	14
City	0.68	11	41	39	18
Fringe	0.44	8	7	—	7
Denver	0.93	34	50	42	35
City	0.49	46	51	54	47
Fringe	0.44	22	—	13	22
Detroit	3.76	29	24	—	29
City	1.67	13	22	—	16
Fringe	2.09	39	42	—	39
Houston	1.42	18	23	11	18
City	0.94	10	27	5	13
Fringe	0.48	31	9	24	28
Kansas City	1.09	17	52	—	21
City	0.60	35	54	—	38
Fringe	0.50	0	—	—	0
Los Angeles	6.04	59	38	71	58
City	2.82	45	26	51	44
Fringe	3.22	69	74	88	71
Miami	0.94	43	95	—	50
City	0.29	95	90	—	94
Fringe	0.64	28	52	—	31
Milwaukee	1.28	19	92	—	23
City	0.74	32	93	—	37
Fringe	0.54	2	—	—	2
Minneapolis	1.48	25	26	—	25
City	0.80	26	27	—	26
Fringe	0.69	24	—	—	24
Newark	1.69	27	71	—	33
City	0.41	68	94	—	77
Fringe	1.28	14	35	—	20

*Dash (—) = base too small for reliable estimate.

Table B continued

Metropolitan area	Population in millions	Percent within commuting distance			
		White	Black	Mexican American	Total
New Orleans	0.91	31	34	—*	32
City	0.63	43	40	—	42
Fringe	0.28	12	4	—	10
New York	10.69	30	21	36[2]	29
City	7.78	30	20	36	29
Fringe	2.91	29	27	31	29
Paterson	1.19	0	0	—	0
City	0.28	0	0	—	0
Fringe	0.91	0	0	—	0
Philadelphia	4.34	26	43	—	29
City	2.00	23	46	—	29
Fringe	2.34	29	32	—	29
Pittsburgh	2.41	27	46	—	28
City	0.60	33	46	—	35
Fringe	1.80	25	45	—	26
St. Louis	2.10	43	60	—	46
City	0.75	68	78	—	71
Fringe	1.35	33	12	—	32
San Bernardino	0.81	43	61	49	45
City	0.22	73	95	99	77
Fringe	0.59	32	36	34	32
San Diego	1.03	38	49	46	39
City	0.57	28	50	42	31
Fringe	0.46	49	—	51	49
San Francisco	2.65	55	55	64	55
City	1.11	36	44	39	37
Fringe	1.54	68	80	63	68
Seattle	1.11	44	54	—	45
City	0.56	31	56	—	32
Fringe	0.55	57	—	—	57
Washington, D.C.	2.08	70	75	—	71
City	0.76	82	81	—	82
Fringe	1.31	67	45	—	65
All major SMSA†	65.81	36	41	50	37
City	32.58	36	42	42	37
Fringe	33.23	37	37	68	37

*Dash (—) = base too small for reliable estimate.
† Standard Metropolitan Statistical Areas.

Table C. Population characteristics of the states[3]

	Population in millions (1967)	Percent population increase (1960–67)	Population per square mile (1960)	Percent urban (1960)	Percent black (1960)
United States	198.0	10%	51	70%	11%
Northeast:	48.2	8	273	80	7
Connecticut	2.9	15	521	78	4
Maine	1.0	0	31	51	0
Massachusetts	5.4	5	657	84	2
New Hampshire	0.7	13	67	58	0
New Jersey	7.0	15	806	89	9
New York	18.3	9	351	85	8
Pennsylvania	11.6	3	251	72	8
Rhode Island	0.9	5	817	86	2
Vermont	0.4	7	42	39	0
South:	61.4	11	63	59	21
Alabama	3.5	8	64	55	30
Arkansas	2.0	10	34	43	22
Delaware	0.5	16	225	66	14
Florida	6.0	20	92	74	18
Georgia	4.5	14	68	55	29
Kentucky	3.2	5	76	45	7
Louisiana	3.7	12	72	63	32
Maryland	3.7	18	314	73	17
Mississippi	2.3	7	46	38	42
North Carolina	5.0	10	93	40	25
Oklahoma	2.5	7	34	63	7
South Carolina	2.6	9	79	41	35
Tennessee	3.9	9	86	52	17
Texas	10.9	13	36	75	12
Virginia	4.5	14	100	56	21
West Virginia	1.8	−3	77	38	5
Midwest:	55.1	7	69	69	7
Illinois	10.9	8	180	81	10
Indiana	5.0	7	129	62	6
Iowa	2.8	0	49	53	1
Kansas	2.3	4	27	61	4
Michigan	8.6	10	138	73	9
Minnesota	3.6	5	43	62	1
Missouri	4.6	6	63	67	9
Nebraska	1.4	1	18	54	2
North Dakota	0.6	1	9	35	0
Ohio	10.5	7	237	73	8
South Dakota	0.7	−1	9	39	0
Wisconsin	4.2	6	73	64	2

Table C continued

	Population in millions (1967)	Percent population increase (1960–67)	Population per square mile (1960)	Percent urban (1960)	Percent black (1960)
United States	198.0	10%	51	70%	11%
West:	33.0	17	16	78	4
Alaska	0.3	19	— *	38	3
Arizona	1.6	24	16	75	3
California	19.2	21	100	86	6
Colorado	2.0	12	17	74	2
Hawaii	0.7	15	99	77	1
Idaho	0.7	4	8	48	0
Montana	0.7	3	5	50	0
Nevada	0.4	53	3	70	5
New Mexico	1.0	5	8	66	2
Oregon	2.0	13	18	62	1
Utah	1.0	14	11	75	1
Washington	3.1	8	43	68	2
Wyoming	0.3	− 5	3	57	1

* Less than 0.5.

Table D. Employment and income characteristics of the states[3]

	Percent of 1960 labor force in:		Percent of state in farms (1960)	Per capita income (thousands of dollars, 1967)
	Manufacturing	White-collar		
United States	27	41	49	$3.1
Northeast:	33	44	34	3.5
Connecticut	40	44	28	3.9
Maine	33	35	16	2.6
Massachusetts	36	44	23	3.5
New Hampshire	40	36	19	3.0
New Jersey	36	45	29	3.6
New York	29	47	44	3.7
Pennsylvania	36	40	41	3.1
Rhode Island	39	38	20	3.2
Vermont	25	38	50	2.8
South:	21	38	64	2.6
Alabama	27	34	51	2.2
Arkansas	20	33	49	2.1
Delaware	33	43	60	3.7
Florida	13	43	44	2.8
Georgia	26	35	53	2.5
Kentucky	21	34	67	2.4

Table D continued

	Percent of 1960 labor force in:		Percent of state in farms (1960)	Per capita income (thousands of dollars, 1967)
	Manufac-turing	White-collar		
United States	27	41	49	$3.1
Louisiana	16	38	36	2.4
Maryland	25	46	55	3.4
Mississippi	19	29	61	1.9
North Carolina	32	31	51	2.4
Oklahoma.	13	42	81	2.6
South Carolina	32	30	47	2.2
Tennessee	26	35	60	2.4
Texas	16	41	85	2.7
Virginia	22	40	51	2.8
West Virginia	23	36	39	2.3
Midwest:	30	40	80	3.3
Illinois	32	42	85	3.7
Indiana	35	37	80	3.2
Iowa	19	37	94	3.1
Kansas	17	42	96	3.0
Michigan	38	40	41	3.4
Minnesota	20	41	60	3.1
Missouri.	25	40	75	3.0
Nebraska	12	39	97	2.9
North Dakota	4	35	93	2.5
Ohio.	37	40	71	3.2
South Dakota	7	34	92	2.6
Wisconsin.	33	37	60	3.2
West:	21	46	30	3.4
Alaska.	7	49	0	3.6
Arizona	13	43	55	2.7
California	24	47	37	3.7
Colorado	16	46	58	3.1
Hawaii.	16	42	60	3.3
Idaho	14	37	29	2.6
Montana	10	40	69	2.8
Nevada	6	41	16	3.6
New Mexico	8	44	60	2.5
Oregon	23	42	35	3.1
Utah.	16	45	24	2.6
Washington.	25	45	44	3.5
Wyoming	8	40	58	3.0

Table E. Ratios representing educational attainment by state[4,6]

	Ratio of high school graduates to all 18-year-olds (1963)	Ratio of college freshmen to all 18-year-olds* (1963)	Ratio of college freshmen to all high school graduates* (1963)	Ratio of college freshmen to all high school graduates* (1968)
United States	.71	.36	.51	.57
Northeast:	.75	.35	.47	.59
Connecticut	.79	.44	.56	.67
Maine	.71	.22	.31	.35
Massachusetts	.77	.43	.56	.66
New Hampshire	.70	.27	.39	.45
New Jersey	.75	.39	.53	.59
New York	.73	.34	.47	.71
Pennsylvania	.77	.30	.39	.43
Rhode Island	.67	.30	.46	.67
Vermont	.79	.28	.35	.34
South:	.60	.28	.47	.52
Alabama	.60	.19	.32	.47
Arkansas	.62	.30	.47	.55
Delaware	.72	.32	.45	.49
Florida	.63	.38	.61	.65
Georgia	.55	.20	.35	.41
Kentucky	.54	.25	.47	.49
Louisiana	.62	.29	.46	.49
Maryland	.68	.35	.51	.52
Mississippi	.54	.28	.52	.64
North Carolina	.60	.22	.36	.41
Oklahoma	.70	.38	.54	.62
South Carolina	.55	.19	.34	.39
Tennessee	.62	.26	.42	.46
Texas	.59	.33	.57	.61
Virginia	.54	.25	.46	.47
West Virginia	.66	.25	.38	.42
Midwest:	.78	.38	.49	.55
Illinois	.74	.47	.63	.68
Indiana	.75	.33	.44	.46
Iowa	.85	.40	.47	.53
Kansas	.85	.46	.54	.64
Michigan	.77	.34	.45	.51
Minnesota	.87	.39	.45	.52
Missouri	.76	.38	.50	.56
Nebraska	.82	.44	.54	.56
North Dakota	.85	.43	.51	.62
Ohio	.73	.32	.45	.51

* College freshmen include only degree credit students.

Table E continued

	Ratio of high school graduates to all 18-year-olds (1963)	Ratio of college freshmen to all 18-year-olds* (1963)	Ratio of college freshmen to all high school graduates* (1963)	Ratio of college freshmen to all high school graduates* (1968)
United States	.71	.36	.51	.57
South Dakota	.80	.41	.51	.56
Wisconsin	.87	.36	.41	.48
West:	.76	.53	.70	.69
Alaska	.42	.20	.47	.46
Arizona	.67	.41	.61	.97
California	.78	.63	.80	.75
Colorado	.69	.38	.55	.61
Hawaii	.73	.35	.48	.64
Idaho	.76	.47	.62	.62
Montana	.76	.45	.59	.59
Nevada	.60	.42	.70	.53
New Mexico	.60	.28	.47	.50
Oregon	.83	.45	.54	.64
Utah	.79	.44	.56	.57
Washington	.77	.44	.57	.73
Wyoming	.76	.48	.63	.70

* College freshmen include only degree credit students.

Table F. Distribution of students to college by state† (fall 1968)[5,6]

	Ratio of college freshmen to high school graduates	Column 1 distributed to:		
		Public	Private	Out-of-state
United States	.57	.39	.09	.09
Northeast:	.59	.28	.15	.16
Connecticut	.67	.26	.13	.28
Maine	.35	.19	.05	.11
Massachusetts	.66	.24	.28	.14
New Hampshire	.45	.21	.08	.17
New Jersey	.59	.20	.09	.30
New York	.71	.39	.18	.14
Pennsylvania	.43	.21	.12	.10
Rhode Island	.67	.30	.19	.18
Vermont	.34	.15	.07	.12
South:	.52	.37	.08	.07
Alabama	.47	.35	.06	.06
Arkansas	.55	.39	.08	.08

† Degree credit students only.

Table F continued

	Ratio of college freshmen to high school graduates	Column 1 distributed to:		
		Public	Private	Out-of-state
United States	.57	.39	.09	.09
Delaware	.49	.23	.08	.18
Florida	.65	.49	.06	.10
Georgia	.41	.28	.06	.07
Kentucky	.49	.35	.08	.06
Louisiana	.49	.42	.03	.04
Maryland	.52	.32	.05	.15
Mississippi	.64	.52	.07	.04
North Carolina	.41	.25	.12	.04
Oklahoma	.62	.49	.08	.05
South Carolina	.39	.18	.13	.08
Tennessee	.46	.31	.09	.06
Texas	.61	.49	.08	.03
Virginia	.47	.26	.07	.14
West Virginia	.42	.31	.06	.05
Midwest:	.55	.39	.08	.08
Illinois	.68	.43	.11	.14
Indiana	.46	.32	.08	.06
Iowa	.53	.30	.12	.11
Kansas	.64	.49	.08	.07
Michigan	.51	.41	.06	.04
Minnesota	.52	.39	.07	.07
Missouri	.56	.41	.07	.08
Nebraska	.56	.42	.07	.07
North Dakota	.62	.52	.02	.09
Ohio	.51	.35	.08	.08
South Dakota	.56	.39	.09	.08
Wisconsin	.48	.38	.05	.05
West:	.69	.58	.05	.06
Alaska	.46	.17	.06	.23
Arizona	.97	.88	.01	.08
California	.75	.66	.05	.04
Colorado	.61	.50	.02	.09
Hawaii	.64	.41	.06	.17
Idaho	.62	.38	.12	.12
Montana	.59	.44	.04	.11
Nevada	.53	.37	.00	.16
New Mexico	.50	.37	.02	.11
Oregon	.64	.50	.06	.08
Utah	.57	.45	.09	.03
Washington	.73	.63	.05	.05
Wyoming	.70	.55	.00	.15

Table G. Some pertinent educational characteristics of the states

| | State appropriations[7] | | New free-access two-year colleges (1958–68) | FTE* in free-access colleges | |
	Per capita	Percent of income		Average	Percent of all FTE
United States	$31	0.8 + %	339	1,090	46%
Northeast:	25	0.7	64	902	22
Connecticut	27	0.6	11	642	34
Maine	27	0.9	0	0	0
Massachusetts	16	0.4	10	909	17
New Hampshire	15	0.4	1	155	4
New Jersey	18	0.4	9	1,171	28
New York	34	0.8	16	984	23
Pennsylvania	21	0.6	15	1,021	20
Rhode Island	33	0.9	1	1,357	13
Vermont	31	1.0	1	316	17
South:	27	0.9	126	833	50
Alabama	21	0.8	13	688	65
Arkansas	24	1.0	1	930	77
Delaware	32	0.8	1	518	17
Florida	32	1.0	21	1,700	79
Georgia	27	1.0	8	560	32
Kentucky	30	1.1	0	472	35
Louisiana	27	1.0	3	1,257	75
Maryland	25	0.6	7	745	51
Mississippi	21	0.9	4	625	71
North Carolina	35	1.3	24	503	33
Oklahoma	24	0.8	0	620	37
South Carolina	20	0.8	11	508	29
Tennessee	22	0.8	5	829	47
Texas	31	1.0	16	1,143	63
Virginia	26	0.8	11	575	23
West Virginia	30	1.1	1	557	44
Midwest:	32	1.0	78	917	34
Illinois	37	0.9	26	1,246	48
Indiana	30	0.8	0	0	0
Iowa	37	1.0	5	437	26
Kansas	35	1.0	3	622	51
Michigan	35	0.9	16	1,364	47
Minnesota	35	1.0	9	724	43
Missouri	28	0.8	8	1,067	39
Nebraska	34	1.0	2	527	29
North Dakota	38	1.4	0	604	58
Ohio	22	0.6	5	1,358	11
South Dakota	28	1.0	0	324	13
Wisconsin	39	1.1	4	658	34

* First-time enrollment.

Table G continued

	State appropriations[7]		New free-access two-year colleges (1958–68)	FTE* in free-access colleges	
	Per capita	Percent of income		Average	Percent of all FTE
United States	$31	0.8 + %	339	1,090	46%
West:	43	1.2	71	1,729	71
Alaska	48	1.1	0	301	91
Arizona	39	1.3	5	2,369	67
California	39	0.9	31	2,538	80
Colorado	43	1.2	6	808	49
Hawaii	57	1.5	0	806	44
Idaho	42	1.4	1	1,182	77
Montana	39	1.2	1	535	61
Nevada	33	0.8	0	0	0
New Mexico	37	1.3	1	411	40
Oregon	43	1.2	11	1,046	48
Utah	38	1.3	1	906	31
Washington	57	1.4	12	1,675	73
Wyoming	46	1.3	2	642	100

* First-time enrollment.

Reference notes to tables A to G

1. See Chapter 2 for a description of the methods used in producing the estimates in Tables A and B.

2. Estimates of accessibility to free-access colleges in Tables A and B were computed for Mexican Americans in the five Southwestern states in which the 1960 census enumerated that group. Estimates for Puerto Ricans were restricted to New York and Chicago, the only cities with substantial Puerto Rican populations.

3. The first two columns of Table C and the last column of Table D come from the *Statistical Abstract* (U.S. Bureau of the Census, 1968). The other data in these two tables are for 1960 (U.S. Bureau of the Census, 1967).

4. The first three columns of Table E contain ratios of educational attainment for 1963. These data were reported by Rice and Mason (1964). The last column of Table E comes from two sources: data collected in the residence and migration study of fall 1968, and estimates of 1968 high school graduates by state. I am indebted to Messrs. F. C. Nassetta, T. H. Drews, and W. V. Grant for providing this information prior to publication. Ratios for educational attainment of 18-year-olds is not included for 1968 because current inter-census estimates of the size of various age groups in the 50 states do not appear stable enough to separate individual age groups and form reliable ratios.

5. In Table F the ratio of college freshmen to high school graduates for 1968 is broken down according to the type of college attended. All these ratios are based on the unpublished data mentioned in note 4 above.

6. It seems clear that there are some distortions in the 1968 ratio of college entrants to high school graduates shown in Tables E and F. The New York ratio is probably high by .15 because that state reported all nondegree credit students as degree-credit to USOE in fall 1968. Arizona is probably high by .10 because one large institution reported nondegree credit students as New York did. Even at that, the Arizona ratio is still extremely high (.97 as compared to .61 five years earlier). Various inquiries did not yield any satisfactory explanation for this unusually high access rate, but it may relate to the large immigration and the many adults in Arizona colleges.

7. State appropriations for higher education refer to the 1969–70 academic year (*Chronicle of Higher Education*, 1969c). In order to express this figure as a percentage of income, it was divided by per capita income for 1967 (U.S. Bureau of the Census, 1968) adjusted upward by 15 percent to account for inflation.

6. Implications of state profiles

As institutions and culture become increasingly standardized, variety is worth seeking. Perusal of the 50 state profiles in the foregoing chapter does not go unrewarded. Despite a frequent sameness in the solutions that educators promote, the picture of accessibility of higher education does vary a good deal from state to state. Indeed, it is because of this variation that the data describing the access situation in each state serve a useful purpose. How can these variations be characterized? What have we learned that can be generalized beyond purely local situations? This chapter outlines prototype models and problems that may be useful in efforts to improve educational opportunity in systems of higher education.

A principal difficulty in grappling with such relatively recent and complicated ideas as "equal opportunity for higher education" is the fact that we are not sure what all the problems are and at what level they can be dealt with most effectively. Glenny (1970) has documented the tremendous impact federal legislation can have on access to higher education over the next decade. It is equally clear that, in the last analysis, real educational opportunity will be provided only by the institutions and their faculties. The role of state and urban systems is still developing. Palola et al. (1970) credit state planning with helping higher education cope with quantitative expansion, but seem in basic agreement with Mayhew (1969b) who holds that state agencies have had little success in working on problems of cultural minorities and the educationally disadvantaged—not that there has been much success in any quarter.

Nonetheless, the state profiles suggest a variety of problems that seem to be basically state or metropolitan problems. Furthermore, educational opportunity has been historically a state responsibility and, in particular, matters connected with location of public colleges have been typically state prerogatives. This tradition may stem from the federal constitution, but its present rationale is more appropriately connected with political realities and the comprehension of local affairs that development of accessible higher education implies.

It is, in fact, the need for efficient systems of higher education operating in the broad public interest that has generated the remarkable growth of planning and coordinating mechanisms in the past decade. If, as Miller (1962) states, a major function of such agencies is to coordinate the location of colleges, then the characteristic ways in which institutions are and are not accessible to potential students must necessarily be a matter of primary concern. The following sections depict the most common models of state organization of accessible higher education, describe 13 important restraints on accessibility, and outline several complementary ways in which state or local systems might interpret and gauge accessibility.

Six state models

As we have seen the free-access colleges are almost exclusively public. Still, the nature and organization of those colleges that provide accessible higher education vary considerably from state to state. In some cases the term "model" is too specific, implying an organization and purpose not really present. Nevertheless, there are several fairly distinct models — whether they result from extensive planning or a situation inherited from a previous generation. The important fact is that the nature of the colleges and the way they are governed have a critical bearing on what kind of educational opportunity they are able (or likely) to provide for how many people.

It seems reasonable to assume that the six models described below are differentially effective because the various local circumstances and purposes differ. In actual fact most states tend to rely largely on one model and when they do use a combination, there is frequently little overall coordination. Variety may not be a virtue in itself, but Gardner (1969) has written compellingly of society's urgent need to maintain diverse institutions — be they social, political, or educational. System planners should carefully examine the strengths and weaknesses of these and other models and relate them to specific local conditions and needs.

Comprehensive community colleges

It is widely assumed that the comprehensive community college, having both transfer and terminal occupational programs, is the most promising means for meeting the social expectation of universal opportunity for higher education. There are some 15 states that rely on this model almost exclusively. These tend to be the states that have been the most active during the past decade in expanding educational systems, developing master plans, and strengthening statewide coordination. The best known examples are California, Florida, and Illinois.

Other states, such as Michigan, New York, and Washington, have developed strong community colleges but with somewhat different governance patterns from those of California, Florida, and Illinois. Connecticut, Massachusetts, and New Jersey illustrate the very recent move of some Northeastern states to expand postsecondary opportunity by means of community colleges.

The community college movement has had a fervent and, at times, uncritical following, though the early vision of this institution's vital social role has certainly been vindicated. The purpose and conception of this institution have increasing validity; in fact, the analysis of changing conditions of college admissions outlined in Chapter 1 dramatizes the extent to which social attitudes and conditions have caught up with the original purpose of the community college. Even sympathetic observers recognize, however, that these colleges have a way to go in solving some fundamental problems: high attrition rates, insufficient interest in occupational programs, and difficulty in meeting the needs of disadvantaged students.

Right now the community college is undoubtedly the most generally useful answer to the need for more free-access institutions, though it may have progressively limited educational and political viability as a two-year college in urban areas. This is one way to say that other existing models should not be discounted—first because they probably represent components of long-range solutions, and second because they amount to a substantial investment that will provide much of the educational opportunity for the foreseeable future in many states.

Senior institutions

Some eight or ten states rely mainly on senior institutions to provide accessible higher education. These range from states like Louisiana and Tennessee, which have free-access senior colleges located in proximity to a substantial proportion of their population, to states like Maine and Nevada, which have no free-access institutions at all but do have somewhat less-accessible senior colleges in the main population centers. This group of states tends to share two common characteristics. Most have not emphasized state coordination and planning, and they have not given much attention to the goal of comprehensive postsecondary education.

A strong case can be made for the four-year free-access college, particularly when it is conceived as a comprehensive, community-centered institution in an urban area containing enough population to justify it. Ironically, most of the states that have continued their emphasis on free-access senior colleges are not urbanized. The major drawback of most senior colleges with respect to the free-access function is, of course, the fact that their offerings are largely restricted to traditional baccalaureate programs for traditional students.

Comprehensive community colleges and senior institutions are examples of somewhat different approaches to the whole question of access to higher education. As indicated, the development of systems of higher education is typically much more advanced in those states that use the first model. There is another group of some 10 states that has maintained aspects of both models—some free-access senior institutions plus a larger number of comprehensive community colleges. These include Alabama, Colorado, Maryland, Texas, and Virginia. The coordination of higher education in these states ranges from well-organized to almost nonexistent.

Technical institutes

Eight or ten states have substantial enrollment in postsecondary technical institutions, which are of two distinct types. North Carolina and South Carolina have a number of technical institutes that are listed in *Opening Fall Enrollment* by the U.S. Office of Education and are included here as free-access colleges. Several other states—notably Georgia, Louisiana, Minnesota, and Wisconsin—have large numbers of students in postsecondary area vocational schools. The exact situation is hard to assess because, for some reason, it is very difficult to obtain accurate information about vocational enrollment beyond that supported by the federal government (Swanson, 1968).

Many of these institutions have developed strong and diverse programs in technical and vocational education. Even though the absence of traditional transfer programs is a weakness, it is also a strength because these institutions are thereby free of some of higher education's problems and are consequently able to devote their energies to a single job. The technical institute model has not received the attention it merits and this neglect is symptomatic of a major problem: in most states there is very little evidence that this type of vocational education has been integrated into statewide planning. Until it is, the students, the institutions, and the states seem very unlikely to realize technical education's full potential in equalizing educational opportunity.

Transfer institutions

In a few states free-access higher education is provided largely by junior colleges that stress the transfer function. Most also have occupational curriculums, but enrollment in terminal career programs is relatively small. Georgia, Kansas, and Minnesota are examples of states emphasizing transfer institutions. This model is frequently, but not always, accompanied by the development of postsecondary vocational schools. A principal weakness is the limited number of alternatives available to the transfer-oriented junior college in helping students find acceptable and useful alternatives to unrealistic academic aspirations.

Extension community colleges

The free-access colleges in Alaska, Hawaii, and Kentucky are examples of a unique situation. In each of these states accessible higher education is provided largely by a system of community colleges that operates as an extension of the state university. It is an important departure in governance. The principal advantage would appear to be the direct connection between the resources of the university and the service commitment of the community colleges. The principal disadvantage probably is the danger of the community colleges taking on the coloration of the university. The systems in each of these states are quite new, and it is too early to say whether their experiments will develop a strong new breed of community colleges or a set of somewhat unusual branch campuses.

Branch institutions

Branches of public senior institutions have been a traditional means of providing broad opportunity, but this group now includes practically no free-access institutions except in the three states just mentioned. There are several states like Ohio, Pennsylvania, and South Carolina with extensive branch systems that could have a substantial effect on the accessibility of higher education in those states if the units were more accessible. An important part of the rationale of the branch institution is improving accessibility. The fact that branches — except those set up as community colleges — perform this function to a very limited extent would seem sufficient reason for educators to reexamine the objectives of individual branch campuses. There is certainly a variety of important and unique functions that branches do or can serve—including professional retraining in urban areas or utilization of unusual facilities for special programs. It is less certain that branches can retain the policies and style of the parent institution (as most do) and extend educational opportunity to many additional students not now continuing beyond high school.

Thirteen restraints on accessibility

As the state profiles suggested characteristic models of accessibility, they also suggested characteristic restraints on accessibility. Incidentally, and perhaps symbolically, there are more than twice as many restraints as models. These restraints represent problems in various states suggested by the relationship between demography and educational resources. Consequently, they are all associated with the nature or location of institutions. There is no intent here to include other obvious restraints on access that are normally associated with students (that is, motivation, deprivation, and so forth) or to suggest that those problems are any less critical than they are usually assumed to be.[1]

The 13 restraints described briefly in the following paragraphs tend to be problems that act indirectly to deprive students of equal opportunity. Also, most tend to transcend the interest and authority of individual institutions. A few are quite familiar, but many have either not been recognized or have been too frequently ignored. Most are the kinds of problems that require systemwide attention and planning. Data provided in the profiles of those states cited as examples should be sufficient to identify the nature of the restraint. Beyond this, useful discussion of the problems depends very much on careful consideration of local conditions in individual states.

1. Insufficient colleges

The most common and obvious reason for geographic limitation in the accessibility of higher education is the simple fact that most states do not have enough public colleges to offer proximal education to most residents. As indicated in Chapter 4, solving the problem could require as many as 1,000 new institutions. So, it is safe to say that almost all the states will get along in the near future with fewer colleges than the number equal opportunity might imply as optimal. Some with low coverage like Indiana, Nebraska, and New Mexico have a more difficult immediate problem.

2. Selectivity

There are several states where selectivity has a critical effect on estimates of accessibility. For example, in Maine and Nevada accessibility is rated very low

---

1. Folger and Nam (1967) have assembled a variety of useful census information on factors related to access.

because major state institutions in populous areas are moderately selective. As another illustration, moderate selectivity of branch institutions has a noticeable effect on the overall accessibility of higher education in Pennsylvania and Wisconsin. Because of the fact that selective public colleges are more prominent than they are numerous, selectivity has less effect on the national estimate of accessibility than one might guess. If, for example, all inexpensive but moderately selective colleges were included as free-access institutions, the national percentage of the population living near an accessible college would advance only from 42 to 49 percent.

3. Tuition expense

Cost is obviously a major factor in access to higher education, but in this study much of the cost factor is translated into the differential expense associated with proximity. There are some states (Maryland, Nebraska, Ohio, and South Carolina, for example) where tuition restrains accessibility more than it is typically restrained in public institutions. In most states, however, the public institutions were largely under the 1968 tuition limit of $400 set for free-access colleges, and the private institutions were considerably above that level. Consequently, in the nation as a whole, estimates of the proportion of the population living near a free-access college would not be affected much by including institutions with tuition $100 or so above that level. New methods for studying the effect of cost on accessibility are described on page 216.

4. Shortage in the cities

It has been noted in Chapter 4 that the cities are frequently shortchanged with respect to free-access higher education. Three-quarters of the largest urban areas have a major deficiency in accessible higher education. More than 100 principal cities have no free-access college at all. The profiles of Chapter 5 provide numerous examples — see California, Michigan, New York, and Texas.

5. Competing colleges

A subtle and very frequent restraint on accessibility of higher education in many states is the disinclination to place a free-access college in a city where a major public institution is already located. As is usually the case, that major institution is relatively inaccessible, so the population does without a free-access college. Atlanta, Knoxville, and Salt Lake City provide illustrations. A special case is the selective state university with a nonselective general college. It is not at all clear whether such institutions can have a comprehensive free-access role, but current admissions pressure on urban colleges suggests that the model should and will be studied carefully.

6. Minority balance

As indicated in Chapter 4 there are numerous examples of individual states and cities where blacks are less likely than whites to live near an accessible college—or vice versa (see California, Maryland, and New York). They simply illustrate one more general type of potential bias in accessibility. In different metropolitan areas or states there may be various racial, ethnic, or socioeconomic minority groups that deserve specific attention in system planning.

7. Segregation

Like minority balance, there are many forms of segregation—de facto and otherwise. The racial segregation of many colleges, particularly in the Deep South, is perhaps the best known and most critical form. More generally, segregation can mean any representational imbalance in the actual enrollment of institutions. Such imbalances may result from many causes; they may be rational or irrational, obnoxious or innocuous. The main point is that social pressure for universal and equal educational opportunity does not allow such imbalances to be simply ignored.

8. Inadequate programs

If the idea of equal opportunity for higher education has any teeth to it at all, one must assume that a free-access college should offer enough curriculum choice to attract a wide variety of students. For this reason many specialized institutions were immediately excluded from this study. But of the colleges classified here as free-access, there are several types whose offerings limit the extent and nature of the access they provide. Examples include the county teachers colleges of Wisconsin, the technical institutes of North Carolina, and the transfer-oriented junior colleges of Georgia.

9. Limited coordination

There are now only three states (Delaware, Indiana, and Vermont) that have no coordinating body for higher education; but in those states that do have such agencies, many have been formed quite recently and, in general, they operate with uneven effectiveness. The quality of statewide coordination can have a critical bearing on various aspects of access to higher education. It is particularly critical in integrated educational–vocational guidance, program articulation among institutions, and the development of mutually beneficial relationships between education and the business community.

10. Underdeveloped colleges

A very important restraint on the accessibility of higher education is the fact that many colleges are entirely too small and poorly developed to serve their commuting areas effectively. There are a few such colleges in many states; in some it approaches a statewide problem (see Iowa, New Hampshire, and New Jersey). Speaking more generally, the impression is that inadequate development of the existing colleges (that have small enrollments) has often been a more serious restraint on educational opportunity than the absence of accessible institutions.

11. Sparse population

States like Alaska and Montana pose special problems because it is not geographically possible to put a college near a large proportion of their populations. A more general problem not usually appreciated is the fact that rural youth have a low rate of college attendance (Cowhig and Nam, 1962), and some 10 percent of the nation's population live in counties too sparsely populated to support a college. Sparse population poses the very real problem of how to provide equal opportunity when most prospective students are destined to mature in areas distant from any higher institution.

12. Transfer problems

Another critical problem is that of maintaining continued opportunity for individual development of aspirations encouraged by free-access to the thirteenth year. Transfer opportunity is a necessary concomitant to free-access two-year institutions, but there are serious problems. Dropout rates are high (Sanders and Palmer, 1965; Florida Research Council, 1969); space and financial aid are often lacking for those who do persist (Willingham and Findikyan, 1969; *San Francisco Chronicle,* 1969). It seems imperative that state planning boards recognize the full implications of widely available junior institutions. These institutions must be backed up with adequate transfer opportunity if free-access higher education is to be more than a lukewarm cooling out.

13. Inadequate information

This final item may not be a restraint in the same sense as the preceding ones, but it is a point worth noting. Since social and political forces provide much of the impetus for what is and is not done in extending educational opportunity, relevant information in the public domain can have an important bearing on legislative and administrative decisions that determine the accessibility of higher institutions. It is doubtful, for example, whether some of the Midwestern states would have allowed creeping inaccessibility to overtake their public institutions if the facts had been well known. It is also doubtful that a progressive state like Connecticut would have overinvested in new community colleges in recent years if there had been a factual basis for giving higher priority to program development. These observations provide a convenient introduction to the following section on developing factual bases.

Ways to interpret and gauge accessibility

This report is, in effect, a detailed exposition of one way to interpret and gauge the accessibility of higher education. It emphasizes a necessarily limited but standard measure — percentage of population within commuting distance of a free-access college — which can be applied to various regions, populations, and so forth. This measure provides a useful frame of reference, but the data should be of greater benefit in provoking questions than in providing definitive answers.

The reader who wishes to insist, for example, that a free-access college should have an annual tuition no higher than $300 may well be correct, but he will have successfully missed the point.

It has been shown that there are wide variations in how states handle and fail to handle the responsibility of providing educational opportunity beyond high school. There is also a wide variety of imbalances and restraints on accessibility that a standard measure, like the one used in this study, helps to reveal. Rather than give undue attention to the data reported here, interested administrators and researchers should focus attention on the problems suggested and on ways to collect pertinent information that will clarify the real conditions of educational opportunity in the context of local circumstances. In other words state systems should monitor and evaluate accessibility in a variety of ways that go beyond the data and scope of this report. Some of the possibilities in evaluating accessibility are as follows:

Local analysis of accessibility. An obviously desirable first step might be to undertake an analysis of accessibility generally similar to the procedure of this study but using current information and various alternate definitions of a free-access college. Detailed local analysis can and should take into account future plans and unusual circumstances not widely known. Local studies can provide a variety of more useful and realistic estimates of accessibility than is possible in a national study, but a primary benefit is the understanding gained through the process of developing such methods of evaluation.

The effect of proximity. Since proximity is so dependent on local circumstances, any analysis of accessibility is greatly improved by study of actual commuting patterns and residence of students such as those carried out at Chicago City Junior College (Willis, 1958 and 1964). There is also a great need for additional work on the effect of proximity upon the rate of college attendance—particularly of marginal students, minorities, and others of various socioeconomic conditions.

Enrollment. There are many reasons why an inexpensive, nonselective college may not provide educational opportunity for the people in its immediate area. One simple and objective measure of the extent to which it does is the institution's enrollment compared to the number of potential students within commuting distance. Enrollment breakdowns of a college can be related to a variety of appropriate baselines in the surrounding area: high school graduates, minority populations, special occupational groups, the adult population, and so forth.

Varieties of selectivity. The actual details of the admissions process at an institution are often difficult to obtain even with legal sanction, but any study of accessibility in a system of higher education is likely to be incomplete without understanding admissions criteria. In addition to formal policy, it is just as important to know the number and nature of those students actually admitted and those turned away. There is, for example, the selection that results, even in California, from gross inadequacies of space in relation to number of applicants (*San Francisco Chronicle,* 1969) and the bottom-half students who never apply to a nominally open-door college because the freshman flunk rate is too well known.

Financial aid deficit. A useful method of evaluating the effect of cost on access to college is to estimate the total financial aid deficit in a given system—that is, total college cost minus total funds available for all anticipated students or any particular subgroup of students. By using various components and parameters it is possible to estimate financial restraint on accessibility under a wide variety of hypothetical conditions and aid programs. A computer-based Financial Aid Study Tool (FAST) based on this method has been developed by the College Board and has been used in connection with state planning in Florida and California.

Positive attraction. The social reality of marginal college students suggests that accessible higher education must be more than passively available. Many thriving community institutions project a positive attraction based partly on aggressive public relations and local recruiting. Another important element is the administrative flexibility in procedures, scheduling, awarding credit, and course requirements, which makes college attendance practical for the student with special problems and little interest in academic tradition.

Student migration. The extent and nature of student migration within and outside a state can provide valuable information concerning the relationship of educational resources and student demand. Recent studies in Georgia (Martin, 1969), Utah (Grant, 1968), and Virginia (Clear, 1969) illustrate how access to college is reflected by student migration in those states.

Availability of programs. Whether a college does offer access to educational opportunity depends, in the last analysis, on the students' interest in its programs. An important element in gauging the accessibility of postsecondary education in a system is the extent to which there is sufficient variety to appeal to the interests and talents of most prospective students. For example, one minimum rule-of-thumb for a comprehensive free-access college might be to include one or more associate or baccalaureate programs in each of the following major areas: education, technical fields, business, health professions, and public service. Availability of relevant curriculums brings us full swing into the question of what the student seeks access to. The following chapter moves a step beyond this study in exploring briefly the implications of that question.

7. Making access equal and relevant

This report has emphasized quantitative problems. It contains data that help to describe the availability and accessibility of institutions to people. Of course that is the purpose of the study, but it is also necessary to ask: Access to what? Having colleges where they are needed is important, but equal opportunity implies a great deal more.

As higher education moves out of the convulsive 1960s, its most critical problems deal directly with this matter of opportunity. Rebellious students cast doubt on the value and relevance of the educational experience; minority demands for open admissions raise perplexing questions concerning the very nature of opportunity; and everyone questions, not where the money has to come from (Washington), but when it will be available and how it must be packaged. Simplistic solutions that involve merely opening a number of free-access colleges or creating completely open admissions at all existing institutions are not likely to prove genuinely useful over either the long or short range.

Open admission to all programs and institutions of public higher education is not viable at present under any imaginable conditions short of general revolution. There is the obvious fact that completely open admissions to all colleges would erode the value of the opportunity sought and undermine public confidence in higher education—and probably much of its value as a national resource. Of more significance is the fact that individuals will always differ greatly in the nature and extent of their competence, and those differences have to be harnessed in a sorting and striving process that is vital for the effective operation of a modern society in competition with other modern societies.

It is undoubtedly true, however, that this nation has exaggerated the competitive instinct and, both willfully and inadvertently, has managed to subjugate broad groups of people to social indignity and economic tribulation. The urgent necessity is to expand educational opportunity in ways that will be truly useful to the individual and to society. This will require a greatly broadened basis of opportunity including a variety of institutions and programs within institutions, well-known avenues for seeking opportunity, articulated means for moving to higher levels that demand more competence and offer greater reward, and ready means for continuing intellectual and career self-renewal. This means having some institutions and programs that are selective in various ways and a great many to which access and continued enrollment is determined primarily by interest and progress toward an educational or career goal.

No matter what directions higher education takes over the next decade, there is ample evidence that more of the same is not enough. A central problem is the fact that many young people are not intellectually oriented; typically only 30 to 40 percent have a positive attitude toward various school subjects (Tillery et al., 1966). There is good reason to believe that we have already fanned a desire and expectation that traditional colleges cannot meet. Many minority youth attend college reluctantly and only out of a feeling of economic necessity (Jaffe and Adams, 1969; Knoell, 1966). Middle- and upper-class youth have additional reasons for their alienation from traditional institutions. Keniston (1965) cites such social tensions as the separation of work and family, the shattering of conventional community, and chronic social change.

So while there is an obvious need to increase the number of accessible colleges and to increase the level of financial support to students and to institutions, there is an equal or greater need to make opportunity real—to make it relevant to the needs of individuals and the problems of society. This ultimate outcome of education—its worth to the individual and to the nation—is just as much the responsibility of community leaders as of educators. The following sections suggest ways in which education must be relevant and means whereby institutions, systems, and states can foster relevant opportunity.

What is educational relevance?[1]

The relationships between higher education and the rest of contemporary society are far too complex to permit capturing in simple and durable terms the relevance of higher education to society. It is particularly true since the most fashionable and comprehensible examples may be ephemeral and unreliable indicators of authentic long-range needs. But it does seem reasonable to assume that relevance refers to whether or not higher education is serving its basic functions on behalf of its primary constituencies. Further, it seems straightforward enough to imagine the primary constituencies as individuals on the one hand and society on the other. If one then assumes that higher education is mainly concerned with helping to establish social roles and providing modes of action for carrying out those roles, these two functions and these two constituencies suggest four types of relevance: personal, social, educational, and economic.

Personal relevance

Higher education has personal relevance to the extent that it helps individuals find their roles in society. This means first the equal opportunity for individuals to gain access to appropriate educational experiences. Since education beyond high school is a voluntary move to an institution somewhat unconnected with the secondary level, there are many possibilities for de facto imbalances in opportunity associated with race, class strata, economic condition, and so forth. Such differences are extremely important because they carry with them the assumption of underlying social restraints. Those restraints are commonly assumed to inhibit motivation and hamper individual freedom.

Personal relevance also implies an effective and humane guidance and admissions process through which individuals seek opportunity. It means the op-

---

1. This discussion of four types of relevance is based on a much more detailed and somewhat differently organized earlier paper (Willingham, 1970).

portunity for students to understand their strengths in the context of a wide assortment of competencies and career possibilities. Of course such understanding must be built upon a coordinated plan of educational opportunity and continuing guidance information. It is hard to overstate, however, the importance of maximizing the individual's sense of free choice, new alternatives, and control of his destiny.

Perhaps, most important of all, personal relevance is reflected in the quality of the educational process. As stated so well by Axelrod et al. (1969):

"For most people, getting an education appears to be a matter of acquiring units of information; how much one acquires is in direct proportion to the number of semesters spent in college. There is rarely any suggestion that a college education might improve the individual, that it might broaden his horizons, liberate him from dogma, from prejudice, or from internal conflict that limits his humanity. Seldom does any member of the general public visualize a college education helping a student to find himself, and rarely does he think of education as consisting of a total experience embracing not only courses and examinations, but also opportunities for students to try new styles of life, to learn from each other, or to form their beliefs through involvement in controversial issues."

The question is whether the educational experience will contribute to the growth of a mature and competent adult, able to contribute to society and support its basic values. There is urgent need to give much closer attention to the development of the student — the development of his career, his competencies, his personal interests, and his view of the world. Renewing the faculty's traditional interest in the student is commonly regarded as the key to this difficult set of problems. There is also the more concrete need to develop improved bases for understanding what a student knows and doesn't know when he leaves secondary school. The concept of setting specific objectives to work toward has much merit in meeting the here-and-now needs of disadvantaged youth and the middle-class objections to irrelevancy. Bloom (1968) and Popham and Husek (1969) have recently described different aspects of this new approach to curriculum design and evaluation.

Social relevance

In performing the basic function of defining social roles and responsibilities, higher education serves the broad interests of society by providing pressure-release mechanisms in times of stress. The pressure-release mechanism works in one way to marshal national resources and apply them where they are needed. Kerr (1963) and Galbraith (1967) give considerable emphasis to the marshaling function; Galbraith calls higher institutions the most important resource of the modern industrial system. There are other times of stress that call not so much for application of resources as for adjustment of roles throughout society. As Gardner (1968) has described the educational system, it is the indispensable instrument of the revolution in social organization.

A striking period of social adjustment occurred during the return of veterans to civilian life after World War II. The country is now faced with a far more serious task of social reorganization involving a substantial proportion of the minority and majority population. Perhaps the best line of evidence concerning current problems of social relevance may be found in the nature of student protests. Peterson's (1968) study is particularly revealing. Of 27 types of protests included in his survey, the notable fact is that every one of the six most frequent types involved moral issues such as the Vietnam War or racial discrimination. One interpretation of the student rebellion is that it is the acting out of needs felt deeply by students but not sufficiently channeled by the existing educational framework. The blasé indifference that angers and turns off students is by no means the whole story, but it provides substantial challenge for improving the social relevance of postsecondary education. There appear to be two major problems.

The first is the inadequate sense of community and social commitment that students find on most campuses. The fact that much discipline-oriented coursework is removed from real problems causes students to agitate for action and this agitation, in turn, convinces many observers that the university is best kept far away from any issue of real consequence. A second major problem, not unrelated to the first, is the fact that expanding educational opportunity has brought the reality of new types of students and the difficult job of providing relevant education for them. Most innovations have been of three types: minority culture programs, compensatory programs in conventional settings, and the New Careers movement (Riessman and Popper, 1968) that emphasizes education coordinated with work in a definite career line.

These forms of social relevance—a social commitment and the flexibility to serve new students—have a direct bearing on educational opportunity in fairly obvious ways. Inadequate commitment to problems of society or the immediate community reinforces an impression of institutional detachment hardly attractive to educationally marginal youth.

Educational relevance

In the present framework educational relevance refers to teaching individuals effective modes of action. If educational opportunity is to mean anything, it must last through to a useful outcome. New matriculants who end up as resentful dropouts or apathetic accumulators of dubious credits amount only to deceptive statistics. Two principal issues are what the colleges teach and how they teach it.

There has been a continuous debate on what the colleges should teach in order to lead to the most useful outcomes. Hutchins (1968) constructs an eloquent defense of liberal education as the individual's best preparation for a career and protection from intellectual obsolescence. Though the argument contains much validity, it runs against the current of increasing emphasis on vocational education and professional specialization. It may be that the debate has largely run its course for a relatively simple reason.

The pace of technological change makes it increasingly important that education keep pace with career requirements but insures that it can never really do so. Consequently there is reason to expect more and more emphasis on retraining and continuing education, all of which means that relevant education will have to be more rather than less sensitive to the reality of the working world. In time this may necessitate a radically different relationship between work and education— one in which the social norm involves intermittent periods of each with both being equal parts of an integrated life course. But in the meantime there is special need for follow-up studies of graduates in occupational programs in order to better articulate the curriculum with the intended job (Little, 1969).

A second important aspect of educational relevance is how the faculty teaches. In recent years there is wide implicit agreement among various writers that education can be made more relevant by broadening the conception of instruction. First, Katz and associates (1968) suggest that instruction should be broadened to modes other than the traditional academic-conceptual (for example, esthetic-artistic, people-oriented, motoric expression, and the art of sociability). Second, Mayhew (1969a) argues persuasively that most students can profit from a variety of experiences such as independent study, understanding of a different subculture, a sustained off-campus experience, and experience with the use of new media. Third, it is possible to broaden the methods of instruction through a wide variety of technological innovations already developed at a limited number of colleges (L. Johnson, 1969). It is also suggested that instruction should take place in situations other than the class and laboratory whenever possible in order to "reflect the world beyond the campuses in every feasible way" (Hazen Foundation, 1968). Fifth, new kinds of faculty need to be recruited from among the skilled and dedicated people in nonacademic professions (Katz and associates, 1968). Finally, student resentment of the grading system (Muscatine, 1966) is one more reason for developing additional methods for evaluating student accomplishment (see, for example, Davis, 1965).

Economic relevance

Education has economic relevance to the extent that it develops modes of individual action that are beneficial to society at large. That is, economic relevance stems from the relation of education to work. Most observers readily agree that the development of human resources is a vital national objective— as most agree that education is a primary route to a better job. Most of the interesting and important questions are somehow more complex than these two truisms. For example: What is the economic value of education? How much education is needed at what levels? How are manpower requirements matched with educational specifications?

Becker's (1964) provocative theory of human capital suggests that the rate of return for individual investment in education is substantial. It must be noted, however, that this pioneer analysis is concerned almost completely with monetary gain and does not include indirect effects on the economy, social benefit, or nonmonetary gain to the individual, each of which may be judged a more critical outcome of education.

There are a good deal of data available but few empirical grounds for agreement on how much education the economy needs. Various writers have suggested that additional vocational training may be necessary to reduce unemployment among youth (Arnow, 1968). Jaffe and Froomkin (1968) point out, however, that the number of jobs dropouts can perform is increasing faster than are the number of dropouts. These authors argue that higher unemployment rates of blacks and youth generally must be attributed to the fact that employers give preference to better educated applicants, which implies, in turn, that the principal effect of additional training would be to place different people at the end of the unemployment line.

The Mediterranean Regional Project is one of the first attempts to develop educational plans on the basis of comprehensive manpower requirements. Hollister's (1967) empirical evaluation of this model verifies that manpower requirements have a considerable effect on the educational system, but two problems loom large. Small errors in estimating technological change have significant effects on the occupational structure and consequently wipe out careful estimates of manpower requirements. But the weakest link and most serious problem in the manpower estimating procedure is the lack of precise knowledge regarding educational needs associated with each occupation.

If these problems are to submit to useful solutions, it is important to develop better means of anticipating what skills and competencies society needs. Only through a broader view can the educational requirements of the economy be protected from the vagaries and parochialism of professional interest. It should be added that fluctuations in national priorities can have a tremendous impact on manpower requirements (Lecht, 1969). These complicated questions of economic relevance are simply one good example of an overriding problem. A guarantee of equal and relevant educational opportunity implies a number of responsibilities at the institutional, state, and national level. It is advisable to consider briefly the nature of those responsibilities and some of the means for meeting them.

Fostering relevant opportunity

The foregoing discussion of relevancy in higher education suggests a number of specific problems. It is also evident that the idea of equal and relevant opportunity implies some very broad operating objectives. These may be described as: insuring unbiased access to appropriate programs for all individuals; developing and maintaining an integrated and continuing guidance and admissions system that emphasizes individual choice; maintaining a coordinated and efficient system of postsecondary education including all levels and types of programs; utilizing human resources so that the educational system effectively matches manpower need with individual interest and competence; enhancing career and personal development in a manner that is relevant to each student's needs—particularly those who have experienced social disadvantage.

These implied objectives are awesome in their complexity, their scope, and their potential impact on people's lives. While all these ideas exist in theory, there are precious few practical models. It is also clear that these objectives do not necessarily reflect the interests of the faculty and often not individual institutions. They are primarily public interests; and public interests typically must be guarded by public action. The conclusion is a simple one. If students and society want relevant educational opportunity, then some degree of "central" planning and organization naturally follows. What "central" means depends on where one sits in the overall scheme — student, faculty, institution, educational system, state government, or federal government.

In any event it is not simply a question of whether there is enough good in an objective to overcome the disadvantages. In part, the objectives just outlined are incompatible with one another. And there are several important sources of tension that are likely to affect any planned program of educational opportunity. Some are primarily political relationships: institutional interest versus system control; meritocratic versus egalitarian selection (partially a question of distribution of privilege); and individual choice versus governed social welfare. Other tensions have more substantive foundation. There is the long- versus the short-range view of the utility and function of higher education — the short view more likely being associated with a cost-benefit justification of occupational training and the long view with interpreting liberal education as a humane institution and a vital national resource. Closely related would be the academic-professional versus the social-political interpretation of the role and function of higher education.

Furthermore, programed means of utilizing human resources and influencing people's lives are socially dangerous because they can easily result in exploitation rather than real opportunity and genuine social benefit. It is for this reason that it is important to build in mechanisms that give the individual an upper hand in dealing with systems so large and complicated that they are necessarily impersonal.

It seems perfectly predictable that these tensions will continue to characterize the governance and planning of higher education. The philosophical and social issues will remain. The states will not be bulldozed by the federal government; the institutions are too strong to take very many orders from many state boards; and everyone knows the faculty is not easily controlled. But there is tremendous social pressure and tremendous individual initiative to undertake reform and to expand educational opportunity. What are the means for working toward these goals?

The discussion in this and the previous chapter suggests a wide variety of ways to foster relevant educational opportunity. The following brief outline contains many familiar items and some suggested by this study, though none deal with the background problems of educational disadvantage. These 60-odd means of fostering opportunity may be appropriate for any or each of the three levels: institution, educational system, or state.

Educational programs

Minority culture programs to improve the relevance of education for socially different students.

Community action projects to involve the institution in social problems that are meaningful to students.

New programs to foster a broadened interpretation of student accomplishment and evaluate their progress.

Programs to encourage the involvement of faculty in the career development of students.

Maintenance of adequate college guidance services to meet the needs of all students.

Experiments in student governance to share authority and teach responsibility.

Formal coursework devoted to modes of learning, social coping, and how to be a professional.

Service and cultural programs to make the institution a familiar and integral part of community life.

Maintenance of a strong job placement service for recent and older graduates from the institution.

Access programs

Expanded work-study programs (for example, New Careers) to integrate economic and educational opportunity.

Broadened instructional methods that are appropriate for new and different students and new content.

Programs to assist unprepared students in achieving mastery of specific skills that are vocationally or socially useful.

"Search" programs to identify unrecognized talent.

"Reach" programs to serve students in sparsely populated areas.

Special admissions programs for students who cannot qualify and succeed without extra assistance.

Special aid programs for students who cannot afford college costs or the foregone income that attendance entails.

Maximum administrative flexibility in order to serve students who have special needs or odd schedules.

Institutional and system research

Flexible models of freshman placement in order to maintain continuity between secondary and higher learning.

Attrition studies to identify ways in which students and institutions may have failed to convert access into opportunity.

Analysis of the incidence and conditions of altered career plans — the process and its effect on the student.

Studies of the effect the institution has on the values, aspirations, and competencies of its students.

Analysis of the financial aid and admissions decision-making process to determine what values are reflected in the institution's administrative actions.

Examination of transfer policy and student movement among institutions to reveal possible irrational barriers.

Evaluation of programs designed to expand relevant opportunity for disadvantaged students to improve their effectiveness.

Resource studies to project needs for adequate facilities, funds, and faculty.

Surveys of business and industry to determine new programs needed for emerging occupations.

Projections of manpower needs over a period of several years in order to anticipate demand in existing programs.

Monitoring of economic changes and the labor market to support current placement activities.

Studies of the accessibility of programs and institutions to students in different demographic groups.

Studies of commuting patterns and the effect of proximity on access rates of various minority and socioeconomic groups.

Studies of enrollment in relation to surrounding population to assist in determining the extent to which institutions serve constituencies.

Analysis of the total aid deficit for various groups of applicants under various assumptions of income, cost, and aid sources.

Operational programs

Early guidance programs to develop realistic aspirations before poor achievement in school turns the student off.

Computerized educational-vocational information systems to help integrate the vast quantities of necessary information in a form students can easily interpret.

Cooperative admissions systems that would reduce cost and confusion to the student while spinning off retrievable data of great value in planning.

Testing programs to describe the background, interests, preparation, and special potential of individual students.

Programs to administer financial aid efficiently and monitor its effect.

College locator-recruiter services that help colleges and students find one another.

Financial need analysis to help colleges and students justify equitable need.

Prediction systems for estimating the likelihood of student success in different courses, programs, and institutions.

Information systems that help the student to estimate the probability of admission and receipt of aid.

Improved information that will tell the student what higher education is really like and how it varies from campus to campus.

Programs of credit by examination that recognize the accomplishment rather than the auspices under which it was achieved.

Programs of advanced placement that give talented students credit for their preparation and continuity to their study.

Planning and coordination of educational systems

Development and revision of master plans to provide direction, public justification, and broad principles of access to higher education.

Development of guidelines for coordination of relevant programs among units of a system.

Development of current bilateral state agreements that maximize opportunity for career training at minimum cost.

Development of detailed guidelines regarding specific policy issues, such as transfer admissions, without imposing unjust barriers.

Introduction of comparable criteria, statistics, and definitions that encourage fair planning across institutions.

Introduction of planning and budgeting that support efficient operation and justify expenditures in the broad public interest.

Development of management information that supports rational planning and budgeting.

Representation of students and faculty in planning in order to balance fiscal and political forces with social and academic interests.

Enhancement of the accessibility of individual colleges to the fullest extent provided by a system plan.

Funding and development of comprehensive programs at existing institutions to at least a minimum level that attracts students.

Addition of free-access institutions to maximize the coverage of all populations within the state.

Development of effective information services to inform the public, trustees, and elected officials of imbalances in educational opportunity and the need for programs and the means to fund them.

Surveys of students

A periodic local or state census of student interests, achievement, competencies, and aspirations to form a benchmark for planning and assessing equal opportunity.

Studies of the educational needs of special groups of students: minorities, rural youth, students who discontinue education, adults who come back.

Brief annual or biannual surveys of high school seniors to monitor trends in the education–career plans of various groups and the problems they face in seeking education or work.

Social bookkeeping on the admissions process: annual and institutional variations in applicants, rejects, no shows, enrollment, aid applicants, and aid recipients.

Surveys of student reactions to policies, programs, and services.

Longitudinal analysis of attrition and accretion in the number of students originally interested in a given career and those who end up there several years later.

Follow-up surveys to evaluate the relevance of occupational curriculums to job conditions and demands.

Migration studies to monitor the flow of students from school to different colleges within and outside the state.

Follow-up studies of graduates to examine the relevance of the college experience.

8. A summary of findings and conclusions

Access to higher education has been affected by several developments of major significance during the past decade. Extensive federal funding has supported a quantum leap in the rate of college attendance. The civil rights movement and the student rebellion have brought into serious question the academic values that underlie restrictive admissions and discipline-oriented curriculums. Accelerating public expectation now demands that equal opportunity for relevant education beyond high school is a right not a privilege. The assumption of public responsibility in order to meet these public interests is reflected in the rapid development of state planning and coordination. Greatly expanded research and technology are becoming an integral part of the whole process of planning and monitoring access to higher education.

These developments have changed the fundamental nature of access to higher education in three ways. They reflect a marked shift from a scholastic to a societal view of the admissions process. Proximity has been added to cost and selectivity as an essential consideration in determining the accessibility of higher education. And most important, social change has created a new level of commitment and accountability that requires public demonstration that opportunity is equal and education is relevant.

What colleges are accessible?

In order to determine the accessibility of higher education as of fall 1968, each college in the country was rated on a five-point scale based jointly on tuition and selectivity. For the purposes of this study, the two lowest levels were designated "free-access" or simply accessible colleges. Of some 2,600 colleges, 789 or about 3 in 10 are free-access—meaning they accept most high school graduates and charge no more than $400 in annual tuition.

Of those colleges that are not free-access, 500 are special purpose or heavily religious; the remaining 1,300 or so institutions are inaccessible in roughly equal measure because of cost or selectivity—but more often both. Free-access higher education as defined here is almost exclusively public; it constitutes 60 percent of the public and 1 percent of the private sector.

Accessible higher education is also heavily represented by two-year colleges; they constitute three-quarters of the total free-access group. Three out of ten public senior institutions are free-access; the same proportion holds for their branches. Sharp regional variations in accessibility are indicated by the percentages of first-time students who enter free-access colleges: Northeast 22 percent, Midwest 34 percent, South 50 percent, and West 71 percent.

People and colleges

The 789 free-access colleges were plotted on detailed maps with commuting perimeters ranging from 2½ to 25 miles in radius, depending on the population density of the area. Estimates of the number of whites and minorities living within those commuting areas provided the basic data for describing the accessibility of higher education.

Slightly more than 2 out of 5 people live within commuting distance of a free-access college in the United States. Potential students are least likely to live near an accessible college in rural areas or in the largest cities. In general, the larger the metropolitan area the smaller the proportion of people living near an accessible college. There is, in fact, a serious deficiency of accessible higher education in 23 of the 29 largest metropolitan areas in the country. In each case less than one-third of the central or fringe population lives within the commuting perimeter of a free-access college. In all, there are 102 metropolitan areas in which the principal city has no free-access college.

The most serious urban deficiency is in the Northeast, but that region has also been slow to develop the accessible colleges it has. The West has the most accessible colleges and the highest rate of college attendance, but it is the only region where the major central cities have less accessible higher education than their fringe areas. The striking fact about the West is not so much the existence of accessible colleges as the liberal funding, advanced development, and heavy enrollments typical of the region.

A high proportion of the South is covered by free-access colleges, though segregation of institutions makes some of that accessibility illusory, and limited resources have retarded development of colleges in some states. The Midwest was the surprising region of this study. Despite its tradition of accessible higher education, a smaller proportion of Midwesterners live near a free-access college than is true of any other region.

The analyses undertaken did not reveal gross racial imbalances, though these estimates of the accessibility of higher education for minorities are undoubtedly inflated, and there is evidence of racial imbalance in some cities and states. The largest groups of people who do not have ready access to a college are whites in the metropolitan Northeast, the rural South, and throughout the Midwest. Blacks in the South are undoubtedly another such group, though these data are insufficient to show it.

The various factors that determine college location only infrequently result in new colleges being placed where they can serve the most people. Assuming no great improvement on this score, the 550 new colleges recommended by the Carnegie Commission (1968b) would have the approximate effect of raising the proportion of the population covered from 4 in 10 to 7 in 10 — that is, if the colleges were opened immediately.

State models of access

Various types of educational and demographic data were brought together in order to characterize the accessibility of higher education in each state. This analysis indicated that the states have used primarily six models of free-access higher education:

Comprehensive community colleges. In some 15 states free-access higher education is almost synonymous with the comprehensive community college. States like California, Florida, and Illinois have been very active in expanding systems, developing master plans, and strengthening statewide coordination. This model still has weaknesses, but the results of this study definitely support the assumption that the community college is the most generally useful approach to expanding educational opportunity in the 1970s.

Senior institutions. Some 8 or 10 states rely mainly on senior institutions to provide accessible higher education—usually with little emphasis on coordination. These range from states like Louisiana and Tennessee that have many free-access senior colleges to states like Maine and Nevada that have only a few moderately accessible colleges. There are about 10 other states like Colorado and Virginia; although they have some accessible senior colleges, they have moved in varying degrees toward state coordination and community college systems.

Technical institutes. Some 10 states have substantial enrollment in either postsecondary area vocational schools or in technical institutes. These are highly developed in some states like South Carolina but are often inadequately coordinated with other forms of educational opportunity. In general the very poor integration of vocational education with other forms of postsecondary opportunity is a serious national problem.

Transfer colleges. In a few states like Georgia and Kansas the free-access institutions are junior colleges that emphasize the transfer function—sometimes but not always accompanied by a separate system of area vocational schools.

Extension community colleges. Alaska, Hawaii, and Kentucky are undertaking a significant experiment in governance and coordination of resources. Their free-access institutions are community colleges that operate as extensions of the state university.

Branch institutions. Historically, some seven or eight states like Ohio and Pennsylvania have used branches of senior colleges to extend educational opportunity. In 1968 very few branches were free-access except those formally organized as community colleges.

Restraints on access

The data of individual states indicate 13 ways in which the availability of free-access colleges is restricted:

Most states have insufficient colleges to cover the population.

In several states selectivity of public institutions has a noticeable effect on accessibility.

In some states cost restricts access, but most public colleges have lower tuition than the $400 guideline of this study.

Many major urban areas are seriously shortchanged in accessible colleges.

Smaller cities with a prominent but relatively inaccessible senior institution frequently lack a free-access college.

There is a wide variety of potential and obvious minority imbalances, though these particular data revealed relatively few.

Segregation is a major and general type of restraint reflected in enrollment patterns.

Lack of comprehensive programs is an important restraint on the student's interest in higher education and its value to him.

In many states inadequate coordination restricts opportunity in a variety of ways; inadequate articulation of vocational education is a major problem.

In many states underdeveloped colleges are a more serious restraint on opportunity than the lack of free-access colleges.

Sparsely populated areas are a major problem; they cannot support conventional colleges but have many poor students.

Inadequate space and aid for transfer students are serious restraints on the spirit and reality of free-access higher education in even the most progressive states.

Inadequate information concerning the conditions of educational opportunity has acted as an implicit restraint when inequities have not been revealed.

Problems of quality

The quantitative problems of providing accessible higher education make it also clear that there are serious qualitative problems in converting access to opportunity. These can be grouped under four general types of relevance: personal, social, educational, and economic.

Personal relevance implies an effective and humane guidance and admissions process that results in truly equal opportunity regardless of race, socioeconomic condition, or academic preparation. There is an urgent need to give much closer attention to the development of the student — his career, his competencies, his interests and attitudes, plus concrete and useful educational outcomes.

Social relevance is the capacity to marshal resources and reorganize social roles. One critical problem is the fact that students often fail to find on the campus a sense of community and social commitment that they regard as essential for the national welfare. A second major issue is the fact that expanding educational opportunity brings the reality of providing appropriate education to culturally different minority and majority students who often have little interest in traditional academic life.

Educational relevance includes the partially incompatible goals of teaching a currently useful skill while emphasizing a liberal education to protect the individual from intellectual obsolescence. It also implies flexible use of methods of instruction that respect individual differences, fit different content, and recognize the values of educational experiences beyond the purely academic ones.

Economic relevance requires a reasonable fit between educational specifications and manpower requirements. Critical unsolved problems include the general level of education needed at present, the educational requirements of different occupations, and reliable means of projecting manpower needs.

Fostering relevant opportunity

If equality of opportunity has any real meaning, it must be relevant to individual and social needs. The problems of providing it are awesome in complexity and scope. These are matters of vital public interest that frequently transcend the primary concerns of faculty and often even individual institutions. As such, they require extensive planning, coordination, and evaluation by colleges, systems, and states. There are many ways in which relevant educational opportunity may be fostered:

Access programs to locate and bring in new students under conditions that meet their needs.

Educational programs to move the institution closer to society, the faculty closer to the student, and the student closer to an understanding of himself and the adult world.

Institutional and system research to evaluate procedures, resources, and programs and how they are related to the desirable outcomes of the educational process.

Operational programs to assist the student in planning his education, the institution in operating effectively, and the educational system in efficiently managing its operations.

Planning and coordinating to enhance comprehensive opportunity, utilize human resources effectively, protect the individual and public interest, and justify the commitment of resources.

Surveys of students to support the planning function, improve programs, monitor the quality of educational opportunity, and inform the public.

Some general impressions

Writing in 1960 on educational goals for Americans, John Gardner stated:

"In dealing with students, the first goal is equality of opportunity. By 1970 we should have achieved a deeper understanding of this phrase than ever in the past. We should have become keenly aware of all of the forces that limit individual growth, and should have learned much about how to cope with these forces. We should insist that regardless of the individual's economic level, regardless of his color, whether he lives in a modern suburb or the backwoods or a city slum, he should receive the best we can give in the way of opportunity and encouragement to develop whatever abilities he possesses."

Certainly no one can deny that we have reached a deeper understanding of the meaning of equality of opportunity during the past decade. But the data of this study amply illustrate how far we have to go in meeting the national goal of providing higher education within commuting distance of most of the population (Eisenhower Commission, 1960; Carnegie Commission, 1970). Less than half of all Americans live near an accessible college, and there is good evidence that this condition puts them at a distinct disadvantage. It is a conservative estimate that each year more than 500,000 youths do not continue education beyond high school simply because they happen not to live near an accessible college.[1]

We have not provided with this statistic, or with others included here, any sort of definitive answers to the question of accessibility of higher education either nationally or particularly in local areas. It is important to say again that the definitions used here can give only the most general indications of accessibility. Much of the intent of this study is to urge closer local attention to the real conditions of college going as outlined in the latter part of Chapter 6. Furthermore, Chapter 7 goes into some detail to say that living near an accessible college does not guarantee access to genuine opportunity, a useful education, or an enriching experience. The data do, however, provide clear indications of some serious problems, and they also relate to matters of general educational strategy.

There are many geographic imbalances in the availability of higher education, but the inadequate coverage of major urban areas is a general case so serious as to require special emphasis. Considering the urban problems of physical decay, deprived populations of poor minorities, and the constricting lack of individual alternatives, the addition of inadequate educational opportunity in many cities is best described as repressive.

There is no doubt that the country needs far more community institutions than it has at present, but in many states the development of existing colleges is just as urgent a problem if not more so. There are many colleges with quite a small enrollment, limited programs, and a narrow view of their responsibility to the world around them. In any community that has a free-access college, a primary question is whether that college has been developed sufficiently to actually provide relevant opportunity to a significant proportion of the local population. Over the long range, it seems entirely likely that community service and continuing education are even greater needs in development of local institutions.

As with most complicated social problems, these matters depend very much on commitment and leadership, but one cannot escape the impression that a massive increase in funding is a critical necessity. New levels of expenditure will surely be rationalized in legitimate educational and economic terms, but the basic goals are social and the motivation is political. It seems not at all a simple question of massive funding in order to meet quantitative demand and to carry on the development of an increasingly expensive enterprise, but rather resources that will be required to achieve the metamorphic transition of higher education into a rather different social institution.

The evolving expectation, not fully articulated, is that higher education will serve new functions including the support of a radically different life style, the

---

1. Studies by Koos (1944a), Trent and Medsker (1965), and Bashaw (1965) all indicate that the proportional rate of college attendance is higher in those communities with an accessible junior college than in those without one. The proportionally higher rate can be estimated from data reported in those three studies at 2.4, 1.6, and 2.1, respectively. Assuming the most conservative differential of 1.6 and some 65 percent of high school graduates eventually attending college, one would estimate an additional 540,000 college entrants if all (rather than 42 percent) of the current 3 million high school graduates lived near an accessible college.

reestablishment of community identity, and a calculated redistribution of privilege. Such mind-boggling change does not come about easily or quickly, but such possibilities suggest the need to understand the process of change a great deal better. Many of the problems we are dealing with here are subtle processes of social organization and individual growth. There is no simple cost-accountable index of career development, equal opportunity, or utilization of talent. They are process phenomena that have to be organized and evaluated through time in a complex network of people, programs, and policies. Higher education is not expert in these matters, and therefore it is vital to develop the competence and the values in institutions and systems that will be necessary to work toward the social expectations developed over the past decade. Recently proposed legislation (*Chronicle*, 1969d) may support such development by strengthening statewide coordination and programs of career education.

The prospect of additional structure in an overly organized society suggests a good measure of sober caution and a careful scrutiny of what values may become institutionalized in the process. Doermann (1968) has urged flexibility in the mechanisms by which students distribute themselves to college. McConnell (1962) warns that we know far too little about "fit" to even consider assigning students to programs or colleges. Gardner (1969) describes the essential need to maintain a broad diversity among social institutions and how they operate.

Perhaps the root problem of access to higher education in the 1970s is how to expand equal and relevant opportunity as rapidly as possible without slipping into one or both of the alternate chasms — stiffling individual choice or crippling higher institutions. There must be quality institutions with sufficient autonomy to develop the advanced academic disciplines or to meet local needs as the college and its community see them. There must be mechanisms which guarantee that students retain control over their decisions so that utilization of talent does not mean exploitation of the individual and more steps toward a mechanistic society.

There can be added brief notes of pragmatic pessimism. The problems of unequal opportunity stem from a variety of social conditions. Jencks and Riesman (1968) have written persuasively on the tendency to exaggerate the role of higher education and its social effects. Bowles (1969) goes further in expressing doubt that real equality of educational opportunity can be achieved without a major and improbable redistribution of political power. An important implication is the need to mobilize individual communities in support of the new meaning of equal opportunity for higher education.

These various impressions are similarly directed. The aspiration of expanded educational opportunity requires much greater effort, though it will not be quickly realized. Grand solutions deserve the caution they receive, and when all else fails, there is much virtue in treating symptoms.

Bibliography

American Association of Junior Colleges, *Directory American Association of Junior Colleges.* Washington, D.C.: American Association of Junior Colleges, 1968.

Arnow, Philip, "Bridge the Gap from School to Work." *Occupational Outlook Quarterly,* Vol. 12, No. 4, 1968, pp. 28–31.

Axelrod, Joseph; Freedman, Mervin B.; Hatch, Winslow R.; Katz, Joseph; and Sanford, Nevitt, *Search for Relevance.* San Francisco: Jossey-Bass, Inc., Publishers, 1969.

Baird, Leonard L.; Richards, James M. Jr.; and Shevel, Linda R., "A Description of Graduates of Two-Year Colleges." *American College Testing Research Reports,* No. 28, 1969.

Bashaw, Wilbur L., "The Effect of Community Junior Colleges on the Proportion of the Local Population Who Seek Higher Education." *The Journal of Educational Research,* Vol. 58, No. 7, 1965, pp. 327–329.

Bayer, Alan E., and Boruch, Robert F., "The Black Student in American Colleges." *American Council on Education Research Reports,* Vol. 4, No. 2, 1969.

Becker, Gary S., *Human Capital.* New York: National Bureau of Economic Research, 1964.

Berdahl, Robert D., *Study of Statewide Systems.* Washington, D.C.: American Council on Education, 1970, in press.

Bloom, Benjamin S., "Learning for Mastery." *Evaluation Comment,* Vol. 1, No. 2, 1968.

Blumenfeld, Warren S., "Some Characteristics of Finalists in the 1966 National Achievement Scholarship Program." *National Merit Scholarship Corporation Research Reports,* Vol. 2, No. 4, 1966.

Bowles, Frank H., "Observations and Comments," in McGrath, Earl J., ed., *Universal Higher Education.* New York: McGraw-Hill Book Company, 1966.

Bowles, Samuel, "Towards Equality of Educational Opportunity." *Harvard Educational Review; Equal Educational Opportunity,* Vol. 38, No. 1, 1968, pp. 89–99.

Bowman, Mary J., "The Human Investment Revolution in Economic Thought." *Sociology of Education,* Vol. 39, 1966, pp. 111–137.

Burckel, Christian E., *The College Blue Book.* Los Angeles: College Planning Programs, 1968.

Carnegie Commission on Higher Education, *A Chance to Learn: An Action Agenda for Equal Opportunity in Higher Education.* New York: McGraw-Hill Book Company, 1970.

Carnegie Commission on Higher Education, *Federal Aid to Higher Education: An Essential Investment in the Nation's Future.* Berkeley, Calif.: Carnegie Commission on Higher Education, 1968a.

Carnegie Commission on Higher Education, *Quality and Equality: New Levels of Federal Responsibility for Higher Education.* New York: McGraw-Hill Book Company, 1968b.

Cass, James, and Birnbaum, Max, eds., *Comparative Guide to American Colleges,* 1968–1969 ed. New York: Harper & Row, Publishers, 1968.

Chandler, Marjorie O., *Opening Fall Enrollment in Higher Education.* Washington, D.C.: U.S. Department of Health, Education, and Welfare, Office of Education, 1968.

Chronicle of Higher Education. "Negro Enrollments This Year on the Nation's Campuses," Vol. 3, No. 16, 1969a, p. 3.

Chronicle of Higher Education. "Nixon Administration Seen Giving High Priority to 2-Year Colleges," Vol. 3, No. 17, 1969b, p. 1.

Chronicle of Higher Education. "What States Spend Per Capita," Vol. 4, No. 5, 1969c, p. 1.

Chronicle of Higher Education. "Two-Year Colleges Would Get Larger Share of Aid," Vol. 4, No. 9, 1969d, p. 2.

Clear, Charles E., *A Study of Educational and Occupational Aspirations of Virginia's 1966–67 High School Seniors.* Richmond, Va.: Division of Educational Research and Statistics, State Department of Education, 1969.

Cleveland Plain Dealer, "Ohio Regents to Oppose Rhodes Bill," January 17, 1970.

Cole, Charles C. Jr., *Encouraging Scientific Talent.* New York: College Entrance Examination Board, 1957.

Coleman, James S.; Campbell, Ernest Q.; Hobson, Carol J.; McPartland, James; Mood, Alexander M.; Weinfeld, Frederic D.; and York, Robert L., *Equality of Educational Opportunity.* Washington, D.C.: U.S. Department of Health, Education, and Welfare, Office of Education, 1966.

Coleman, James S., "The Concept of Equality of Educational Opportunity." *Harvard Educational Review; Equal Educational Opportunity,* Vol. 38, No. 1, 1968, pp. 7–22.

Comparative Guidance and Placement Program, *Program Summary Statistics—1968.* New York: College Entrance Examination Board, 1968.

Cowhig, James D., and Nam, Charles B., "Factors Related to College Attendance of Farm and Non-Farm High School Graduates: 1960." *Current Population Reports* Series P-27, No. 32. Washington, D.C.: U.S. Department of Commerce, Bureau of the Census, 1962.

Creager, John A.; Astin, Alexander W.; Boruch, Robert F.; and Bayer, Alan E., "National Norms for Entering College Freshmen—Fall 1968." ACE *Research Reports,* Vol. 3, No. 1, 1968.

Davis, Junius A., "What College Teachers Value in Students." *College Board Review,* No. 56, Spring 1965, pp. 15–18.

Doermann, Humphrey, *Crosscurrents in College Admissions.* New York: Teachers College Press, 1968.

Educational Policies Commission, *Universal Opportunity for Education Beyond the High School.* Washington, D.C.: National Education Association, 1964.

Egerton, John, *State Universities and Black Americans.* Atlanta: Southern Education Foundation, 1969.

Eisenhower Commission, *Goals for Americans: The Report of the President's Commission on National Goals.* Englewood Cliffs, N.J.: Prentice-Hall International, Inc., 1960.

Eskow, Seymour, *Barron's Guide to the Two-Year Colleges.* New York: Barron's Educational Series, Inc., 1967.

Ferrin, Richard I., *An Analysis of the Changes in Free-Access Higher Education in the United States from 1958–1968.* New York: College Entrance Examination Board, in preparation.

Flanagan, John C.; Davis, Frederick B.; Dailey, John T.; Shaycoft, Marion F.; Orr, David B.; Goldberg, Isadore; and Neyman, Clinton A. Jr., *The American High School Student.* Pittsburgh; Project TALENT, University of Pittsburgh, 1964.

Florida Community Junior College Inter-Institutional Research Council, *A Follow-Up Study of First-Time In-College Freshmen in Florida's Community Junior Colleges in Fall 1966.* Institute of Higher Education, Gainesville, Fla: University of Florida, 1969.

Folger, John K., "The Balance Between Supply and Demand for College Graduates," *Journal of Human Resources,* Vol. 2, 1967, pp. 143–175.

Folger, John K., and Nam, Charles B., *Education of the American Population.* Washington, D.C.: U.S. Department of Commerce, Bureau of the Census, 1967.

Galbraith, John K., *The New Industrial State.* New York: Houghton Mifflin Company, 1967.

Gardner, John W., "National Goals in Education," in Eisenhower Commission, *Goals for Americans: The Report of the President's Commission on National Goals.* Englewood Cliffs, N.J.: Prentice-Hall International, Inc., 1960.

Gardner, John W., *Excellence.* New York: Harper & Row Publishers, 1961.

Gardner, John W., *No Easy Victories.* New York: Harper & Row Publishers, 1968.

Gardner, John W., "What Kind of a Society Do We Want?" *Reader's Digest,* September 1969, pp. 74–78.

Gleazer, Edmund J. Jr., *American Junior Colleges.* Washington, D.C.: American Council on Education, 1967.

Glenny, Lyman A., "Impact of Certain Federal Aid Programs on Statewide Planning for Higher Education." Speech at College Entrance Examination Board Invitational Conference on Financing Higher Education, Atlanta, 1970.

Glover, Robert, *Cooperative Admissions Information System.* New York: International Business Machines, 1967.

Gossman, Charles; Nobbe, Charles E.; Patricelli, Theresa J.; Schmid, Calvin F.; and Steahr, Thomas E., *Migration of College and University Students in the United States.* Seattle: University of Washington Press, 1968.

Grant, Claude W., "A Follow-Up Study of Spring, 1966, High School Graduates in the State of Utah." *The Personnel and Guidance Journal,* Vol. 47, No. 2, 1968, pp. 157–162.

Hawes, Gene R., *The New American Guide to Colleges.* New York: Columbia University Press, 1966.

Hazen Foundation, *The Student in Higher Education.* Report of the Committee on the Student in Higher Education. New Haven, Conn.: Hazen Foundation, 1968.

Higher Education Act of 1965. Public Law 89–329. Washington, D.C.: U.S. Government Printing Office, 1967.

Higher Education Amendments of 1968. Public Law 90–575. Washington, D.C.: U.S. Government Printing Office, 1968.

Higher Education and National Affairs. "Community College Bill Introduced by 28 Seniors," Vol. 18, No. 6, 1969a.

Higher Education and National Affairs. "Higher Education Bill of Rights Introduced by Three Senate Members," Vol. 18, No. 14, 1969b.

Higher Education Facilities Act of 1963. Public Law 88–204. Washington, D.C.: U.S. Government Printing Office, 1967.

Holland, John L., and Whitney, Douglas R., "Career Development." *Review of Educational Research,* Vol. 39, 1969, pp. 222–235.

Hollister, Robinson, *A Technical Evaluation of the First Stage of the Mediterranean Regional Project.* Paris: Organization for Economic Co-operation and Development, 1967.

Huddleston, Edith M., and Poole, Hazel C., *Opening Fall Enrollment.* Washington, D.C.: U.S. Department of Health, Education, and Welfare, Office of Education, 1958.

Hutchins, Robert M., *The Learning Society.* New York: Frederick A. Praeger, Inc., 1968.

Jaffe, Abram J., and Adams, Walter, "Trends in College Enrollments." *College Board Review* No. 55, Winter 1964–65, pp. 27–31.

Jaffe, Abram J., and Adams, Walter, *American Higher Education in Transition.* New York: Bureau of Applied Social Research, 1969.

Jaffe, Abram J.; Adams, Walter; and Meyers, Sandra G., *Negro Higher Education in the 1960's.* New York: Frederick A. Praeger, Inc., 1968.

Jaffe, Abram J., and Froomkin, Joseph, *Technology and Jobs.* New York: Frederick A. Praeger, Inc., 1968.

Jencks, Christopher, "Social Stratification and Higher Education." *Harvard Educational Review,* Vol. 38, 1968, pp. 277–316.

Jencks, Christopher, and Riesman, David, *The Academic Revolution.* Garden City, N.Y.: Doubleday & Company, Inc., 1968.

Johnson, Charles E. Jr., and Reed, Ritchie H., "Characteristics of Students and Their Colleges: October 1966." *Current Population Reports* Series P-20, No. 183. Washington, D.C.: U.S. Department of Commerce, Bureau of the Census, 1969.

Johnson, Charles E. Jr., and Zappolo, Aurora A., "Factors Related to High School Graduation and College Attendance: 1967." *Current Population Reports* Series P-20, No. 185. Washington, D.C.: U.S. Department of Commerce, Bureau of the Census, 1969.

Johnson, Lamar, *Island of Innovation Expanding.* Riverside, N.J.: Glencoe Press, 1969.

Katz, Joseph, and associates, *No Time for Youth.* San Francisco: Jossey-Bass, Inc., Publishers, 1968.

Keniston, Kenneth, *The Uncommitted.* New York: Harcourt, Brace & World, Inc., 1965.

Kerr, Clark, *The Uses of the University.* New York: Harper & Row, Publishers, 1963.

Kirp, David L., "The Poor, the Schools, and Equal Protection," in *Equal Educational Opportunity.* Cambridge: Harvard University Press, 1969.

Knoell, Dorothy M., *Toward Educational Opportunity for All.* Albany: State University of New York, 1966.

Koos, Leonard V., "How to Democratize the Junior-College Level." *School Review,* Vol. 5, 1944a, pp. 271–284.

Koos, Leonard V., "Local Versus Regional Junior Colleges." *School Review,* Vol. 5, 1944b, pp. 525–531.

Lecht, Leonard A., *Manpower Needs for National Goals in the 1970's.* New York: Frederick A. Praeger, Inc., 1969.

Life Insurance Agency Management Association, *1968–69 College Costs.* Hartford, Conn.: Life Insurance Management Association, 1968.

Little, J. Kenneth, *Review and Synthesis of Research on the Placement and Follow-Up of Vocational Education Students.* Columbus, Ohio: Center for Research and Leadership in Vocational and Technical Education, Ohio State University, 1969.

Lovejoy, Clarence, *Lovejoy's College Guide.* New York: Simon & Schuster, 1968.

Martin, Edmund C., *College Enrollment of Georgia's 1968 High School Graduates.* Atlanta: Georgia Educational Improvement Council, 1969.

Mayhew, Lewis B., *Contemporary College Students and the Curriculum.* Research Monograph No. 14. Atlanta: Southern Regional Education Board, 1969a.

Mayhew, Lewis B., *Long-Range Planning for Higher Education.* Washington, D.C.: National Institutes for Mental Health, Contract PH-43-66-1166, May 1969b.

McConnell, Thomas R., "A Reply to the Critics." *Journal of Educational Sociology,* Vol. 22, 1949, pp. 533–550.

McConnell, Thomas R., *A General Pattern for American Public Higher Education.* New York: McGraw-Hill Book Company, 1962.

McGrath, Earl J., *The Predominantly Negro Colleges and Universities in Transition.* New York: Columbia University Press, 1965.

McKendall, Benjamin W. Jr., ed., *Statewide Seminar on Race and Poverty in Higher Education.* (California). New York: College Entrance Examination Board, 1968.

McQuitty, John V., and Tully, G. Emerson, *Plans Beyond High School.* Tallahassee, Fla.: Office of the Board of Regents State University System, 1969.

Miller, James L. Jr., "The Two Dimensions of State-Wide Higher Education Coordination." *Educational Record,* Vol. 43, No. 2, 1962, pp. 163–167.

Muscantine, Charles, *Education at Berkeley.* Berkeley, Calif.: University of California, 1966.

Nash, George, *A Description of the 1,144 Accredited Four-Year Institutions of Higher Education.* New York: Bureau of Applied Social Research, 1969.

Palola, Ernest G.; Lehmann, Timothy; and Blischke, William R., *State-Wide Planning in Higher Education.* Berkeley, Calif.: Center for Research and Development in Higher Education, 1970.

Perrella, Vera C., "Employment of High School Graduates and Dropouts." *Monthly Labor Review,* Vol. 92, No. 6, 1969, pp. 36–43.

Peterson, Richard E., *The Scope of Organized Student Protest in 1967–68.* Princeton, N.J.: Educational Testing Service, 1968.

Popham, W. J., and Husek, T. R., "Implications of Criterion—Referenced Measurement." *Journal of Educational Measurement,* Vol. 6, No. 1, 1969, pp. 1–9.

Rice, Mabel C., and Mason, Paul L., *Residence and Migration of College Students, Fall 1963.* Washington, D.C.: U.S. Department of Health, Education, and Welfare, Office of Education, 1964.

Riessman, Frank, and Popper, Hermine I., *Up from Poverty.* New York: Harper & Row, Publishers, 1968.

Sanders, Edward, and Palmer, Hans, *The Financial Barrier to Higher Education in California.* Claremont, Calif.: Pomona College, 1965.

San Francisco Chronicle. "State College Campuses Overflow," October 2, 1969.

Seibel, Dean W., "Follow-Up of a National Sample of High School Seniors: Phase 2—One Year after Graduation." *College Entrance Examination Board Research and Development Reports,* RDR-65-6, No. 1. Princeton, N.J.: Educational Testing Service, 1965.

Sewell, William H., and Shah, Vimal P., "Socioeconomic Status, Intelligence, and the Attainment of Higher Education." *Sociology of Education,* Vol. 40, 1967, pp. 1–23.

Simon, Kenneth A., and Fullam, Marie G., *Projections of Educational Statistics to 1976–77.* Washington, D.C.: U.S. Department of Health, Education, and Welfare, Office of Education, 1968.

Singletary, Otis A., *American Universities and Colleges,* 10th ed. Washington, D.C.: American Council on Education, 1968.

Swanson, J. Chester, *Leadership Role, Functions, Procedures of Vocational-Technical Education Agencies at the State Level.* Vol. I. A Nationwide Survey of Status and Organization 1966–67. Berkeley, Calif.: University of California, 1968.

Tiedeman, David V., "The Organization and Intention of a Proposed Data and Educational System for Vocational Decision-Making." *Information Systems for Vocational Decisions* Report No. 1. Cambridge, Mass.: Harvard University, 1965.

Tillery, Dale, *School to College: Distribution and Differentiation of Youth.* Berkeley, Calif.: Center for Research and Development in Higher Education, 1969.

Tillery, Dale; Donovan, Denis; and Sherman, Barbara, SCOPE *Four-State Profile Grade Twelve— 1966 (California, Illinois, Massachusetts, North Carolina).* New York: College Entrance Examination Board, 1966.

Trent, James W., and Medsker, Leland L., *The Influence of Different Types of Public Higher Institutions on College Attendance from Varying Socioeconomic and Ability Levels.* Berkeley, Calif.: Center for Research and Development in Higher Education, 1965.

Truman Commission, *Higher Education for American Democracy.* Washington, D.C.: U.S. Department of Health, Education, and Welfare, Office of Education, 1947.

U.S. Bureau of the Census, *County and City Data Book 1967.* Washington, D.C.: U.S. Department of Commerce, 1967.

U.S. Bureau of the Census, *Statistical Abstracts of the United States—1968.* Washington, D.C.: U.S. Department of Commerce, 1968.

U.S. Bureau of the Census, "Income in 1967 of Families in the United States." *Current Population Reports* Series P-60, No. 59. Washington, D.C.: U.S. Department of Commerce, 1969.

U.S. Office of Education, *Education Directory, 1948–49: Part 3, Higher Education.* Washington, D.C.: U.S. Department of Health, Education, and Welfare, 1949.

Warga, Richard G., *Student Expense Budgets of American Colleges and Universities for the 1968–69 Academic Year.* College Scholarship Service Technical Report. Princeton, N.J.: Educational Testing Service, 1968.

Western Interstate Commission on Higher Education, *Progress of the Management Information Systems Program.* Boulder, Colo.: Western Interstate Commission on Higher Education, 1969.

Willingham, Warren W., "The Importance of Relevance in Expanding Post-Secondary Education." *Trends in Post-Secondary Education.* Washington, D.C.: U.S. Department of Health, Education, and Welfare, Office of Education, 1970, in press.

Willingham, Warren W., and Findikyan, Nurhan, *Patterns of Admission for Transfer Students.* New York: College Entrance Examination Board, 1969.

Willis, Benjamin C., *The Second Report on the Chicago City Junior College to the Chicago Board of Education.* Chicago: Chicago Board of Education, 1958.

Willis, Benjamin C., *Higher Education. Part I: The Chicago Teachers Colleges; Part II: The Chicago City Junior College.* Study Report No. 10. Chicago: Chicago Public Schools, 1964.

Yarrington, Roger, ed., *Junior Colleges: 50 States / 50 Years.* Washington, D.C.: American Association of Junior Colleges, 1969.